Forewords by
Karen Curry Parker

Stop Overworking and Start Overflowing

25 Ways to Transform Your Life Using Human Design

Kristi H. Sullivan

Featuring: Jen Allen, Connie Aramento, Lauren Armstrong, Amber Clements, Ashley Ashida Dixon, Janette Gallardo, Alana Heim, Rev. Bamboo Ilana, Julianne Joy, Linda Landon, Sandra Lee, Kristy Martin, Jacqueline Martinez, Sabine Messner, April Novoa, Nancy OKeefe, Maggie Ostara, Sally Gamboa Parihar, Mary Jo Rathgeb, Catherine Rivers, Cat Skreiner, Christa Timil Keyes-Venson, Tonia Twigger, Rachael Weaver, Robin Winn

Stop Overworking and Start Overflowing

Kristi H. Sullivan

Published by Brave Healer Productions

FOREWORD ONE

Asha D. Ramakrishna

Kneeling on the floor of my office crying, I remember asking God to save me from the soul sucking job I was enduring. It was not even the job itself, it was the people and the expectations that were pulling at me: a working mother of two young children managing the complexity of being the primary kale-winner, conscious mother, responsible immigrant daughter, unsettled wife, a brown woman in a white male-dominated science world, and a human trying like hell to have a spiritual experience among the human chaos.

Life can be very full, especially when you live according to the demands of others. In Human Design, we call this *conditioning*. We are all conditioned by the system of oppression, and are impacted from it from a very early age. Luckily for you and I, there are ways to acknowledge the programs that run through our society and our nervous system and yet access the power within to thrive; Human Design being a beautiful doorway to this uplevel.

Human Design began to infiltrate my life a couple years before that desperate plea I shared and my attempt to better understand my spirited daughter, whom I discovered was a Reflector; merely showing our family and our community the dissonance we were experiencing. I was struggling to be present as a mother, unfulfilled in my career, and not knowing if I was in the right marriage for me. Knowing the ultimate purpose of the Reflector types which is to reflect back to us how well or not we are doing and to flow through the transits, ideally in joy and exuberance, forced me to look within.

Know thyself, the ancient Kemetic teaching, resounds at certain points in my life, and this moment was a pivotal one. Perhaps, you find yourself there right now?

Human Design has been the most elegant way to help me to first know myself, know my partner, know my children, and then the ripple effect of being able to train healers and mystics to help other humans. What I most love about Human Design is that it is a roadmap to better embody our unique way of making decisions, and understand the nuances of how we each process energy, from the cosmic field, our planet, our communities, and our people.

Flourishing in life and business is our birthright, and let's not forget that.

Fast forward many moons from that desperate moment in my office, praying to Goddess. I am grateful for the many years of teaching others about their astrology themes, their seasonal process, and yes, their Human Design. I believe that when we not just know ourselves, but also each other, we can allow for more compassion, more liberation of each individual in the way they choose to express, with the foundation of *Ahimsa* (Yogic concept for *Do No Harm*). When we understand that an open Throat needs to be recognized, so we ask them open-ended questions, or when we can harness the emotional waves of a defined Solar Plexus, or even learn from the questions of the open Head & Ajna, we all win.

Liberation of the individual can be forged by the individual themself, but when a community and an entire society is devoted to space for everyone to be themselves, then we have a chance of evolving as a collective. The ethos of my work is *Feel Good, Be Wealthy, Give Back,* and everything I do and support must align with that. Human Design has been that for me, my family, my students, and the companies I have supported.

Every esoteric teaching comes alive when it runs through the nervous system of humans, when it is practiced through day-to-day challenges, and when it is proven in the laboratory of life. When we can identify with the lived experience of another, it becomes possible for ourselves, and that is the exact opportunity you have here today; to swim in the possibilities of your own thriving. The stories and experiences of some of my students, colleagues, and new friends and their embrace of Human Design is an honest anchoring of what you wish to pick up and expand in your own life.

Kristi Sullivan understands just this. Kristi has such a big heart and is truly vested in disseminating the power of Human Design to those who want to go deeper. She sees this system as a way to know ourselves and as a roadmap to create a life that is fully lived.

Kristi is as much a Human Design enthusiast as I am, and has channeled that devotion of this tool by bringing together diverse stories from seasoned teachers and top experts. These teachers share their wisdom, their fascinating journey to unravel their internalized conditioning, and ultimately to their personal liberation.

Kristi curated such rich stories in this book; The challenges many humans face in the ways we are unconsciously asked to fit into a box are universal. Ultimately the authors here aim to liberate all humans, and they deliver! The collection of authors here give us numerous tools and easy to implement perspectives so that each one of us can truly stop being machines of the system and use our creative genius to overflow, no matter our background. When the most oppressed are liberated, we are all liberated.

The honest experiences and wisdom of the authors in this book can help you to see yourself between the lines of their stories. Ultimately, I invite you to be honest to your own conditioning, and the opportunity to overcome the expectations of others, knowing you are worthy, no matter what anyone says, to be fully yourself.

It may be a process to arrive there, so honor your process, honor that depending on your Design, it will have a different way of unfolding, and you are up for the task.

Most importantly, do not be fooled by the present-day post-colonial system that tells you to buckle up and do it yourself; we are not created or neurologically wired to do life alone. Community, mentorship, and support are imperative to our thriving. We are in it together.

May the stories and the tools in this book open your inner doors back home to your most precious connected Self. Thank you, Kristi, for heeding the call to bring such beautiful Human Design experts together in this book that can become a resource unto itself.

Asha D Ramakrishna is a #1 Best Selling Author of the book "The Priestess Code: Awakening the Modern Woman," where Yin Principles are revealed for a more organic and harmonious approach to life. With a background in Molecular Biology and Business Development, she breaks esoteric teachings into practical logical approaches to living. Asha is a Minister of Spiritual Peacemaking & incorporates philosophies such as Feng Shui, Karma Healing, Human Design, to name a few. She is the founder of the Dharma School: Modern Priestess School & Sacred Commerce Program. She is originally from Venezuela and South India. She currently lives in occupied Nipmuc Land (Harvard, MA) with her soul mate, two human daughters, and a 50-pound Portuguese Water Dog.

To learn more about her work visit https://www.ashaisnow.com/dharma/

FOREWORD TWO

Karen Curry Parker

I could begin this foreword with my story of how I "discovered" Human Design, or rather how it "discovered" me. I could tell you how, three weeks after first seeing my Human Design chart, I put my house on the market, packed up my four children, and moved to Sedona, Arizona, because every cell in my body just *knew* I had to learn everything I could about Human Design as fast as possible.

I could share with you, how through a series of strange and serendipitous events, I came to work at the international headquarters for Human Design and had the privilege of learning directly from the founder of the Human Design System, Ra Uru Hu, and how I went on to teach and write about Human Design for 22 years.

Those are the components of my story with Human Design. But I want to start your journey with this beautiful collection of stories by telling you how Human Design is for you.

You see, you are a once-in-a-lifetime-cosmic event. There has never been anyone like you before, and there will never be anyone like you again. Not only are you a unique and irreplaceable phenomenon because you're one-of-a-kind, you probably didn't get an instruction manual to help you discover how to maximize your potential and create a life that is a true reflection of who you are.

Living a rich and authentic life is your true purpose on this planet. You really didn't come here to "do" anything. You came here to be yourself, the full expression of a human story that, ultimately, adds beauty, abundance, and growth on the leading-edge of consciousness to the entire story of humanity.

The story of Human Design includes a prophecy that informs us that we are standing on the edge of a massive creative revolution, and you are part of this big leap in human history.

And yet, as we stand on the cusp of this revolution, we are facing a global creativity crisis in a time when we need to be able to tap into expanded collective creativity to resolve the challenges facing humanity today. Our job is to create an equitable, just, abundant, sustainable, and peaceful world by first becoming who we were born to be.

The metrics for creativity have been significantly declining since 1990. Researchers used the Torrance test for decades to measure creativity. It is a better predictor of real-world success than traditional IQ tests. Researchers at the University of William and Mary analyzed 300,000 Torrance Test scores since the 50s and found that creativity scores began to nosedive in 1990.

That sounds alarming, but the good news is that scientists have a pretty good idea about what's causing our collective creativity to tank. Research shows that our hurried, over-scheduled lives and ever-increasing amounts of time interacting with electronic entertainment devices negatively impact our creativity.

We're too busy and electronically entertained for creativity to blossom. Gone are the days where childhood was spent outside, immersed in nature and imaginary play. Children are often just as over-scheduled and overstimulated as adults.

Ask any Projector; most of us are too busy and overwhelmed with life's pandemonium to keep up with emails and healthy self-care, much less find creative time to daydream, ponder and tune into our authentic selves.

Creativity demands downtime, time to simply think, contemplate and daydream. Science shows that being bored increases creativity. Einstein instinctively knew this, spending hours floating in his sailboat contemplating the wonders of the cosmos and integrating his brilliant ideas that revolutionized our understanding of how the world works.

To be more creative, we need to stop and get off the perpetual motion machine and wait for the epiphanies, the downloads from our muse, and the right timing to share what we've discovered.

We also need downtime so that we can shut out the noise and reconnect with our authentic selves. Of course, knowing your Human Design can facilitate this process.

When people first learn their Human Design, the most common questions about their Type and Strategy are about waiting. Why do they have to wait? How long? What will they do while they wait?

All Types have to wait to a certain degree. The Manifestor has to wait for inner timing. The Generator Types have to wait for their Sacral response. The Projector has to wait for the right invitation and recognition. The Reflector has a rich and practiced relationship with waiting and experiencing the energy around them.

We wait because it's a vital part of remembering who we are.

You are the soul expression of life's intelligence living in a human story. Your every breath is sacred. Conditioning makes us forget who we are and how we are designed to engage with the world. Waiting and living true to your Human Design helps you reconnect with your soul curriculum so you can better serve the world at your highest level.

The entirety of your human story is a cosmic gift, and you, deliberately steering your life and crafting the narrative of your life, in partnership with Source, is the purpose of your life. That partnership won't necessarily involve dramatic spiritual events such as the visitation of an angel or a kundalini experience.

The experience of the rightness of your unique life story is in the sensual alignment with what feels good and correct, following your unique Human Design Strategy and Authority. When you are living true to the expression of consciousness through you, you experience a wave of joy, harmony, and sweetness, subtle as it is at times, that lets you know you're headed in the right direction, towards the fulfillment of whatever you need to experience next to fulfill the narrative that is your unique story and part of your cosmic journey.

This is why you must wait. Understanding your Human Design helps you wait in the way that calls your destiny to you.

Waiting is essential for the deconditioning process. Our conditioning around doing is so powerful that waiting seems like torture and a direct antithesis to getting things done in the world.

There is fear and tension around the idea of waiting. *How long? What if nothing happens? What if I "miss the boat"? Where will the money come from? How will anything in my life happen?*

The root of this worry is about our self-worth and the artificial value society confers upon us when we're busy. *Who am I if I'm not "doing"? And what is my value in the world if I'm not busy "doing" something?*

The very real and tangible benefit of waiting is that it gives us time to heal our self-worth, divorce our value from our doing, and remember that we are inherently valuable simply by virtue of our existence. We wait so we can remember who we are and find the path back to our irreplaceable and vital role in the cosmic plan that only we can play.

Waiting bears tremendous fruit if you sink into it and allow it.

I'm a gardener, and I live in Minnesota. This season of the year is a time of enormous tension and waiting in my garden. The plants are unfolding and blossoming; baby fruits emerge on the vines and between the leaves. I'm eager and anticipating the harvest, but there's work to be done in the meantime. I have to pluck those darn beetles off the leaves, make sure the squash doesn't get moldy if I overwater it or let it dry out too much, train the vines to grow in the right direction, and tie up the tomatoes and eggplants so that the weight of their bounty doesn't cause them to topple over and break off.

Waiting is a gift; it helps us prepare; it allows us to evaluate our personal story and decondition it, look at our old stories and assess whether we want to continue to use them to define us or whether it's time for an upgrade, a new story that creates a stronger, more aligned template for what we want to bring into the world as the full expression of our potential.

Waiting also affords us time to heal our bodies. When we push too hard, too fast, too much in the wrong direction, using our vital energy to hold up masks and maintain facades that demonstrate to the world who we think we should be to be loved, feel valued, or successful, we burn ourselves out.

We use our life force energy to try to be someone we're not, saying "yes" when we want to say "no," denying our connection to life's intelligence trying to express itself through us. As a result, we burn out and can't connect to the energy necessary to implement our creative ideas.

When you have a lifetime of being told it's not okay to be who you are or how you are, even if the advice you've received about "fitting in" and "being successful" was well-intended, your body and spirit experience it as trauma.

I define trauma as any event, experience, or perception that has caused you to lose connection to your value and your right place in the world. (If you want to learn more about this, watch my TEDx talk:

https://www.ted.com/talks/karen_curry_parker_a_better_job_won_t_help_the_truth_about_burnout)

Understanding your Human Design can help you heal this trauma.

The trauma of a lifetime of being told you can't be who you are and that who you are and how you are is somehow wrong keeps the body in a constant state of adrenalized preparation for a fight for survival. We react to life as a result of our adrenaline and cortisol high. We lose our ability to create consciously, deliberately, and in alignment with our true potential, failing to activate the beauty of the human story we were born into.

Lastly, the process of waiting, that coming into alignment with the cosmic pause that Human Design invites us to embrace, makes us more receptive to life's intelligence, reconnecting us to our inherent creative essence and positioning us to activate the elegant solutions to the challenges facing the world today.

Waiting invites us to reclaim our natural inventiveness. Actively scheduling time to think, reflect, and experiment, putting reasonable boundaries on your use of passive tech, varying your routine and your company, and getting out for more long walks, resting, regenerating, and playing all serve to help you connect more deeply with your innate creativity.

And the more creative we are, the easier it will be for us to find elegant solutions to the challenges facing humanity today.

I hope that as you read the stories shared with you here, that you will find yourself in between the lines, that your eyes will light up with recognition, and you'll be inspired by the possibility of transformation and find hope that you, too, can live life as you were designed to and fully express the true story of who you were born to be.

From my Heart to Yours,
Karen Curry Parker

Karen Curry Parker is one of the world's leading experts on using Quantum Human Design, the power of archetypes and personal narrative to activate peak performance potential. She's developed a system that explores the relationship between Quantum Physics and Human Design. Karen works with C-Suite leaders and helps build creative initiatives for entrepreneurs. Karen is currently working on her Ph.d in Integrative Health and exploring the impact of personal narrative and language on gene regulation and function. She is a multiple best-selling author and has written more than 17 books, including Understanding Human Design, the New Science of Astrology: Discover Who You Really Are. Karen is the mother of 8 children and a proud Grandma of two Generators. She lives in Minneapolis with her family.

TABLE OF CONTENTS

INTRODUCTION

Do you believe that we are spiritual beings having a human experience?

I am guessing you might (like me), which is why you're here and why this book found you at the right time and place in your journey.

Do you believe that you are unique, like a cosmic star?

This is also true for me, and in this book you will meet 25 authors who share their stories of how they discovered and embraced their uniqueness, leading to positive shifts and transformation in their lives, using a cosmic system called Human Design.

SHIFTING FROM OVERWORKING TO OVERFLOWING

"I don't get it," he said after I tried to explain the latest business success I was experiencing by working less hard. "I think we just need to agree to disagree."

"It's okay if we see things differently," I replied, trying not to get defensive. "I know this concept is not the old programming of work-hard-to-be-successful that you're used to. This new way of working may not make sense, but it is paying off for me in ways I couldn't imagine."

He rebuked, "But you are living with rose colored glasses, it's not real life. And is it really sustainable?"

I was all too familiar with the doubts, fears, and worry that silently whispered *what if this doesn't last, what if this is just a sham?* My lifelong programming questioned these concepts as well, but I knew it was time to shift. The first step was faith and trust that something greater is at work, like a cosmic power or our higher self, and the magical outcomes of aligning to who I truly was meant to be.

Rewind from this scene to a few years back, I was checking my email and noticed one with a subject line that read *3 Lies and 1 Life-changing Truth* from my coaching friend. It immediately grabbed my attention, and I opened a video she attached.

"We're all taught to work hard to be successful, but only a small percent of us are naturally wired to do this. The others are trying to adapt, except that we're trying to act like someone we're not naturally built like," explained her video. The hairs on my arm stood up, and I immediately knew I had to learn more.

I grew up in the 1970s-80s (technically, Generation X) in a family whose background was Eastern European. My ancestors believed in working hard and that to achieve success, you had to work even harder. This doctrine has been passed down through many generations in my family—and perhaps yours too.

At an early age, I entered the 'work force,' first pulling a wagon door-to-door to sell veggies from our garden, then visiting the neighbors who wanted to buy wrapping paper and cards out of a catalog so I could earn my first boom box (a little pink AM/FM radio and cassette player which I have to this day). In my teenage years, I had not one, but two paper routes and proudly earned the prestigious title of Papergirl of the Month. Working hard was in my blood.

My life was destined to follow the typical American dream formula: Go to school, get a job, work hard until you retire. So after graduating high school, I entered a four-year college, completed several internships while studying, received my bachelor's degree, created a robust resume, and found my first 'dream' job. Life was on track.

In 2000, I got married, and soon after, settled into our first house as well as a new job with my new last name. For fun (or perhaps because 9-to-5 employment wasn't enough), I also started a side gig teaching fitness at the local YMCA. That same year, I took my first yoga class and discovered a new spiritual journey (different than my traditional church upbringing). You could say I was hooked on the mind-body-spirit experience. Within a few years, I was studying and teaching yoga exclusively while still climbing a career ladder with my full-time job.

As years went on, my spiritual interests evolved as did my personal and professional growth. In addition to other side gigs for income, I explored things like essential oils, reiki energy, Ayurveda and nutrition, astrology, and other non-Western, holistic modalities. Perhaps my mother's background in nursing influenced my initial interest in health and wellness, and my passion was growing.

A few years prior to 2020 (a pandemic year that none of us will forget), I faced some personal crises, but I was able to use tools that I acquired on my journey to help me transcend these challenging times. I can claim now, looking back, that I certainly grew in mind, body, and spirit, and perhaps can say, even thrived.

One tool that helped me greatly was Human Design, which I discovered during a year-long coaching program with a mentor of mine (remember that video I mentioned?). I learned that I had a unique energetic blueprint based on my birth, that in a sense, was my natural programming. It was a life-changing concept for me and opened my awareness up to understanding that I also had a lifetime of conditioning and unnatural programming that perhaps didn't always benefit me or my energy. Human Design also connected me more deeply to my inner wisdom to help me make decisions for my particular design and navigate life in a whole new way.

I came to realize that my previous work ethic trapped me on the hamster wheel with limiting beliefs and self-doubts (and not always my own) swirling through my brain. I had been under the impression that the harder I worked, the more satisfied and successful I would feel, and that eventually I'd receive and feel more love and appreciation. But the truth was, something was out of alignment for me. I wasn't living as my true design.

I eventually realized I didn't have to work so hard to create my success (even as a Generator, one of the Human Design types) and I learned how to Stop Overworking and Start Overflowing!

I applied this knowledge to my daily life choices and activities, experimenting with what is called "living your design." The profound changes not only positively impacted the success in my career (particularly the new solopreneur business that I started last year), but also positively affected my mindset, relationships, wellness, and abundance both financial and non-monetary.

Since learning about Human Design, I've been on a mission to help others learn about their energetic blueprints and how to live in their design, and I'm excited that the opportunity for publishing this book came to me. I hope to help others get off their hamster wheels, overcome their conditioned programming, self-doubt, and limiting beliefs, and instead see and embrace their uniqueness, potential, and true life purpose.

I'm so glad you're here, and that this book was birthed to share the Human Design system with you!

ALIGNED BY DESIGN

To give you a short background about Human Design, in case this is your first time reading about this topic, the system was "revealed" in the 1980s. It brings together ancient and modern sciences like the Hindu Chakras, the Chinese I Ching, and the Jewish Kabbalah and astrology, which have all been around for thousands of years across many different cultures.

The founder, Alan Robert Krakower (known as Ra Uru Hu), channeled the information when he was on vacation, and shared the data and lessons before he passed away. You can find them through his organization, Jovian Archive at www.jovianarchive.com. Ra's teachings are considered a self-help/ self-discovery method or "navigation tool" without any religious component.

Maybe you have taken personality or communication tests like Myers-Briggs, DISC or the Enneagram. Or perhaps you've studied astrology, or various other human dynamic interpretations. Consider the Human Design system as another tool to understand yourself, but it runs much deeper than other assessments. It shows your unique energetic blueprint based on your birth day, time and location. And I have heard there are approximately two billion combinations!

Human Design is like a rabbit hole, and this book may be your first peek inside. You can find lots of resources on the Internet to discover and explore this complex system. I always recommend you start with a guide to help you understand your chart. This can be helpful at any stage. These authors are just a few of the many practitioners who teach in the space of this rabbit hole.

Some helpful phrases you may hear:

Type - This is the first "layer" of Human Design. I think of it as the car manufacturer or model. We fit into one of five design types, but yet we are further unique when you look at the interior of the car and what lies under the hood. We don't look the same on the outside, so we don't on the inside either! The five types are: Generator, Manifesting Generator, Manifestor, Projector, and Reflector.

Strategy - This is the guiding principle to help each type be most aligned with their uniqueness. The strategy for the majority of the types (three out of five, or approximately 90% of the population) is either to wait for an invitation or respond to an opportunity, which is very different than the "just do it" programming that we all are taught to do. In my analogy, think of this as proper maintenance and gasoline to help your car run most efficiently and effectively.

Authority - This is the decision-making process that is unique to each individual, sometimes based on type. Human Design teaches that your authority resides in your body, perhaps in your gut or emotions, not in your mind as most of us are conditioned to think. In my analogy, think of this as the map to help you pinpoint and get to a destination, like a GPS that provides guidance and navigation for your life.

Understanding your Human Design, as well as the design of others, can help you with many aspects of life, like improving relationships, shifting your mindset, creating better wellness, or bringing you more abundance both in your personal life and career/business, and generally providing you with more awareness, acceptance, and alignment with how you were born and who you are meant to be.

In this book, you will find a variety of authors who have studied with various teachers. I liken it to learning yoga. Someone (or group), somewhere, at some point in time, developed the system and passed it down through different lineages, through which the students basically learn similar information. Here you will find teachings in different styles. I teach the foundations of Human Design and your basic blueprint, for example, versus another practitioner who is gifted with revealing your deep soul purpose, or others who use the system to coach parents, provide business consulting, or even guide financial decision-making.

We all have a common mission here: to share this amazing information that literally has transformed our lives and help others learn how Human

Design can be used as a tool for transformation, evolution, manifestation, and so much more. In these chapters, you'll find personal stories of each author as well as a technique that can help you on your journey to being your unique self.

Enjoy reading this book, whether cover to cover, or just by flipping to a random chapter. May you find a story that resonates with you, an author that inspires you, and information that motivates you to be your unique self, embrace others as different, and yet know that we are all on the same journey to live our best lives!

With gratitude and love,

Kristi

CHAPTER 1

HOW TO BE IN A 'JUST DO IT' WORLD

RECOVER FROM BURNOUT AND IGNITE YOUR LIFE

Linda Landon, PCC, Human Design Specialist
& Ignite Your Joy Coach

MY STORY

Have you ever felt like you're absolutely spent - like you can't and don't want to ever get up again? There's nothing seriously physically wrong with you, and yet, everything feels terribly wrong?

That was me 15 years ago.

I was on my hands and knees, and I couldn't get up. The truth is, I didn't want to get up. I was sick and tired of being sick and tired and felt like all I wanted to do was lie down and die.

This is what burnout feels like. Not only is it a physical state of collapse, but it's also accompanied by depression, a feeling of hopelessness, and a sense of being utterly lost. Then you worry that there's something terribly wrong with you and that you'll never get better. Which, of course, makes you feel worse.

I felt absolutely hopeless, alone, and lost. I had just purchased a beautiful condo close to the ocean in Los Angeles and committed to making a life for myself in Southern California. The thing is, this sprawling metropolis was the last place on the planet I had ever wanted to live, and now here I was. I had no idea where I belonged but figured that I might as well put down some roots since I was here. In a very competitive market, I looked at dozens of homes and managed to find a condo that felt like an oasis in a harsh and arid city.

Now don't get me wrong. I had a decent life in LA: Rewarding work as a Recovery Coach, a few friends scattered around this vast city, and many professional colleagues. But I was lonely and so so tired all the time. And I kept getting sick.

So I did what a misguided Projector does – I got up off the floor and went to work. Even though my body was screaming at me to rest, I turned on my computer, worked on some marketing materials, met with clients, set up some meetings, and then again, collapsed.

Fortunately, I managed to find a great naturopath who got me back on track physically, and reconnected with my former spiritual coach and mentor, Robin Winn, who, along with a spiritual community, taught me how to start filling myself up from the inside out.

Over the next few years, I crawled back to health and regained the ability to function well enough to keep going. It even looked like I was getting better. I immersed myself deeply in spiritual practice, learning how to fill my whole being with essence; I embarked on an incredible journey of sexual exploration that opened up my capacity to experience full body orgasm, I toured the country teaching a process called The Release Technique, and I expanded my coaching business to include sexual healing for couples.

Yet, I still felt like I was pushing against some invisible wall. Whenever my business started to increase in revenues, clients would leave, or worse, I'd get sick with a cold or flu or some random infection. Then I'd have to rest, and my income would plummet.

Though I was experiencing more sexual pleasure than I imagined was possible, I couldn't seem to attract a partner who was really into me. I honestly felt like Sisyphus, condemned for eternity to push a boulder up a hill, only to have it roll back down again.

The operative word here was *push*. I didn't know how to not push or pressure myself. I followed the guidelines of all the best marketing gurus, yet I felt like something was seriously wrong with me. While my colleagues were surging ahead with seemingly boundless energy—filling classes, making time for family and friends, and cramming one more thing into an already busy schedule—I just wanted to lie down and plan my next vacation. I can't tell you how many fabulous workshops I promoted that never launched. It's embarrassing to admit even now.

I was beginning to wonder if I wasn't cut out to be an entrepreneur. Yet, the thought of re-entering the workplace and working for someone else felt like death. My life was at a serious crossroads.

Then a miracle occurred: My coach invited me to check out Human Design, and my whole life changed.

I was shocked to learn that I am a Projector, and Projectors need to *wait* to be recognized and invited. Projectors are here to guide others to do the heavy lifting when they are invited! We are not meant to initiate, and we are not designed to go, go, go and *just do it*. We are designed to *be* wise guides and leaders of those who have the sustainable energy to build and do. That was my first 'wow.'

Then I learned that all but two of my centers are open. This really blew my mind.

In the world of Human Design, energy centers govern how we think, feel, love, and interact with others, in short – how we navigate the world. Some centers, which are called *defined*, provide us with consistent energy that originates from within us and radiates outwards. Centers that are *undefined* are completely different. In these centers, we receive energy from those around us.

Having so many open centers meant that I am an empath – one of those highly sensitive people who is strongly affected by other's feelings, emotions, and thoughts! I learned that those of us with many open centers not only feel, but without awareness and proper skills, *absorb* energy from people close to us, a stranger across the room, our city, and our whole world!

Living in a densely populated city like Los Angeles can be exhausting for an empath, and especially a Projector. No wonder I felt trapped, beaten down, and unable to find my way out.

Finally, my life started to make sense. I began to review my past and discovered that the few opportunities that had worked out came through invitations.

For example:

When I was 19, I was invited to work as a cook on Martha's Vineyard, and I had a magical summer. The following year I actively sought another job on the island as a cook, and it was hell.

My move from New York City to the Bay Area in California came from an invitation. I had ten glorious years there before I moved to Los Angeles.

It became clear that all my failed relationships were ones where I was the pursuer, yet it was hard to trust that someone would invite me in.

The biggest ah-ha was my business. When I was invited into a collaboration, it always worked out. Yet, most of the time, I was the solopreneur, pushing and pushing and getting nowhere. My friends used to say I worked harder on my business than anyone they knew. My profession became my main relationship, and it was not a happy one.

My mantra was, "push through until you meet your goal, and then you can rest." I had it all backward. It seemed the more I pushed to attract clients, the more I pushed them away.

As I began to unhook myself from old patterns and surrender into my Projector-ness, my life transformed. I mean, *it really transformed.* Trust me, I kicked and screamed along the way, but I was burned out and desperate enough to give it a try. So my new mantra became, "rest, play, and then, work."

I stopped working on my business and instead started working on myself. Mornings became dedicated to self-love: Instead of getting on the computer as soon as I woke up, I would luxuriate in bed and self-pleasure, then get up and meditate, take a walk or go to a yoga class, and have breakfast. After I felt filled up, I'd see a few clients, meet with a colleague or friend, or go to a meeting, and then take a nap! Later, I might do a bit more *work*, but only if I felt like it.

I took classes in Human Design because I felt like it and became a Human Design specialist. Introducing my clients to Human Design transformed their lives and made my coaching much much more fun. I even wrote a book for my clients: *Ignite Your Vitality using Human Design.*

Want to receive a free copy of the book? Use this link:

http://igniteyourjoy.us/human-design-2/

I started to tune into how my body responds to pushing. It was incredible to track that fine line between what I call *intuitive action* and pushing. When I overrode that inner voice that said, *enough, it's time to stop* and did one more thing, my body would immediately respond with the old symptoms of tiredness, depression, and hopelessness. My body became my trusted teacher.

It wasn't easy to make this adjustment and undo over 40 years of old habits. And yet, my desire to heal helped me overcome my resistance to change, and gradually transformation happened.

Today, six years later, I live in a beautiful home on the side of a mountain in Western North Carolina, and I love my life. Surrendering to my Human Design made this possible. I live in a state of flow, and everything is so much easier.

Over the last few years, as I've stopped pushing and promoting, my business has doubled in income. This business sustained me as I remodeled and sold my condo in Los Angeles and drove cross country to Asheville, NC, during the pandemic.

I was invited to move to Asheville, and since I accepted that invitation, doors keep opening. A couple I met at the Asheville airport offered me their recently remodeled apartment as a place to live. I have more close friends here than I had in over 20 years in LA in less than one year. And I was able to purchase a magical home amid a very hot market because the sellers invited me to be their buyer. I'm completing a remodel in record time because excellent workers have been referred to me, and, as it turns out, Projectors make excellent general contractors!

At age 68 I am finally living my dream. The biggest miracle is that I'm as healthy, happy, and energized as that young woman 50 years ago on Martha's Vineyard. I am more resilient, capable, and clear-headed than I can ever remember and so much wiser. My life flows from moment to moment, and there is no push. I have learned to trust that joy is truly your birthright if you follow your strategy and allow the universe to support you.

Are you wondering, *how can I transform my life too?* Perhaps you're at a crossroads like I was. Do you want to give in to the story that you're too old, too tired, and it's too late to go for your dream? Or, are you willing to try something that may seem a little crazy and radical?

Here are the steps I have been taking, in no particular order, since I was introduced to Human Design. At first, I had no idea what I was doing. All I knew was that I had to save my life.

I invite you to try some of these tools out – and unleash the brilliant and joyful light you are designed to be.

THE TOOL

DO WHAT YOU LOVE TO DO FIRST

Make self-care and self-love your top priority. This gives you the energy to engage in what our 'just do it' culture considers essential (like work). In other words, make what you used to consider unessential or luxurious essential.

No matter what, my mornings are dedicated to me: I wake up without an alarm, practice yoga, go for a walk or hike, eat and meditate. Only when I feel filled up, do I venture into the world of doing.

GET HUMBLE AND ASK FOR HELP

Projectors need people! The worst thing a Projector can do is try to find solutions on their own. Alone with myself, listening to my thoughts spinning around and around in my head is futile and a living hell. We need people to guide and direct us–and to know ourselves!

Most Projectors need to speak their thoughts out loud with someone who can listen without offering advice. Then they get clear and know exactly what to do.

ASK GENERATORS TO DO THE HEAVY LIFTING

Ask someone to clean your house and help with the kids, even if you're a part-time mom or dad. As a business owner, one of the best decisions I ever made was to hire a Generator to rebuild my website and handle my marketing. Maybe your neighbor might like to mow your lawn! Barter if you don't have the financial resources. You have plenty to offer in return for another's assistance.

SPEND TIME IN NATURE

Walking and hiking or just laying in the grass looking up at the trees is a lifesaver. Gaia can absorb and digest all the excess energy Projectors take in through their open centers. I've already taken two breaks in my writing today to lie on my back and look up at the clouds.

PAUSE AND WAIT BEFORE YOU TAKE ACTION, EVEN IF YOU'VE BEEN INVITED

This is a big one. The more open centers we have, the more it's likely that we have been *conditioned*, meaning, propelled to do things that are not in alignment with our true nature.

Conditioning is a complex and interwoven web of patterned behaviors we adopted in the past (and sometimes in the present) to keep us safe in an environment that didn't recognize and support our true nature. An unsupportive environment wasn't necessarily anyone's fault, and conditioning was a brilliant strategy we used to survive.

Unfortunately, these patterns got wired into our neural pathways. We keep on repeating them, believing that they are still who we are. In truth, these conditioned patterns prevent us from *being* our beautiful Projector selves.

Taking time to pause, be mindful, and check to see if you're following your Human Design strategy, as well as getting support from a trusted listener, can help you unwind these old patterns and align with your true self.

STOP PUSHING

This is probably the biggest lesson for me. If you're a Projector, it's crucial that you wait for an invitation before you *do* anything, especially something major. Invitations can come in all kinds of interesting ways, including a calendar reminder!

When you've received an invitation, ask your inner wisdom if it's the right invitation for you and if it's the right time to take action or not. As I have the Gate of Love for the Body in my Earth, my body is my wise guide. It always tells me when I'm about to cross the subtle line between doing something because it feels good and doing it because I *should*.

FIND A WAY TO DEEPLY LISTEN TO YOURSELF

Discover your way. For me, as I have the Gate of Stillness, and the Gate of Love for the Body in my Incarnation Cross, spiritual practice is key, as well as plenty of fresh air and exercise. What is your way to really tune in and hear yourself?

KNOW WHEN TO KEEP YOUR MOUTH SHUT!

I can't tell you how invisible I used to feel in group settings. If I was chatty or offered my suggestions, people would either not hear me, call me bossy, or worse, adapt my suggestion as their own and ignore me.

Here's what I suggest you try out: When you're with a group of people, *listen* and don't talk about yourself. Be open and curious about the others; draw them out. When, and only when they ask about you, feel free to open up and be your lovely chatty Projector self.

REST, PLAY, AND THEN...WORK

This is the new mantra for my life. What might happen if you start allowing yourself to enjoy your life? Spend more time in bed, playing alone or with your lover, take long walks without your phone, lie on your back and watch the clouds pass by.

Rest is much much more than sleeping, though Projectors do need plenty of sleep to discharge other's energy and replenish. It's whatever makes you feel good!

Once you feel filled up, then do some work, which, if you're doing what is correct for you – guiding and directing others – can be a total pleasure.

Linda Landon, PCC, is an International Coach Federation certified business and life coach, trained recovery coach, certified Human Design Specialist, Deep Coaching facilitator, Somatic practitioner, and experienced seminar leader. She is the author of *The Power of Pause: simple meditations for complicated lives* and *Ignite Your Vitality using Human Design*. She is also the creator of the Wellness Sexuality Practice for individuals and couples.

Go to this link to receive your free copy of Linda's book:

http://igniteyourjoy.us/human-design-2/

A life-long entrepreneur and president of Linda Landon and Associates, LLC, Linda is passionate about guiding people to maximize their vitality and wellness, especially as they grow older. Her clients learn how to alchemize their particular life challenges into pure love, brilliance, and success beyond anything they have imagined.

She has trained with dozens of master teachers and teachings, including Rosen Method Bodywork, Somatic Therapy, the Release Technique, Don Miguel Ruiz's The Four Agreements, the Work of Byron Katie, Enneagram-based Coaching, and the Diamond Logos. She has traveled around the country teaching the Release Technique, presented to audiences of up to 500 people, and worked with hundreds of clients worldwide. For the last six years, she's studied Human Design with Karen Curry Parker and is now a certified Human Design Level 4 Specialist.

Linda has synthesized her mindfulness-based trainings and life experience to create a powerful and effective approach that is unprecedented, transformative, and overflowing with love. To learn more about Ignite Your Joy, please visit her website: http://igniteyourjoy.us

In 2020, during the Covid pandemic, Linda followed her heart and moved to Asheville, NC. She now lives on a hillside overlooking the Blue Ridge Mountains and is practicing her new mantra as a Projector—Rest, play, and then work. One of her many pleasurable pastimes is expressive painting.

Would you like to learn all about your Human Design chart? Receive a free copy of Linda's latest book, *Ignite Your Vitality using Human Design*.

http://igniteyourjoy.us/human-design-2/

CHAPTER 2

SHOWING UP IN OUR GIFTS

(RE)DEFINING WHAT IT MEANS TO BE IN RELATIONSHIP WITH GOD

Christa Timil Keyes-Venson

MY STORY

Human Design changed my life, and since you've taken the time to read this book, you've probably come across more than a few stories that share this sentiment. And yet it's true; Human Design has changed my life by permitting me to be myself, by showing me the value of being myself and embracing my innate gifts. Gaining permission and recognizing the value I bring may seem like weird concepts, but with parents, family, friends, teachers, media, and society telling us who we should be, it is very easy to forget who we are and chase who we've been told we need to be.

In my case, permission to be myself brought me back home to God. It gave me a framework to see who God really is and who I get to be in Him. It has helped me show up more fully in my gifts and build a healthy, productive relationship with God.

When I first learned about Human Design, it didn't stick. I couldn't make peace with what I read. *A channeled voice? Chakras? Astrology?* Much of it didn't sit right with me. It sounded too mystical to me. Don't get me wrong, I'm all about the woo woo being a Christian, but it needed to be filtered through what I already knew about God.

I grew up in a very religious and strict household and was taught astrology, among other things, was demonic. Astrology, fortune-telling, and the likes were "playing with the devil" because "your future is in God" and "you're welcoming in demons." At that point in my life, I was too scared to question anything I was taught growing up. I just existed at the edge of the knowledge I was taught, trusting my future was indeed "in God" but not truly knowing what that meant.

As an adult, I still believed in God, but I was less active in the church because I had a skewed perception of who God was. I kept thinking; *When I get my act together, I'll come back to God. When I'm doing all the right things, then I'll be ready.* I thought God wanted my perfection. And looking back, that couldn't be further from the truth.

So back to Human Design. I'd heard of it but was weary because I thought it was going against God. However, when I encountered it again a few years later, it was different. When I was exposed to it this time, it was being applied in a business context and didn't seem so mystical, and let's keep it real, spiritually questionable.

So, I decided to give it another chance. I got a reading, pulled my chart, and Googled every possible thing I could. *Oh my goodness! This is wild.* There were so many descriptions of how I thought, even private things that I never shared. *How did it know!?* It seemed too accurate to be a fluke. And too helpful to be wrong. But I wasn't convinced yet. I was still uneasy. *What about what I was taught in church? I know God is real but what if they weren't teaching me right!?* The thought of being misled was uncomfortable. *How would I know what the truth was? How would I know where the line was? How would I know what to trust?* So I decided to take the only action I could. I had to talk to God about it and see what He had to say.

I researched all the scriptures I could about using the stars, divination, design, and the gifts God gives us. Above all of them, there was one that stood out to me:

> *For we are His workmanship [His own master work, a work of art], created in Christ Jesus [reborn from above—spiritually transformed, renewed, ready to be used] for good works, which God prepared [for*

us] beforehand [taking paths which He set], so that we would walk in them [living the good life which He prearranged and made ready for us].

Ephesians 2:10 AMP

OMG! God intentionally designed us. We are His art. He designed us in a specific way for a specific purpose. He's given us gifts to use and a path to take.

This revelation ushered in a new perception of who God was and who I get to be in Him. It highlighted that 1) I did have a path that was specifically created for me, and 2) I was intentionally crafted to handle whatever was on this path.

But that still left me with my need to perfect. *If God intentionally designed me, why can't I get it right?* I wanted to do all things God instructed me to do. I wanted to be perfect, so He could accept me. I thought that once I had it together, then I could be in relationship with God. But I happened upon another scripture:

Concerning this, I pleaded with the Lord three times that it would leave me. But he said to me, "My grace is sufficient for you, for my power is perfected in weakness." Therefore, I will most gladly boast all the more about my weaknesses so that Christ's power may reside in me. So I take pleasure in weaknesses, insults, hardships, persecutions, and in difficulties, for the sake of Christ. For when I am weak, then I am strong.

2 Corinthians 12:8-10 CSB

I got this whole thing wrong. God doesn't need me to be perfect. He's the perfect one. He gives me grace because He knows I have weaknesses. When I surrender to Him, He takes my shortcomings and transforms them.

My mind was seriously blown. I know now that God's guidance, His word, His commandments aren't arbitrary. He's not trying to rain on our parade and keep us from having fun. But rather, He's trying to expand us. He's trying to show us the very best way to live so that we can continually be expanded into new levels of peace, joy, and love. Sins are sins because they disrupt our relationship with God. Some things always disrupt our relationship with God (i.e., blasphemy), while other things are dependent upon the context (i.e., sex). I believe astrology and, by extension, Human

Design is in the latter category. It's a tool that can be used in combination with our faith, or it can be used in place of our faith. As a Christian, it comes down to prioritizing our relationship with God over anything.

In learning Human Design, I began to come into a different understanding of who I get to be in God. All of my flaws, shortcomings, weaknesses, all the things I thought I needed to fix before coming to God were the very gifts God had given me. They were the things God wanted us to work on *together*. He wanted to show me how to use my gifts.

All the time I spent looking to others for who I needed to be and how I could "get it right" was time spent running from God and the intended use of my gifts. For a long time, I was self-obsessed. I was hyper-focused on who I was being and judging myself for who I wasn't. And as it turns out, that ability to see me—my skills, talents, faults, and way of being—so distinctly from those around me and recognizing how I could be better was the exact superpower God gave me. As I said, I just didn't know how to use it.

Through Human Design, I learned the gifts of each gate are neutral. That how it's expressed is dependent on me and not the gift itself. It's like when a superhero first starts learning about their powers, they mess a lot of things up and even accidentally hurt people sometimes. They don't fully understand the responsibility of the gift, and they don't know how to control it. They let their emotions, namely fear, get the best of them. It's no different with the gifts God gives us.

Realizing the gifts God gives us are neutral, and it's really about how we use the gift, gave me a sense of agency. It allowed me to do the work of unlearning who the world told me I needed to be and embrace who God designed me to be by showing up in my gifts. And when I started showing up in my gifts, it helped me recognize that the way God talks to me and through me is unique to me. My relationship with God is my own.

Remember how during this whole process, I was hypercritical of myself? That is me operating my gifts in a spirit of fear. My unconscious sun gate is 18, The Gate of Correction. And my conscious sun gate is 10, The Gate of Behavior of The Self. In low vibe (aka fear-consciousness), I'm afraid of not behaving the way I'm supposed to and being unable to make the corrections that can help me improve. *The very thing I've stressed my whole life about.* But in high vibe (aka love-consciousness), it's about knowing and appreciating that God has intentionally designed me and the path I'm on to continually expand me in each new level I grow into.

When I started to shift my perspective into love-consciousness, I opened the door to a relationship with God. I allowed Him to come in and change me and show me a different way of being. Being in relationship with God teaches me a different, better, loving way to show up in my gifts.

> *And we have come to know and to believe the love that God has for us. God is love, and the one who remains in love remains in God, and God remains in him.*
>
> 1 John 4:16 CSB

THE TOOL

Being new to Human Design, you may have yet to experience the magic of permission to be yourself it provides, but I want to prepare you for it. And if you have, this exercise I'm about to share is a wonderful opportunity to anchor into the remembrance of your greatness. To get the most out of this exercise, I want you to grab pen and paper (or the notes section of your phone works too). Writing it out can help us to better articulate our feelings, emotions, and opinions.

First, I want you to identify and write down a personal struggle you often have with yourself. This personal struggle is something you may keep beating yourself up about; it keeps playing over and over in your mind. It's something you wish you could be better about or maybe even completely change. For me, this is when the shame, fear, and anxiety of *not being good enough* start to overtake me. For you, it could be the inability to resist peer pressure, resentment towards boundaries, being crossed, fear of not knowing enough, or being unprepared. Whatever this personal struggle is for you, it takes you out of your power and causes you to doubt yourself.

Once we have this struggle identified, I want you to think about and write out the narrative that plays in your head when it comes up. When I fail to accomplish what I set out to do, my personal struggle gets triggered: *I should have done more. I'll never get to where I need to be if I don't step it up. I need to be more focused. But I don't know how to. I don't know if I'll ever figure it out. What if I never live up to my potential? I'm such a screw-up. I should have known better. Everyone will be so disappointed.*

The stories in our heads feel real. How we are talking to ourselves and what we are saying feels like the truth. Our view of our effort and potential outcomes feel reliable and accurate. But they aren't. These narratives are our mind's attempts to make sense of what we are experiencing. They are defense mechanisms that are trying to protect us but are built on faulty logic. They are based on the assumption that you are alone and powerless.

Once you write out the narrative of your personal struggle, I want you to pick one sentence that speaks the loudest and circle it and write an affirmation that counters it. 'What if I never live up to my potential?' screams the loudest to me, so I circle it and write the following: *I am ever-expanding into my full potential.*

When writing your affirmation, it is helpful to structure it as an "I am" statement and keep it brief. For this exercise to be the most effective, we want to clearly and easily identify and speak into who we get to be. Having too wide a focus or weighing it down by too many details is counter-productive and takes us out of our power.

I invite you to take your newly created affirmation into prayer. You can use the structure I provide below to get you started, or feel free to speak from your heart.

Dear God,

I thank you for designing me with unique gifts and a path all my own. I invite you into my life and thank you for showing me how to effectively use my gifts. Help me to live into my affirmation and deeply resonate with the fact that I am (insert affirmation). I know when I feel weak, I know that your grace covers me and that showing up in a spirit of love will help me release the negative narrative I tell myself and propel me forward in my purpose, to a state of abundance and overflow. In Jesus' name, I pray.

Amen.

We've taken three amazing steps towards showing up in our gifts. We've identified the narrative, highlighted a new way of being, and surrendered to God. Any time you're triggered, I challenge you to return to this process and repeat your affirmation until you start to feel better and push the negative narrative out of your mind.

As a next step, you can use Human Design to start identifying your gifts and how they can be used to breathe life into the affirmation you've created here. Learning about and nurturing your gifts is one of the best ways I've found to be in relationship with God. You are intentionally designed for a unique purpose, and God just wants the opportunity to guide you through it.

To help you in this process, you can grab a free copy of my Purpose Starter Guide that shares more about what it means to show up in your gifts and offers a simple activity to introduce you to your gifts.

https://view.flodesk.com/pages/5fda5d6b432f5b89be33521e

Christa Keyes is a Human Design Educator who pairs her experience as a teacher, therapist, brand strategist, and designer with her love for Jesus to be an advocate for soul-centered leaders. She teaches how to recognize and refine your gifts pairing Human Design and Biblical principles so you can show up as an embodied leader in your field. Her practical, down-to-earth, yet inspiring teaching style is a hallmark of her personal philosophy of meeting people with love where they are to help them get to their next level of purpose. She's an avid DIYer and loves to bring life to all she touches, no matter if it's a DIY project, family, friends, or clients. You can find her sharing her journey on IG @human.designed.by.god

CHAPTER 3

TURN DREAMS INTO SUCCESSES

HUMAN DESIGN AND BIOFIELD TUNING FOR YOUR BUSINESS

Sandra Lee, BS, LMT

I never do anything right. I'm always wrong.

I'm only six years old, but already I feel trapped in playing an endless mental loop tape. Today was miserable. I compress the air back in my chest to keep a flood of tears from bursting out. Sitting on the floor of my room, I make crooked angry pencil marks on the half-filled page of a little spiral notebook. Each tally mark adds to the evidence of my failures.

Everything I say is wrong too. I promise myself; *I'm never going to speak again.* Of course, I always fail utterly in that oath.

My entire life, I have gotten angry about big things and meaningless things. Anger was triggered with ridiculous frequency.

When I was eleven, my mother said, "Everyone in the family avoids asking you to do things because you always get angry." From then on, I believed *I'm bad, and I hurt people.*

'Anger' equated with 'bad,' and both applied to me. *There is something wrong with me. I shouldn't be angry. When I am angry, I should be able to turn it off.*

MY STORY

I met Karen Parker in a teleseminar about Human Design. She wasn't talking to me personally, yet she revolutionized my world.

In the Human Design system of personality types, I am a Manifestor. Karen explained that Manifestors frequently experience anger. It's normal for Manifestors to feel angry, and there is nothing wrong with that. My ears perked up; *what did she say? It's okay to be angry?*

I purchased Karen's practitioner training. The next day, I inhaled the entire first-level class, learning about the five types.

I learned about being a Manifestor, and in one day, I had a new life. I had flipped from despising myself for having uncontrollable anger to being peaceful about this anger.

When I start running endless self-critical loop tapes, what I learned about being a Manifestor gives me a new pathway out of the trap.

There is nothing wrong with me or with this anger. I didn't do anything wrong. No one else did anything wrong. I can't turn the anger off, and I can't prevent it. I can learn how to manage anger and choose to be peaceful about it.

This is a miraculous gift. *Whenever I am judging myself, I can choose to be peaceful.*

Understanding anger was my first Human Design transformation.

Awareness of the Conscious Sun was my second life-altering lesson. Where the sun was at the time I was born represents what I do in all areas of life. In my chart, the sun sits in the Gate 26.

The Gate 26 is energy for truth and integrity and the absence of truth and integrity. Learning this was another *of-course-that's-me* moment. I always seek to make things better, to increase the truth and integrity. However, there's a flip side. I'm a perfectionist, forever noticing where things are 'wrong' or lacking in integrity, then striving to fix them.

BIOFIELD TUNING

Seven years into my Human Design journey, I learned biofield tuning. Using tuning forks and sound, I focus healing intention on the energy field or aura. The sound shows me where energy is blocked, so I can help reestablish the natural flow.

In thirty years as a licensed massage therapist, I learned many energy healing modalities. Yet, I wasn't using those techniques because they weren't giving the physical changes I expected.

When asked about my intuitively guided bodywork, this is what I say. "People's bodies talk to me, asking for what they need." When I get stuck energy moving, my clients feel and function better.

In 2019, I was introduced to biofield tuning. It was like turning on a whole new light switch. Tuning fork sounds lit a pathway that gave me access to significantly more accurate intuitive information for my clients. *This all feels so right. It is divinely guided.*

Sound is the most foundational and powerful creative force. Doing biofield tuning, I shape energy with sound and intention. From this place of power, anything can be created.

From the perspective of the Gate 26, doing bodywork and biofield tuning together increases the health and well-being of my clients. Their biofields show me where energy is blocked, and integrity is needed.

Energy movement in the biofield is context-dependent. When my client is happy and inspired by their work, their energy flows smoothly. They can think clearly, make wise decisions, and take effective action. They are cruising, and truth and integrity are high. Business is thriving.

I call this state "being in the flow."

When my client is upset, afraid, or stuck, their energy is chaotic. Thinking is confused. Decision-making is difficult. Actions are more likely to go sideways. The flow is blocked, as are truth and integrity: my client's health, relationships, happiness, and business struggle.

Every single thought or feeling controls the energetic system. I see this with every person.

One day, I learned a lesson about energetic shutdowns. It fascinates me because I simultaneously experienced this from two perspectives. In one, I'm all in, emotionally and physically. In the other, I'm calmly and objectively observing myself and my reactions. Until this happened, I'd never witnessed a panic attack, much less experienced one.

A large credit card bill is due, thanks to some sizable business purchases. Aware that the money isn't in my checking account, I open the statement. *Freak out!* My pulse is racing, my breathing is rapid and shallow, and I'm sweating. It's intense.

I transfer money and pay the bill. Unaware that the danger is over, my body continues racing as if a bear is chasing me. *I am still panicking! Breathe. It's time to rescue myself with biofield tuning.*

I strike a tuning fork and bring it into my aura. The sound hits a steel wall. My entire energy field is contracted, and the chakras are slammed shut. I am ungrounded and energetically disconnected from the earth. *Wild. I've never seen this before.*

I tune myself for several minutes and return to feeling calm and balanced. My energetic system is grounded, and the chakras are flowing. *That state of emergency is over. Breathe. What an experience!*

Breathe. My dear reader, after that story, you may benefit from a nice, deep breath. My heart races just reading it.

I saw how powerfully thoughts and emotions affect not just my energy field but everyone's. Fortunately, complete shutdowns like this are rare.

In today's fast-paced business world, most people are accustomed to 'normal' levels of stuck energy. Persistent stress has become a norm that is worn like a badge of honor. Unfortunately, consistently stagnant energy leads to muscle tension and pain and eventually to declining health.

I love how biofield tuning and sound restore the integrity of the energy field, reestablishing energy flow. The most immediate response is relief from stress and overwhelm. My clients feel calm, centered, and balanced. They have increased mental clarity and ease in making decisions. They reevaluate negative beliefs and make empowered choices.

For decades I searched for an energy healing modality that would produce obvious physical results. *Finally, I found it!* Biofield tuning restores integrity to the energy field and the body. Sometimes this produces obvious physical changes. This happens whether my client is in my office or seeing me online from across the globe. Everything is energy, and we are all connected!

One day, I was working with a client on Zoom. After fifteen minutes of biofield tuning, I say, "Move your ankle. Can you stand on it?"

"Yes! And my shoe is too big now!" She sounds shocked. The circulation has increased, and her foot is less inflamed and painful.

When these seemingly miraculous things happen, I used to feel stunned. Having this kind of physical impact now feels 'normal.' I love that kind of normal! Making things more 'perfect' through the integrity of the Gate 26 is truly a gift.

HUMAN DESIGN AND BIOFIELD TUNING

While doing biofield tuning one day, I saw the Human Design chart overlaid on the biofield. A lightbulb came on. *Let's do Human Design and biofield tuning together!*

Just like charts and readings support individuals in being happy and successful, Human Design offers tremendous insights for businesses. Each business has its own unique and powerful design, and can be successful or not, in integrity or not.

I love combining Human Design and biofield tuning for a business. The chart describes its gifts, challenges, and purpose. Understanding its purpose enables a business to be more intentional in how it contributes to the world. Biofield tuning brings integrity to the energetic alignment, and the business more effectively attracts those they are designed to serve.

The Gate 26 is one of the energies associated with sales in the chart, spreading truth and integrity to the world through business. I facilitate this with Human Design and sound.

TURN DREAMS INTO SUCCESSES

My friend Vena's story illustrates the benefits of using Human Design and biofield tuning for small businesses.

Putting her personal chart on the table, I ask Vena, "What do you want for your life?"

"I've always wanted to run my own school of aesthetics."

"You've never told me about wanting a school!" I feel a deep, resonant knowing inside my heart space. It's like a tiny flame is waiting to be nourished. "Look at your chart, Vena. A school would be a perfect expression of your Human Design and your life purpose!"

"Well, I've been thinking about it more seriously lately."

Roll forward two years. We are sitting at Vena's school, The Academy of Aesthetic Arts.

"I have students, and they are happy. But I need more. My instructors count on me, and I have to pay them next week. Plus, rent is due. I'm stressed out and exhausted." Vena wonders, "Is keeping the school open worth the hassle and money?"

I respond, "Let's look at the school's Human Design chart."

Something unique about this school is its nurturing environment and personal touch. Vena's dream is to support students who struggle to succeed in large, impersonal schools.

"Vena, according to the school's chart, these are the perfect people for you to serve. You teach women how to build dream businesses and create freedom. This school and its purpose are perfect expressions of your purpose."

This was my first deep look at the chart for a business. It struck me that Human Design for businesses is as accurate as for individuals. *This works!*

I explain, "Understanding the purpose in your chart gives you language for talking about what you do. Aligning your awareness, marketing, and communications with the school's purpose powerfully attracts your ideal students."

This was just before the start of the government's 2020 coronavirus shutdown. The reading confirmed for Vena; *you're traveling the right path.* When business came to a standstill, holding that in mind encouraged her to keep going.

The timing was perfect. Women were at home with money available to invest in education and creating fulfilling businesses. When occupational training and salon services were approved to reopen, Vena was ready.

Biofield tuning smooths the flow of Vena's energy and the energy of the business, so she can release stress and stay balanced. Starting and expanding the school brought financial pressures and big decisions that felt risky and overwhelming. Biofield tuning clarifies Vena's priorities. We identify directions and aligned actions that are consistent with her goals and her purpose.

The Academy of Aesthetic Arts is thriving. Vena has enough students to support more comprehensive programs, providing her graduates with better skills and increased earning potential. Outgrowing their space, the school relocated to a larger site and is considering adding another location.

Vena drew upon insights provided by Human Design and energetic integrity from Biofield Tuning. Her dream of having a school of aesthetics has grown into a tremendous success.

BIOFIELD TUNING AND YOUR BUSINESS

Whether you are seeking to get your business thriving or things are already terrific, consider biofield tuning. Tuning fork sounds help find energetic blocks and then clear them, so energy and integrity flow through your business and life.

What happens when you stub your toe? Energy gets blocked in your foot and ankle, and you limp. Pain keeps you from walking properly, much less running.

Is your business limping? Where do you lack integrity? Do you have a stalled business project or a difficult situation? Are strained interpersonal relationships wreaking havoc?

Whenever things are not going smoothly, chaotic or stuck energies are holding you back.

With biofield tuning, you can get back to strolling.

Perhaps your business is already cruising and productive. Integrity and energy flow are strong. Your business is grounded, connected, and effective.

Is it time to stretch and provide even better service? What about expanding into new markets and offerings? When you start something new, there are barriers to overcome.

Biofield tuning can ease the way.

Look at my friend Vena Marie Villanueva. The Academy of Aesthetic Arts was already successful, and it was time to grow. Biofield tuning smoothed the way.

THE TOOL

ENERGY FLOW & AWARENESS

Apply this tool when you have something to accomplish; when things are not progressing, integrity is lacking, and energy is stuck. Reestablish the flow, and the bindings will fall away.

This tool draws on concepts from several modalities.

What you'll need: A notebook, pen, and quiet, undisturbed time.

You'll be grateful later that you took notes.

Think about your business, situation, project, or relationship.

Is the project's energy moving, or are you stuck? Does it feel like you're progressing? Is something out of integrity?

If things are not progressing smoothly, take these steps: NAB, QED, Visualize, IFS, Breathe, Breathe, Visualize, Gratitude. Make sure to take notes throughout.

1. (N) Notice. Notice that something is not going as intended. What is it?
2. (A) Ask, awareness. What do you need to know? What does your consciousness have to say? Is integrity missing? *This is incredibly valuable information. Take notes!*
3. (B) Body. Is there a body sensation or feeling? Is there tension, pain, or something else?
4. (Q) Qualities. Describe what the energy block looks and feels like. Does it have density, weight, color, temperature, texture, emotion? Movement or lack of movement?

5. (E) Energy. Everything is energy. Be aware that blocked energy can move.
6. (D) Desire, decide. Do you want this to shift?
7. Visualize. 'See' or 'feel' the blocked energy however you can in your mind's eye or body. If you don't think you 'see' it, then imagine that you see it.
8. (I) Intention. Set an intention to shift the energy block.
9. (F) Flow. Allow the energy to flow in whatever way that it wants to move.
10. (S) See the energy flowing away from the area.
11. Breathe the blocked energy away.
12. Breathe fresh, clean energy into the area, allowing energy and truth to flow.
13. Visualize. Visualize your intended outcome.
14. Gratitude. Notice what changed and what you learned. Give thanks.

Do this for yourself. Everything is energy, and your mind is a powerful instrument for manipulating it. You are adding truth and integrity to your business and your life.

I created a short biofield tuning audio for you to enjoy to experience its grounding abilities. You can find it and other useful tools at

https://miracleinspirations.com/book-resources

IN CONCLUSION

Thank you so much for engaging with my chapter. I hope it has been rewarding.

The combination of Human Design and biofield tuning can help you in numerous ways:

- Understand your purpose and the purpose of your business.
- Develop language for communication and marketing that is consistent with your purpose.
- Attract the people who value what you offer.

- Be in the flow, and be in the right place at the right time.
- Benefit both your well-being and your business.
- Either support your flow or block it with every thought. It's your choice!
- Let go of stress and overwhelm.
- Increase the truth and integrity in your life and your business.
- Be intentional and turn dreams into successes!

I look forward to the opportunity to help you fulfill your purpose and your big why.

I offer you a short complimentary consultation to see how working with me might benefit your business. See my book resources for this and other tools:

https://miracleinspirations.com/book-resources

Should you decide to experience Human Design and biofield tuning, tuning fork sounds and my intuitive insights will help you be clear and aligned with the integrity of your purpose.

May you Turn Dreams Into Successes!

Breathe.

Sandra Lee, BS, LMT, Human Design Specialist, Biofield Tuning Practitioner.

Sandra is the owner of Miracle Inspirations Inc. and a Human Design 3/5 Manifestor.

A massage therapist for nearly three decades, Sandra says, "People's bodies talk to me." Through Human Design and Biofield Tuning, she produces seemingly 'miraculous' results that surprise even her.

Sandra's healing journey began with a BS in chemistry from Caltech, a top science and engineering university. She helps clients visualize and understand the 'science' of their bodies.

Sandra loves supporting individuals and entrepreneurs like you in thriving through setting intentions for healing, integrity, and success. She helps you fulfill the purposes of your life and your business.

Sandra is a blogger and a best-selling contributing author to *Abundance By Design: Discover Your Unique Code for Health, Wealth, and Happiness with Human Design.*

Sandra lives in the beautiful Okanagan Valley of British Columbia, Canada, with her husband. She also visits friends and does bodywork in Olympia, Washington. She loves whole food cooking and intermittent fasting. Her daily food pictures posted on Facebook inspire her friends.

Want to turn your dreams into successes? You are invited to connect with Sandra at https://MiracleInspirations.com

Please visit my Book Resources for gifts.

https://miracleinspirations.com/book-resources

Request free Human Design charts for individuals or businesses. For the business birth date, use the filing date for licenses or incorporation documents.

Request a complimentary Discover What's Possible Consultation. Let's talk about your needs and how you might benefit from Human Design and Biofield Tuning.

Listen to a short Biofield Tuning Grounding audio.

And more…

Stay Tuned,

Breathe

Sandra

CHAPTER 4

THE SECRET TO MANIFESTING

STOP DOING AND START BEING

Catherine Rivers, CPC

MY STORY

"OMG, I am supposed to be different!" The moment I learned I was a Manifestor and my type is only 8% of the world's population; I was hooked. *Here I am, 54 years old, and I feel like I have been seen for the very first time. I have permission to be me; something was I never allowed growing up.*

At the time I was introduced to my design, I was clawing my way up from a state of total burnout. I'd left a 20-year, high-paying, high-stress job in the tech industry that was killing me. Where driving home from work was tortuous. With each drive home, I would feel my life force drain out of me. Like the air going out of a balloon, I would deflate. It was all I could do to crawl into the house and get myself to the couch. *If my colleagues saw me now, they would think I was the biggest loser/phony/sissy in the world.* This was my inner thought pattern night after night. Calling myself a loser, phony, or sissy were the mild terms. Imagine the others.

Work wasn't the only thing that had taken a toll. *I don't talk about it much; it happened so long ago now. I lost four babies. And then I lost my ability to conceive. Oh, the grief and the constant tears. And if that wasn't enough, my dream house flooded three times, and I was used as a scapegoat by my agency and publically humiliated.*

My personal life was one crisis after another. Yet, after every setback, my response was to aim bigger and try harder.

I can do this. I can fix this. I can prove myself.

And I did.

I moved from the public sector to the private sector and doubled my income. I sold the house that flooded and bought a better property. I gave up wanting to be a mom and realized my husband was not my best friend. We divorced. I found peace in horses and became a breeder. Those foals were my children, and I created a family of my own making.

I made this all happen, but it wasn't enough. I was still utterly exhausted.

I can't do this anymore. My life isn't working. I dread going into the office.

But it was through my high-tech job that I discovered my next career. "What are these letters on your business card? Certified Professional Coach?" As I listened to her talk about life coaching, I realized she described the part of my work I loved most but only got to do 5% of the time. In an instant, I knew. I kept telling everyone, "I am 50 years old, and I finally know what I want to be when I grow up!"

A friend of a friend introduced me to her ontologically based coaching program. *Ontology? What the heck is that? The study of being?*

I took a leap, made a huge investment in myself, and enrolled in a year-long program.

For me, that year of coach training was a deep dive into the nature of empowerment. The fundamentals of personal power. This is where I was first exposed to the philosophy of "being fueling doing."

I remember waking up one morning three months into this coaching program to a life-altering thought. *No one can give me the life I want except me. If I don't take a leap of faith, nothing will change.* When I went into my stress-filled tech job that morning, I gave notice.

Empowerment is an amazing study, yet an event in that coach training program was ultimately disempowering.

It was the second training weekend where we did an exercise getting to the heart of who we are. I did the exercise and came up with my answer, "I am a catalyst." *I can still feel that moment. That answer felt so right to me.* When one of the mentors came by to check on our progress, she responded, "You don't want to be a catalyst. Being a catalyst implies you are working alone. It is better to be a synergist, someone who fosters collaboration and works with groups."

I allowed her to change my sense of myself. I let her interrupt and override my process. Little did I know what this would cost me.

Even though my coach training was primarily about being, I spent the first four years of my practice frantically doing. I was doing everything I could to build my practice and increase my income. I even took three more years of training from other industry leaders.

I can do this. I can make it. I can be successful. I was constantly driving myself.

When shaman Will Whitesmith read my Human Design chart, I felt a deep initiation like a door opened into a new realm, a realm that seemed to know me so intimately. I felt called.

The first thing I remember feeling was utter relief. *I am supposed to be different. I am designed to do life differently than everyone.*

The implication was staggering. For all these years, I followed the advice of thought leaders and struggled to implement my business in a way that wasn't correct for me. *I am not a failure after all. Their advice isn't correct for me. Stop listening to everyone else and start listening to yourself, Cathy!*

I devour Human Design. I can't get enough of it. I read everything I can get my hands on. I study my chart. I do charts for all my horses. *My horses are unique. They each learn differently. I can see this in their charts. What if I adjust my training methods for each horse? Will I get better results? What does Peg need? My rare quadruple split girl? Everything broken into the smallest of steps? And Mia with her logical mind? She just watches her siblings' lessons and then does it perfectly when it is her turn!*

When I tell the story of bringing Human Design into my practice, I share, "Traditional coaching methods of goals, project plans, and milestones work for about 15% of the population. Most people don't flourish with artificial time, such as project plans and deadlines. I had started to feel like I was a crappy coach or I had crappy clients, but I knew that wasn't true. Human Design allows me to support each client in ways that are best for them. When clients work within their own natural tempos, the results are outstanding."

My coaching practice based on Human Design was growing, but I was still not making enough to live on without tapping into my savings. This financial stress keeps me exhausted. Life still isn't clicking. But I can't go back to the corporate world; I feel too weary even to give it a try.

It was time for another leap of faith. *But is it a leap of faith? Or is it my splenic inner authority that guides me? Aren't intuitive, splenic hits akin to leaps of faith? Haven't I always made leaps of faith and landed on my feet? I left government work and moved to the private sector on just one conversation. I signed up for coaching school on a hunch. I left my corporate job after that morning's wake-up call. Doesn't everything good in my life come from out of nowhere? Hasn't my inner authority been guiding me all these years?*

As a Manifestor, I don't have sustained energy. It wasn't correct for me to be working sun up to sundown. To be constantly trying so hard to keep up. I unconsciously recreated my corporate work pace into my private life! I kept resisting the inner voice that was telling me to stop working so hard. Stop doing so much.

Bang! I suddenly knew. I had to put all my eggs into my Human Design basket and commit myself 100% to living my design.

This commitment meant huge change. I mean huge. I sold my farm and all my horses. And again, from out of nowhere, the next home shows up right at the last moment.

Manifestors are human catalysts. We catalyze others. That also implies that we catalyze ourselves. We are self-catalyzing. The spark to act comes from within, not from without. All the other types respond to their world. Not Manifestors. We are not responders. We are initiators. It is an inner spark that prompts us into *correct* action. Deep within us, something sparks, and, voila, we move into action. We manifest.

I still can't believe I did this, but I spent the next year, *an entire year,* only taking action when the impulse came from deep *within* me. *I bet on my design. I wouldn't let my fear of not making money pull me off course! Trust my design, was my daily mantra.*

Slowly but surely, I started to recognize the spark from within me and grew resolve to ignore the chatter coming from my mind. The mental voice that relentlessly badgered me to take action. *I should be working; I should be making money; I should be doing something, anything.*

Do you know how hard that was? How many inner conversations do we all have that are harsh and cruel? Mental conversations urging us into action using shame, blame, and guilt? I knew all of this from my ontological work, but I hadn't conquered it for myself, not completely. Our thought forms hang on with the fierceness of an addict to their drug.

It is a challenge to be energetically and physically ill and still keep pushing forward. But that is what I did over and over every time I faced adversity. I was depleted in large part because I used my energy incorrectly. I can't run on adrenaline. I can't run on my mind. I can't run on anything coming from the outside.

As I stopped being externally driven and started being internally informed and inspired, everything changed for the better. Everything.

Today my life is filled with ease and success. My practice is booming. I thrive financially. My health is restored, and I have amazing work/life balance.

The secret? I stopped doing and started being.

Remember that lesson I spoke about earlier? Where I knew I was a catalyst and let myself be talked out of it?

I allowed my mentor to change my mind. Even in the kindest of environments, environments all about empowerment, we can unknowingly lose our way. I wasn't aligned with my energy. I wasn't congruent, and that made all my efforts fall flat. I couldn't get traction. I could only manifest at the cost of my health and quality of life.

All it took was for me to be me. Not who I thought I should be.

Human Design helped me get clear and connected to myself. You, too, can gain clarity and reap a similar reward in your life by thoroughly understanding and living your design.

Here is what I share with people curious about my journey and when I use myself as an example in classes.

- "I am highly individual. I am energetically imprinted to do things my way, to trod the unbeaten path. The only person that has to believe in my work is me. When I do that, people find me."
- "I am not meant to work with a consistent tempo. When my energy is on, it's on; when it is off, it's off. I no longer fight this. However, when I do get catalyzed, watch out. I might run you over!"
- "I am splenic and must listen to my bursts of intuition. Intuition makes no sense. It can't be explained. It isn't logical or rational. Intuition just knows. My job now is to recognize my intuitive hits, trust, and take action."
- "I've stopped trying to figure out my life, which keeps me in my flow. Mentally trying to figure out life is a waste of time and energy. This is true for all of us."
- "Manifesting is easy. There is no effort in manifesting. It is as quick as the snap of your fingers. It wasn't there, and now it is. None of us should work hard. All of us should be working with joy and ease. And if that joy and ease mean long hours and deep work, great. But it should never deplete our life's vitality or cause suffering."
- "I am highly individual yet interact with others in a deeply personal way. I work through the power of friendship, being open-hearted and available to share my wisdom."

It took multiple iterations, but my business model now reflects who I am at my essence. It is unique yet very successful. All I have is a website where I have painstakingly chosen language that comes directly from my heart and shares what I deeply believe to be true. I have Google business reviews that share client experiences; that is all, no huge mailing list hungry for new subscribers. No pushing out weekly newsletters and offers. No detailed business plan to drive me.

There is no frantic doing in my life these days, only action that comes from the core of my being. People from all over the world find me and work with me. When I ask why they chose me, they express, "You feel right to me. I know I can trust you."

When we get our being right, the doing flows and grows. I credit the art of being and the deep insights of Human Design for all of my success.

THE TOOL

The one tool I suggest is to get to a Human Design reading from an experienced professional. Work with your design information for a couple of months and then get another deeper reading. You and your reader must resonate. Check us all out. I offer free 30-minute consults for this very reason. If we aren't going to click, then I won't be able to transmit the knowledge to you that you're seeking.

But for here and now, I offer this tool and encourage you to 'own who you are.' Own your essence; live from your essence. Choose from your essence.

Remember, when we get the *being* right, the *doing* flows and grows.

1. Below is a list of gifts and qualities that are expressed through our Human Designs. Which ones resonate with you? Mark the ones that you know in yourself. Be mindful *not* to mark the ones you aspire to be.
2. Narrow your list down to the top five qualities.
3. Make big and/or little posters with these qualities. Then, display them where you will see them; on your bathroom mirror; as your screen saver.
4. When you feel frustrated, angry, bitter, or disappointed, meditate on your list of five to find your center of being again.
5. Get back to *being*, and then resume your day.

- ☐ Competent
- ☐ Grace-filled
- ☐ Logical
- ☐ Truth-seeking
- ☐ Refining
- ☐ Realizing
- ☐ Improving
- ☐ Connecting
- ☐ Directing
- ☐ Creative
- ☐ Defining
- ☐ Lawful
- ☐ Joyous
- ☐ Ambitious
- ☐ Patient
- ☐ A Celebrator
- ☐ A Fighter
- ☐ A Stimulator
- ☐ Spirited
- ☐ A Revolutionary
- ☐ Sensitive
- ☐ Genius
- ☐ Adaptive
- ☐ Influential
- ☐ Friendly
- ☐ Wise
- ☐ Aloof
- ☐ Leader
- ☐ Manager
- ☐ Conceptual
- ☐ Focused
- ☐ Visionary
- ☐ Emotional
- ☐ Balancing
- ☐ On to what's next
- ☐ Starter
- ☐ A Storyteller
- ☐ Intuitive
- ☐ Instinctive
- ☐ In the Moment
- ☐ Essence
- ☐ Influential
- ☐ Listener
- ☐ Percolator
- ☐ Energetic
- ☐ Power
- ☐ Inspirational
- ☐ Deep
- ☐ Selective
- ☐ Collaborator
- ☐ Tactile
- ☐ Peace-seeking
- ☐ Organic
- ☐ Universal
- ☐ Detailed
- ☐ Assured
- ☐ Cautionary
- ☐ Mutative
- ☐ Experimental
- ☐ Experiential
- ☐ Synchronous
- ☐ Committed
- ☐ Natural
- ☐ Humanist
- ☐ Catalyzing
- ☐ Tasting
- ☐ Smelling
- ☐ Acoustic
- ☐ Touch
- ☐ Efficient
- ☐ Integrative
- ☐ Precise
- ☐ Ideas
- ☐ Imagination
- ☐ Seeing
- ☐ Sensory
- ☐ Foundational
- ☐ Studied
- ☐ Gifted
- ☐ Change Agent
- ☐ Abundant
- ☐ Flexible
- ☐ Consistent
- ☐ Wondrous
- ☐ Opinionated
- ☐ Organized

Catherine Rivers is a Human Design Master Professional Consultant and a Certified Professional Coach.

In 2005 she left her career in global technology and immersed herself in ontologically based life coaching. She now has 21 years of expertise teaching empowerment and mentoring others to live life from their essence.

When Cathy had her own Human Design reading in 2008, she instantly knew this work was profound. She devoured everything she could get her hands on and hasn't stopped studying. Cathy did her advanced training with Chetan Parkyn and continues to study under his mentorship.

As a Manifestor, Cathy is a human catalyst. Her energetic design is geared towards transformation for herself and her clients. Working with Cathy, change and growth happen in a fundamental way that alters each person, partnership, family, or organization for the better. Her leading-edge techniques and tools, combined with her keen listening and deep compassion, create a powerful and transformative experience.

Cathy offers Human Design readings for individuals and couples and training for coaches and therapists. Do you want to create transformation for yourself? Check out Cathy's year-long Transformation Program to help you integrate your design into daily life and experience the power of living from your being and essence.

You can find her at www.catherinerivers.com and read her Google reviews at Rivers Life and Business Coaching.

CHAPTER 5

RETURNING TO YOURSELF

A PATH TO SELF LOVE AND ACCEPTANCE

April M. Novoa, Human Design Specialist, Lmt

The individual has always had to struggle
to keep from being overwhelmed by the tribe.
If you try it, you will be lonely often, and sometimes frightened.
But no price is too high for the privilege of owning yourself.

-Friedrich Nietzsche

MY STORY

My body was shaking, my heart was pounding, and I was having a difficult time breathing. I had a panic attack. I was no stranger to them. I started having them in college after a car accident 30 years prior. Every so often, one would happen, and I would feel like I had an out-of-body experience. I would witness my body react in ways my mind had no discernible control over. I was helpless to do anything but let it pass. This last year was beyond difficult. I attempted to make everyone around me happy and satisfied and came up short. I was failing, and my life seemed to be falling apart.

At some point in my childhood, I took on the role of a savior. I came to believe that being loved and accepted had to be earned through people-pleasing. In my mind, if I was behaving correctly, I would be treated kindly. If I wasn't measuring up, I would be subject to rejection, emotional and verbal abuse, and disapproval and believe I deserved it. I seemed to attract individuals that reinforced that mindset throughout my lifetime. I was anything but me. I had no idea who I was. I looked in the mirror and saw a shell, not a person. I was whatever anyone needed me to be, and I began to realize it. My body was letting me know something was very, very wrong. The day I understood this was the day things began to slowly change for the better.

Living in a way contrary to who we are is painful. It's like having a pair of shoes that are too tight or just don't fit right. I believe that most of us walk around like that; most people for their entire lives. We hobble around and try to look like we are alright, all the while struggling to stay upright. We imagine that being real and vulnerable will cause others to think less of us, or worse yet, reject us altogether.

Rejection is painful. More painful than tight shoes! It's downright threatening and in the worst possible way. There is an important reason for that. We are wired to fear rejection. It's in our DNA, and we're deeply conditioned to conform to prevent rejection from the time we're born. Most of the time, it's well-meaning and done to us quite innocently. Other times it's not. The need to conform to fit the expectations of our parents or caregivers, families, teachers, peers, and society at large drives us far away from who we truly are. For thousands of years, rejection by the tribe meant sure death or annihilation. The name of the game was survival. Fear of rejection served to keep us alive! A person's physical well-being was more of a priority than their mental and emotional well-being. As a result, we will endure quite a lot for acceptance. We will suffer terribly to be seen as acceptable or worthy in the eyes of our tribe.

There is a certain malleability in a person who figures out they have not been standing on solid ground. In my case, when the dust settled and when acceptance of that fact solidified, an openness and softness took the place of the illusory control I imagined I had. Once very fixed and what I thought to be predictable, my perspective was now receptive and capable of considering any number of possibilities where the nature of reality was concerned. My intention now, every day, is to approach life with a beginner's mind, ready to part with what I believe should better information arise. My journey has taken me to some interesting places. I have a lot of gratitude for what I have picked up along the way and the individuals willing to share their insights with me! I have come to see everyone as my teacher in some way, shape, or form. However, I have learned that the wisest teacher is within. That within me, within you, is a well of wisdom waiting to be discovered. I knew there was some inherent wisdom within me but was unsure, beyond my meditation practice, how to go about recognizing it.

One morning several years ago, I set out to my office. I had a heavy client load that day, so I got an early start. I listened to a podcast on my way to work.

I am quite frankly a little addicted to podcasts, particularly if they are about personal growth. This particular day the host of the podcast I was listening to was interviewing a woman sharing about a system called Human Design. She explained that it was the science of human differentiation and that there were five Aura Types, and beyond that, a tremendous amount of nuance in what constitutes a human being. The Aura Type revealed a particular strategy in decision making. Within each individual was an inner authority that gave the individual an inner knowing as to whether something was correct or not for them. Bingo! This was a clue. This was a treasure map of sorts to this inner guidance I was seeking. I was very excited and reached down to turn up the volume. I didn't want to miss anything!

She spoke about the Generator, which has an open and enveloping aura. They are here to master something or some things. Then of the Projector, the guide, here to manage and direct. Surely, I was a Projector. I had been in some sort of helping profession my entire life! Or perhaps I was a Manifesting Generator? They seemed very exciting! Maybe the Reflector? I did resonate deeply with the moon, and I felt very sensitive to the energy of others and my environment. It was really interesting, and I hung on to every word until she got to the last type. This particular type, the Manifestor, didn't seem appealing to me. Yet, there was something about her description of the Manifestor that was hitting home. I thought to myself, *well, certainly, I am not that type.* So I vowed to run my chart, with the free link she gave, as soon as I go to my office.

Having arrived at my office, I quickly booted up my computer, went to the link given, and ran my chart. My heart pounded a little faster as I input the required information. When the results came up, I stopped breathing for a moment. It was what they very type that I hoped I wasn't. I was a Manifestor! My heart sank. Nonetheless, as I began to read about my type, I found it to be accurate, scary accurate. As I began to investigate, what I learned began to deeply resonate with me in the coming weeks.

I was a Manifestor, but I just didn't want to see myself that way. I didn't see myself as powerful or with an aura that is closed or that repels. I didn't like the idea of informing or initiating, which is the Manifestor strategy. I felt much better flying under the proverbial radar, alone, and avoiding conflict of any kind. Knowing this motivated me to do some deep inquiry as to why I was so uncomfortable with this?

I have learned that the things in life that make us most uncomfortable usually contain important information in our best interest to uncover and pay attention to. The uncomfortable emotions usually point to an area that needs healing and attention. For most of my life, my pattern was simply not to explore certain uncomfortable things, but this got my attention. In retrospect, I don't believe I had a problem with being a Manifestor as much as I had a problem being seen by others in that way.

I sat with this knowledge for a while, uncertain whether I wanted to pursue it, but something about it kept calling me. I began to read up, not only on my type but also on all the types, wanting to understand how this system worked or if it worked. I wasn't 100% convinced, even though everything I was reading confirmed the results I received. Without revealing why I was asking, I questioned friends and family to see if they saw these characteristics in me. Sure enough, those that loved me and knew me very well for years confirmed what I was learning about myself.

What Human Design calls the "not self-theme" of the Manifestor is anger. Through Human Design, I realized I had a lot of repressed anger. I was raised in a time and place that taught me that a good girl did not get angry or show anger. So I became adept at hiding my anger until I was physically ill. Or I channeled it into work and family responsibilities to the point of burnout. Even though I felt like I had done a lot of healing work, I had not looked at it. I had a lot of shame around that emotion and, at that time, still believed my anger was not owed a voice. That was so wrong and so very sad.

Looking back, I truly believe that most of the suffering I experienced was due to this stuck emotion. My anger was not heard, by anyone, especially me. It had not been honored for what it was trying to communicate. So I began to explore the emotion of anger. I began to listen. This was the first gift Human Design bestowed upon me. It permitted me to feel something that was a friend to me that I treated as an enemy. My friend, 'anger,' told me to leave abusive situations and speak up for myself for years, but I would not listen to her. She had been telling me I was working too hard, was too tired, and not taking care of my own needs, but I muted her voice by pushing harder and harder to the point of near collapse.

Manifestors are a minority, only 8-9% of the population, and I had felt different all of my life. I was very resistant to having that confirmed. In my life, I experienced a garden variety of abuse because of how different I was. My way of dealing with that, avoiding that, was people-pleasing and trying to conform to the expectations of others. I worked very hard at it and was perplexed when my adrenal function declined, and I developed other health problems. It all made sense now. I wasn't here to shut down my power for the approval of others or to work as hard as I had been all of my life. I am not for everyone. And that was finally becoming okay with me! My life was fraught with feeling controlled in my relationships and my career. I didn't assert boundaries. I tried harder to please and make everyone happy. As a result, I felt stifled. I didn't feel free. I felt imprisoned. I wasn't respected because I didn't respect myself. At some point, probably very early in life, I stopped creating, stopped being me, and shut down. The resistance and rejection I faced were far too much.

I feel like my story isn't unique among Manifestors. I also believe other types could share a similar story, only flavored a little differently. Conditioning is a reality no matter what aura type a person has. We want to belong. We want to be loved by everyone. So, we get in line with everyone else and march to the beat of another's drum and lose ourselves in the process. It does not have to be this way, and hopefully, it will not be in the future.

Understanding my design has propelled me further down the road to self-love, self-acceptance, and empowerment. I am learning to embrace and love myself and every little thing about who I am. I have only love for others, but I understand that some cannot love back, and they need to be loved from a distance for my well-being. Boundaries are an important part of self-care. We teach others how to treat us, and we don't do them any service by allowing our boundaries to be violated. I feel like I am coming home to myself and I feel deeply inspired to help others do the same. It is exceptional when someone knows and embraces exactly who they are. It is the only way to break self-defeating patterns and live a life full of more joy, satisfaction, and peace.

THE TOOL

So how does one escape people-pleasing and learn to love and accept themselves fully? How does one live a life full of joy, satisfaction, and peace?

- Be radically honest with yourself! Examine and be honest with yourself about your motivations and what drives them. Journaling about this is very helpful. It is also helpful to have a friend that you trust to hold space for you while you process your emotions. The correct kind of support is crucial. Be very particular about who occupies that role in your life. If you need the support of a professional, find one that you are comfortable with and trust!
- Love your wounded parts! Shadow work was a very big part of my healing. Your wounded parts are parts of yourself that were birthed to help you, not hurt you. When you cease resisting them, they transform. They become some of your biggest assets.
- No more comparing! Stop comparing yourself to others. Find out what makes you unique and different by exploring your Human Design and make a decision to love who you are today. Not tomorrow. Today!
- Do not expect 'you' from others. Honor their differences just as you are learning to honor your own!
- Drop approval-seeking! Most people do not approve of themselves, and they cannot give what they do not possess.
- Don't shrink! If you have to 'shrink' yourself, i.e., become less, to be with another person or group of people, they are not for you.

- Stop doing things purely out of obligation! Enact healthy boundaries and expect some pushback. When you apply your unique Human Design strategy and authority, setting boundaries comes very naturally! Keep in mind those who are accustomed to seeing you in a certain way might struggle to adjust. Be patient but be firm and committed to your growth.
- Understand that life is a journey. If you are not where you want to be, that's okay. Just commit to keep going, and do not let temporary setbacks define you. A bad day, month, or even a year or more is not a bad life. Growth is a process, and you are perfectly acceptable and worthy of your love and acceptance wherever you find yourself on the path!

It is okay to be you. You are beautiful. You are unique. You have your own amazing story to live out on planet Earth, and you are the perfect main character in your story! There is no one like you. You have come to this world for a purpose. You are not an accident. You do not take up too much space, so don't shrink yourself in hopes of being loved and accepted. The price you will pay for that is not worth it! Go where you are celebrated!

The work of Human Design is to reveal an inner wisdom that bypasses the conditioned mind. Your inner authority and strategy is an embodied wisdom that is accessible to you. It isn't an easy journey, this returning to yourself, but it is the most exciting journey you can ever embark on! The good news is that setting a course a little different than what is expected of you is no longer fatal. Setting a course that is specifically for you is important if you are going to be fully you. It is crucial if you are to become the truest version of the beautiful being you already are.

There is no design better than any other. They are all beautiful, and the world desperately needs what everyone brings to the table. You have come here, to this earth school, for such a time as this.

April has been a caregiver most of her life, working in the medical industry, alternative healthcare, ministry, and as a foster parent. On her journey, she experienced terrible burnout and health challenges. This led her to a journey of self-discovery, exploring many different philosophies and schools of thought. When she discovered Human Design, she discovered her unique blueprint and began to understand how to manage her life and energy in a more sustainable, authentic, and healthy way. Her goal as your guide and Specialist is to awaken you to the beautiful being you already are and equip you with tools to help you navigate life in a peaceful, successful, and satisfying way! She is a certified Human Design Specialist. April resides in the state of Georgia in the United States. She has been married for 32 years, has four children and one grandchild. You can read more about April and her services by visiting her webpage, humandesignsimplified.weebly.com

CHAPTER 6

RETIREMENT REIMAGINED

AN INVITATION TO LET GO AND CREATE FLOW

Mary Jo Rathgeb, MS, PCC

MY STORY

Retire. Said a voice in my head softly yet firmly. It was a Monday morning in February. The cold and grey sky outside the window contrasted with the steaming cup of coffee in my hands. I was sitting at my desk sipping the hot liquid while perusing the day's schedule. *What the heck? I have too much to do to retire. Look at today's schedule. I am booked from 10 am to 10:30 pm. I am too busy to retire.*

I worked days and nights, sometimes seven days a week for months, years—decades even—to make myself a success. *How can I retire now? I'm too young. Besides, what would I do?*

As I started telling people what I felt I was being directed to do, many people said, "You're crazy!" They echoed my doubts, saying, "What will you do? I can't see you sitting around doing nothing." "I can't either," I admitted, wavering on my resolve to trust this inner voice.

Retire. The potential need for fibroid surgery catalyzed this movement. As I sat in the OB/GYN examining room, admiring the crystals in the mobile suspended from the ceiling, I squirmed, causing the white paper beneath me on the table to crackle. I glanced at the surgeon as she said, "If you do this surgery, you need to clear your calendar for a month. That means coaching calls, too." "I can't even talk on the phone?" "No, that's work and will impact your healing process." *Not work for a month? Is that even possible?*

Back at my home office, I looked at my calendar again, scanning for places where I could take a month off. Next month? Nope. The month after? Nope. Over the summer? Next fall? Nope. Nope. Nope. Wow, I was so busy all the time. A voice then said to me, *have you been* ***invited*** *to be this busy?* I then realized I wasn't living what I learned about myself in Human Design.

I was introduced to Human Design in 2016, and in accordance with the system, I am a 1/3 projector with emotional authority. One Human Design reader told me, "Projectors don't have consistent access to workforce energy. You are not here to work 9-5 jobs. You are here to guide others." I totally resonated, "*Yes! That's what I want to do.*"

They continued to explain, "You also have to wait to be invited. You are not here to initiate." This was confronting. The walls felt like they were closing in as I didn't know any other way to be in the world and make things happen! *I'm doomed!*

I continued to learn that projectors need to wait to be recognized for their talents and invited to share them, or they won't be heard, or their wisdom won't be received. Trying to force invitations doesn't work, and I knew this because I tried. Working harder or staying busy just to feel productive wasn't working either. My heart slumped at the thought of not being in control and especially now because I had even more at stake—my health.

Again, I reflected on my Human Design session, in which he explained, "Once you have an invitation, you then need to wait for *'feeling clarity'* because of your emotional authority. Don't be spontaneous. Sleep on your decisions. Patience is your friend." The resistance to those words was boiling up. *I love being spontaneous! Patient? Isn't that denying myself?* And yet, I was feeling a sense of truth and relief because parts of myself I had judged as bad were just part of how I was wired.

It took several years to start to trust and 'wait for the invitation.' In the beginning, I was questioning everything. *Is this an invitation? How long will it last? What happens when it ends?* My undefined mind was going crazy trying to figure it all out. *I want certainty!*

Worst of all was the question: *What if nobody invites me?*

One of the most liberating realizations I had was: *I'm not lazy! I am just wired differently than most other people and don't have their level of energy to just keep working.* I also realized that invitations sometimes have expiration dates. They don't last forever. I realized there were other times in my life when I "retired early." This call to retirement was not exactly new to me. I now understand these calls to retire as natural endings of invitations and a graceful way to conclude various chapters in my life.

The first time I "retired" was at age 21 from the foodservice industry at my college. Over five years, I worked in every position possible in the college food service, ranging from being a line lady and short-order cook to working the dish room, serving faculty, and working banquets while still in high school. As a freshman in college, I was promoted to student manager and was responsible for hiring and firing peers and upperclassmen, scheduling students, and doing payroll. I even hired and fired a boyfriend during this time.

By junior year, I was winding down. I asked my manager, "Can I step down from the role of student manager and be a checker? "Yes, that's a coveted job, but you've earned it." As I punched meal tickets and managed the line of students who entered the dining hall, I became known across campus as "The Saga Lady." At social events, people would come up to talk to me, saying, "Hey, you're The Saga Lady!" They would invariably glance at the left side of my chest and say, "Where's your name tag?" Haha. Not very funny. Time to retire. Senior year, I retired my name tag and became an ordinary English major.

Once I graduated college and joined corporate, I worked for several decades in marketing. By age 44, I was over it. *Retire*. I hired a financial planner, and we determined that I could retire at age 52—*eight more years to go*. In April 2015, when I was at home, sick from work, I received a call from my boss. She said, "I'm sorry to call you at home when you are sick, but we have restructured the department, and your position was eliminated." *Wait, am I being laid off?* "Blah, blah, blah. . .I will connect you with HR to review your package." As the call was being transferred to HR, I heard Tom Petty's voice in my head singing, *'I'm free!...free falling!'*

Once the relief subsided, the free-fall began. I thought, *Yikes, I have another year to go before retirement. What am I going to do? Get another job in marketing? Nnnoooo.* I was interested in coaching and sat on the idea for five years. I earned a master's degree in grief counseling while still in corporate but never used the degree. I met with a transition coach to determine the next course of action. She invited me to consider ICF credentialed coach training programs, and another cycle started.

Within a week of retiring from corporate, I jumped into entrepreneurship. I busied myself with consulting, coaching, training, working long days, and trying to initiate opportunities. I didn't know about Human Design then. I already started a side business with family members helping people downsize. I learned a lot about myself, business, coaching, and personal development.

I didn't know then that my 1/3 profile in Human Design, the investigator/experimenter, was working to build a solid foundation for myself. In Human Design, 1/3 profiles love learning, researching, and digging deep, while experimenting and learning through trial and error. It took me several years to realize the downsizing work was too physical and draining for me, so I exited the business. I continued coaching private clients and as a success coach.

Over the years, I engaged in social media, created side income streams, and kept taking training classes, adding more and more tools to my toolkit. In 2018, I began studying Human Design with Chetan Parkyn and Carola Eastwood and added it to my practice.

After that fateful visit to the OB/GYN and looking at my calendar to see how I could clear out a month of activities, I acknowledged it was time to retire from all the busyness I had created for myself. The biggest commitment I let go of was the success coaching. It was great for many years, and it was time to move on. I phased out slowly, completing current commitments there and with private coaching contracts as well. I kept good investment income streams, and I stopped other time-consuming side income streams. I minimized my social media activity for a few months. I continued doing Human Design readings though.

One big question I pondered was, *why did I create all this busyness for myself?*

One answer I found in Human Design is my undefined heart/will center. You see, an undefined or open center has inconsistent access to the energy of that center and is easily conditioned by outside forces. A person with an undefined heart/will center doesn't have consistent access to willpower and may feel a need to prove their worth and value to others. *Of course! Part of my busyness stems from trying so hard to prove my worth and value! What took me so long to see this?* I measured my self-worth by my achievements rather than by who I am. Now, I consciously reaffirm to myself: *I am enough as I am. I don't have to do anything to prove my worth. Epiphany!*

Once I got this, I saw the pattern I was living out.

I reviewed the last five years again with this insight. After being laid off, instead of allowing myself to slow down and "retire" until the next invitation came along, I jumped into the first thing I could think of, then the next, and the next, and the next. Some "invitations" were real, and some were forced because I wanted them to work so badly. Instead of achieving the success that I was desperately seeking, I was overworking and running my body into the ground.

In 2016, the same year I learned about Human Design, I also received a Stage I breast cancer diagnosis. I told almost no one except family and close friends. I went through surgery and radiation, continued to work, learn, and power through while also doing alternative healing modalities. I have as a reminder the radiation tattoo, a small blue circle, between my breasts that can be seen when wearing a low-cut top. I recently "graduated" from the breast surgeon's care, being cancer-free for five years. So, when the topic of having surgery for the fibroid came up, I realized that I am still in the same pattern loop. *It's time to stop this loop now.*

The call to "retire" this time around is about focusing on who I am and who I will be. It is about taking care of my physical, emotional, mental, and spiritual wellbeing. I'm aligned with the knowledge that I have abundance. I am supported. I am enough. As I turn my attention to nourishing and caring for myself, I am letting go of the busyness and creating space for what comes next. I don't know what that is, and I am not only okay with not knowing, but I am also looking forward to the adventure of discovery.

I am leaning into my design and trusting what I sense when I tune in to myself. I have learned to discern my "feeling clarity." I experience this clarity as a calm spaciousness in my belly. As a 1/3 projector, I have learned to embrace my insatiable quest for learning and experimenting. While I wait for the next invitation, I am diving deeper into areas of interest, including Human Design Consulting and RIM (Regenerating Images in Memory) facilitation, writing, and more. As I focus on these subjects, I can feel the flow and sense new possibilities on the horizon.

THE TOOL

The process of letting go is simple but not always easy. It requires a level of courage and willingness to look at and see parts of yourself you have avoided acknowledging for various reasons. Then, as you allow emotions, patterns, and parts to surface, you face them, feel them, acknowledge them, accept them, and let them go. Anyone who has cleaned out a closet overstuffed with outfits and shoes you never wear knows how overwhelming it can be to sort through mounds of accumulated clothing to find the keepers and then to bag up the rest and send it off to Goodwill.

Yet, the reward for this examination is immense. Imagine removing all that covers your essence. Imagine knowing that at your essence, you are joy, peace, abundance, and love. Knowing you are enough.

Realization and validation of one's essence results in increased self-worth, trust, and the courage to be yourself. This brings increased confidence and certainty that you can create success by being who you truly are and embodying it wholeheartedly.

To start, I invite you to try a simple and powerful tool I call "Catch & Release." It's a 3-step process that can be done anywhere at any time. It helps you align with what is, so you can see the patterns playing out in your life. The steps are:

1. Catch
2. Allow
3. Release

Step 1: Catch any thought, feeling, emotion, habit, sensation that you judge to be bad, wrong, limiting, or that you're avoiding, denying, or minimizing.

Step 2: Allow it to be in your awareness without doing anything to change it. Acknowledge it with the phrase, "I see."

Step 3: Release it as is. Let it go and let it flow without any judgment about it.

For example, if you are working on anger, 1) Catch when anger arises in you. 2) Notice it and say to yourself, "I am experiencing anger. I see." 3) Let it go without judgment.

Sounds simple, right? However, it's natural to move into judgment when you experience something you don't like about yourself or others. When you stop the judgment, you allow the experience to be, and you can see it for what it is. This is called neutral witnessing or detached involvement. It provides the space for you to experience "what is" without trying to change it, avoid it, grab on to it or control it. Once you accept what is, you can begin to align with the wholeness of who you are.

Aligning with the wholeness of who you are gives you the ability to tap into your innate wisdom more easily. You resonate at higher energy levels, trust your inner knowing, and allow life to unfold as an exciting adventure. We all have unique ways of knowing what's best for us. That's part of the wonder of knowing your Human Design. With this knowing and the acceptance of what is, the process of life alignment and letting go becomes a way of life.

For more resources, visit CreativeDirectionsForLiving.com/resources.

Called the Fairy Godmother of Personal Development, **Mary Jo Rathgeb** takes her clients on a magical journey of re-discovery. With a sense of wonder and curiosity, she supports clients in remembering the truth of who they are so they can reimagine their future. Mary Jo Rathgeb is the founder of Creative Directions for Living, LLC. She is a Professional Certified Coach (PCC), Energy Leadership Master Practioner (ELI-MP), RIM Facilitator, writer, and Human Design Consultant. Prior to her current work, Mary Jo engaged in a 30-year career in media marketing. She has a BA in English Literature and an MS in Grief Counselling. She believes it is never too late to let go of habits you have outgrown, re-align, and evolve into the next version of yourself.

To learn more, visit CreativeDirectionsForLiving.com.

CHAPTER 7

I CHOOSE PEACE

UNTANGLING THE BELIEFS THAT HOLD US BACK

Tonia Twigger,
6/2 Emotional Manifestor, Seeker's Guide

"Today, I break free of a life-long battle with my hair," I say to Karma through the passenger window she lowers from behind the wheel of her Nissan Leaf. "I am done torturing myself about how to make this 45-degree cowlick into a smooth, well-behaved bang. I am done wishing my hair was thicker. I intend to learn to live with, maybe love, my unruly, Woolite hair." *I notice I am talking louder than normal.*

She laughs, and I go on.

"I don't know about you, but I've spent my life blowing, bleaching, perming and rolling—anything to have bigger, better hair. TV commercials conditioned me to believe my "as is" hair isn't good enough. Remember brush rollers or those nasty plastic clamp-on gadgets we used to "put up" our hair before we slept?"

She laughs, and I go on.

"Enough is enough! I have an appointment with a stylist who was recommended to me ten years ago, one that specializes in curly hair. I'm ready to be fully me—not someone's idea of a more perfect me. It's just taken me a while to find the tools and the courage to let go."

As if winded by my enthusiasm, Karma pauses looking forward through the windshield, perhaps to take in my words, perhaps contemplating telling a secret of her own. She turns to look at me with a smirk, "I have a perm!" she exclaims, then pulls away from the curb.

"No one escapes," I call after her.

MY STORY

I meet Will at his office in a big old house on Bainbridge Island in Washington State, a three-hour train and ferry ride from Portland. Tall and thin with a stubble of beard, Will has the ability to introduce me to my spirit guides. It's true. The story begins with a trust writer friend telling me of his dream while traveling with his spirit guides—companions he met through Will. I'm dumbstruck when his dream describes in detail a vision I had in a sweat lodge in New Mexico some months before. I immediately want guided journeys with my spirit guides.

However, Will does not beckon my guides to my side. Instead, he conjures his own agenda using a few deep breaths and long gazes with penetrating blue eyes. He describes the library he sees surrounding my chair, volumes at the ready. He speaks of the breadth of knowledge stockpiled in the leather-bound collection. *So, decades of self-improvement, research on the latest in human dynamics, and teaching classrooms of college students have finally paid off.*

"I sense you have an uncanny intuition for hearing what's behind the spoken word." *I do?* "Why aren't you sharing your knowledge?" Will asks.

"You mean teaching continuing education courses in the business school doesn't count?" I jest.

"Of course," he smiles. "But I suspect there's more for you. I'd like to introduce you to my friend and colleague, Cathy Rivers. She can tell you about your Human Design. I can see your Manifestor energy. You are a rare type." *He has me at "rare type."*

While I am disappointed about the spirit guide thing, I can hear Will's excitement about finding and now nudging me to this calling. What he tells me is not new. I'd known for some time I was meant to do more with the information I'd compiled through two decades of teaching and coaching. I was advised a few years prior by a Peruvian-born, Lakota-trained shaman to stop teaching. Now, eye-to-eye with Will, years of therapy, and accepting responsibility behind me, I am curious. I think I hear him calling me to my next big thing.

Back at my computer, I use my birth information entered into the Jovian Archive website to create my Human Design bodygraph. More graphic than written and busy with colors and numbers, it features a simple body outline with shaded and clear shapes—my personal energy on one colorful page. I know immediately I'll need a guide.

I set up a call, then a series of video meetings, with Cathy.

DISCOVERING MY TYPE

After spending an hour with my body graph, Cathy knows things about me no one else knows. Some of what she tells me is familiar, some isn't. The flattering stuff inflates me like a pufferfish swallowing water. The idiosyncratic stuff hangs in my head—until Cathy is emphatic that all energy is perfect and our focus in thought and language must be on the positive.

"Your energy is powerful and can be felt when you enter a room. But it's not sustainable," warns Cathy. "You must rest before others rest, sleep before others sleep." *Her words are comforting and familiar, and I feel smug. I don't have my office in my bedroom anymore.*

When I tell her I am caring for my toddler granddaughter from Thursday mornings to Friday evenings, she warns I am not built for the sustained energy required of caregiving. *At this point, I figure she doesn't understand the egg connection a grandma has to her daughter's offspring.* She tells me my willpower can push me beyond my limits. *Whatever.*

A few months later, I fall to the flu like I'm not getting up from a fever I can't shake for six weeks. *Note to self: excessive energy outlays can cause a major immune system collapse. I wasn't new to the idea that the really powerful lessons come while we are down and out.*

PIECING TOGETHER MY TYPE MOSAIC

"You're here to find peace," Cathy says. "No other of the Human Design types are here to do that."

"Hallelujah," I say. "World peace?"

"No," she laughs, "peace deep within yourself. Remove obstacles, and choose peace," she urges.

I am known as a peace seeker, writing and taking photos outdoors. I hike and kayak and carry native garden dirt in my fingernails. Jogging for three decades was pretty peaceful; now, practicing yoga is even more so because it is yoga that taught me about my breath.

Getting affirmation from Cathy to seek peace is life-changing. It gives me permission to stop trying to keep up with the energy of the majority around me. I no longer feel guilty when I can't. I can weigh every decision against my body's need for calm in what feels like a reckless, out-of-control world. I can get up early to avoid being rushed. I can schedule three things in a day and not five. I can take time off. I can choose peace.

I'm hooked on eliminating things that aren't peaceful. I order lids to fit every size of oven-proof bowl—no more hunting. I buy a new hose that reaches to the edge of the garden, is a breeze to roll, and is non-toxic. I find the perfect-sized food processor to avoid the battles the Vitamix can't win. And I pat myself on the back for the "no-drama-after-dinner" rule I implemented two decades ago to keep from being drawn into my daughters' 20-something lives before bed. I somehow knew back then that nighttime drama causes me to miss sleep, and insomnia is not peaceful.

Though my grandkids exhaust me (definitely not peaceful), I won't miss an opportunity to hang with them. I've just learned to schedule downtime afterward. A weekend sleep-over might require the entire next week. And I feel peaceful for having had the connection with them that my tribal energy craves.

Cathy tells me I have the power to initiate action, but I must learn to keep people in the loop or they might resist. As a rule, keeping others in the loop is not my forte. I'm more of an "I can do it myself" human, operating as if I need no one. The purpose of me sitting for my granddaughter was to help unburden my daughter. She was working an intense job and overwhelmed by a first child. So, I made things easy.

"She was great, no hassles, no problems," I reported. "See ya later, bye." As predictable with my energy, withholding information causes others to resist me. Over time, my daughter interpreted the vacuum I created with my silence as me being untrustworthy. But by the time she gathered the courage to talk about it, she was hurt and angry. It was the end of babysitting for my beloved granddaughter and the start of a long road to forgiveness. But it was also the start of me stepping up to inform others to choose peace.

"Yours is the most wounded type because people have been trying to control you for a lifetime. Being controlled makes you angry," Cathy shares one day.

I reflect later on the contempt I felt for my mother. I can't remember a time when I wasn't angry at her. Based on what I now know about our combined energies, I can imagine my poor underprepared mom was terrified when she looked through my dense little aura. With the early death of my dad she had no intention of losing me. So she put her head down, worked like a dog, and tried to control the force she could feel inside me. Her favorite showstopper during disagreements, "You're all I've got," only made me madder.

I am no longer angry, and I wish I'd understood the dynamic before her death. As I ease into my true energy, I am becoming a better human.

"You have a defined throat," Cathy announces, "you are here to verbally share with others what it is to be you."

"That's what Will said," I say, puffing slightly. *Plus, I did spend my career sharing from the front of the room.*

"The affirmation feels great," I confess.

It turns out I also have some quirks.

- I'd rather have you give me information than ask me a question.
- I am meant to know a little about a lot of things, but not deep into any one.
- If I don't get my needs met, I am capable of causing a disturbance until I do, or I might distance myself from others' faulty attempts to change. *Two ex-husbands agree.*

- I am body aware and persnickety . . . you might remember the Princess and the Pea—I bet she too was tortured by clothes tags on the back of her neck or was tickled mercilessly by a single hair under her shirt.
- I can hear what's behind your words, which makes me the first in the room to spot a scoundrel.
- I am sensitive to noise, especially concussive sounds like a barking dog.
- I'm supposed to eat cooked food.
- I am reluctant to answer the phone for fear of what I might hear.
- If you violate trust with me, it will be a long road to trust you again.

"If you hope to share what you know and intend to coach others using Human Design, you have to do your own work first," explains Cathy. I can hear her asking if I'm excited enough about Human Design to see me through the time it will take to learn, and with enough tenacity, to adjust my energy as a model for others. After years of consulting with organizations and their people, one thing I do know is even when we're smart and really trying, change is hard, especially trying to integrate new ways of living using a "one-step-forward-two-steps-back" method of change.

EMBRACING EMOTIONAL AUTHORITY

"Fifty percent of all people are emotional decision-makers," says Cathy. "You are an emotional decision-maker. Avoid making decisions in the moment. You must wait through the highs and lows of your emotional waves before deciding. One of your waves is undulating (hope to fear) in the background, and the other builds to a high and then crashes. Do not make decisions in either extreme." *Me? Emotional? I've only recently remembered how to cry. I suck back the tears and figure things out.*

I suspect my emotions went underground after my dad died at 35 of lung cancer contracted in asbestos walls on the Navy ship he served. I paced alongside his casket crying when I was five.

After that, I cried. A lot. I cried when the kids ran too fast and when my allergies kept me from playing in the grass. I cried when kids made fun of me because I didn't have a dad. I cried when Mom yelled. I cried, according to others, without reason.

My depression-era elders—my mom, aunt, and uncle called me "Crybaby." I even remember their exasperation when they finally got to the "I'll-give-you-something-to-cry-about" end of their rope. They inadvertently sent my emotions underground. I practiced for decades—held up through two marriages and divorces, raised two kids by myself, left corporate America to start my own business, not knowing if we would eat. I was the guardian of my declining mother for eight years. Who had time to cry?

As I watched Mom's demise from Alzheimer's disease, when someone asked, "How do you feel about all this?" I was known to say, "No sense crying about it, you just figure it out." I was conditioned to believe my emotions were irrelevant. But as we know, the body long remembers what the mind soon forgets. Beginning when I was 12, under emotional circumstances, my heart felt heavy while I struggled to catch my breath. Over the years I normalized this hyperventilating.

Until one day I open. That is, I stop long enough to breathe and feel. It happens in my herbalist's office. When I mention the pain in my shoulder, he suggests we pause long enough to sit with it and ask about its origin. Sure enough, it only takes a split-second of stillness and silence to notice the sadness and anger lodged there by Mom's regression and the resulting painful responsibilities. My heart spills out in my tears. Seven tissues and a river of tears later, the shoulder pain is gone. My breathing is clear, and my heart is light.

Once I taste the sweet salt of tears, there's no going back. I cry when I share the experience with my husband. I cry when I tell my best friend. I cry when a golden eagle appears in the greenway that surrounds my house. And I cry when I walk out on the deck and see the violets my more-able mom planted in pots years ago. Crybaby's back! Because releasing emotions is delicious and peaceful. And fully embracing my range is key to how I make decisions that are correct for me.

UNTANGLING BELIEFS THAT HOLD US BACK

Dominant family judgments like "Tonia-is-a-crybaby-and-needs-to-toughen-up" are one kind of conditioning that can strangle our own beliefs. Another kind comes through undefined or open centers that appear white on the otherwise color Human Design bodygraph.

"Your open centers are where you will do your lifelong learning," Cathy says. "It's conditioning through open centers that leads us to surrender to the beliefs of others. Part of doing this work is being aware of, and then acting based on true energy and not conditioning."

One of my open centers leaves me afraid (of letting go), one makes me unaware of when enough is enough, and one finds me apt to jump into action to relieve the anxiety of no action.

Notably, letting go is a theme of two out of three of these open centers. Past examples might include staying in a marriage six years after I knew it was over, continuing to drink alcohol long after I knew I needed to quit, exasperating an exercise-induced injury by continuing until I drove myself into the ground, or kidding myself I had any influence over my daughter leaving her disturbing relationship.

The day I met Karma on the street is the day I ended the fight with my hair in an epic gesture of letting go. Now, most mornings, I embrace my cowlicks' choice of the day and go forward in peace.

THE TOOL

Even if you don't have your Human Design bodygraph in front of you (if you're self-aware), you might be able to identify life themes dictated by your own open centers. I've mentioned the challenges I have with my open centers, two of which are about letting go—one of my lifelong learning themes.

How aware are you of your own energy?

How aware are you of your conditioning?

Identify among the following statements the ones that describe you:

- You think about things that don't matter (or have so many thoughts you can't distinguish yours). If so, you may have an open Crown.
- You find yourself (especially when pressed) either seeking or speaking certainty—or both. If so, you might have an open Anja.
- You find yourself trying to attract attention. If so, you might have an open Throat.
- You are on a journey seeking direction, identity, and love. If so, you might have an open G-Center.
- You don't know when enough is enough. If not, you might have an open Sacral.
- You find yourself leaping into action to eliminate stress. If so, you might have an open Root.
- You hold on to things that no longer serve. If so, you might have an open Spleen.
- You avoid conflict and truth. If so, you might have an open Solar Plexus (Emotion).
- You constantly try to prove your worth, e.g., try to be the hero. If so, you might have open Willpower.

Check your awareness by comparing your answers to your body chart. How does the conditioning of these centers affect the quality of your life? What benefit might you find from moving past your conditioning? Who can help?

Tonia Twigger, M.S., is an educator, artist, and seeker. She discovered Human Design after almost three decades consulting with N.W. business leaders, and teaching leadership and communication courses at Portland State University.

It was in a project management class in 2002 that Tonia first recognized a subset of students talking about themselves as successful but not satisfied, surviving but not happy, employed but not engaged. It was for them that Tonia and colleagues Karen Howells and Paul Spindel birthed a series of courses called Creating the Life You Want—a six-week community learning experience. The popular course was archived in 2017 when Tonia found Human Design and realized their course methods appealed to her and other Manifestors, but didn't work as a guide for other energy types.

Tonia is grateful for studying one-on-one and in groups with Cathy Rivers (Rivers Life and Business Coaching), working to align her own energy, and coaching using Human Design for members of the Creating the Life You Want tribe. As often happens, once Tonia began practicing her design and serving her tribe, clients from outside the tight-knit community came calling.

Tonia offers Human Design coaching for seekers looking to define the mission that has eluded them. She loves to inspirit clients to discover what is making them angry, frustrated, or bitter. She welcomes parents interested in fostering the true energy of their children.

Once she felt the gift of "knowing" guaranteed by Gate 57, Tonia surrendered to the Human Design calling, and lives peacefully, coaching from Oregon, USA. If you can't find her, you can bet she's in her native garden, or has wandered off chasing a photo.

You can connect with Tonia using her inbox, tonia.twigger@gmail.com.

Or you can find her @

https://seekersguidetoauthenticliving.blogspot.com

CHAPTER 8

FINDING MY VOICE

HOW HUMAN DESIGN UNCOVERED MY SOUL'S MESSAGE

Rachael Weaver, Creator of the Copy By Design™ method

MY STORY

From the outside looking in, my life has always been ideal. So ideal, my brothers referred to me as Princess because I always seemed to get what I wanted. I met the love of my life in college and got married. We were able to buy a house and have kids. All the markings of "successful" and "happy." And I was happy. I was grateful. But there always seemed to be something missing. *How could I question what we've all been told is the "perfect" life? I should be happy with working hard, climbing a ladder, saving, and retiring with hopefully a few great vacations mixed in. Who am I to want more?*

Every year on New Year's I made the same resolutions to grow my business, make more money and finally find so-called freedom. Yet each new year brought more of the same. I felt stuck in stagnation and the feeling of something missing only grew more intense with each passing ball drop.

From a young age, I knew I would never do the same job for 40 years. That sounded like death to me. Within six months of completing my degree, I knew in my heart I'd leave the field. For what, I didn't know, but I knew life was calling me elsewhere. I felt a pull to something greater, even if I didn't know what that greater thing was. The irony of searching outside of yourself is you never actually find what you're looking for.

Manifesting Generators are said to be multi-passionate creatures that are happiest when they can dip their toes into all the things. And it's true. I'm happiest when I have the freedom to explore and follow my sacral 'yes' down some random rabbit hole. Learn to screen print? Sure! Read for days all about how the subconscious mind works? OMG I can't get enough! So often it doesn't lead anywhere, and other times I only see the "why" years later. Every rabbit hole, though, has built on the last and allowed me to be where I am today.

However, the guilt of being someone that always "quits" right before it gets good has almost stolen all the blessings being a MG have brought. *How can I pivot again, I just did six months ago? How can I "waste" all that money on that hobby I was so passionate about but now feels draining and annoying? Can't I just make up my mind? Commit to something, anything!*

When I discovered Human Design, I was just past 30 and a new mother buried under the weight of trying to be the best mother I could be and build a business all without help, of course. Manifesting Generators can do it all, right? I love my kids, but they have never been my purpose. Building my business and stretching myself creatively has always felt more purpose-filled and expansive. Except our culture says, "my kids are my everything." Shouldn't I find my purpose in changing diapers, shuttling them to activities, and sending them to college?

Who am I to question and not agree with what everyone else thinks? Maybe you've thought that too. *Who am I to want more than just being a mother? Who am I to want a thriving business and life?*

Human Design was the first tool out of thousands I tried that not only made sense and validated what I'd always known to be true, but was also the first one that answered a very deep unyielding question nothing else could.

Does my voice matter? What am I here to say?

My heart always knew there was something I alone could share and no one else, but figuring out what that was eluded me for years. Self-development talks a lot about purpose and finding your purpose. For me though, the purpose didn't go far enough. I wanted to know what I am here to share with the world. If we're all once-in-a-lifetime cosmic events, then how do I fit in?

The answer came through my Human Design chart. Each person's energy works differently, but it's all flowing out through the throat to "make manifest." Understanding how the energy moves allows you to understand what your unique message and perspective is to share. I realized the more you unblock those gates and channels the more your unique gifts, talents, and energy can be expressed. And expressing your energy more fully allows you to be the magnet to all the things you desire. Your unique self can shine for being *you.*

One of my rabbit holes was copywriting. I'm fascinated with why people buy or don't buy. The "know, like, and trust" factor didn't add up in my mind though. And the multiple ways I saw people teach how to do that only served to confuse me more. *How can there be one way to communicate effectively if we're all so different? Why do cold DM's work for some and not others? And why were some people successful with storytelling and for others it didn't work?*

In copywriting it's taught that if you use certain persuasion tactics, you'll sell whatever the thing is. There's a formula for everything. Get enough eyeballs on it and you'll turn a profit eventually. I hated that. Most people can smell a salesman from a mile away. We don't want to be sold; we want to make an empowered decision. We don't want to feel like a profit margin! That way of doing business is the old paradigm. We're moving to a new era that is based on sharing our gifts and talents. Yes, get paid for what you're passionate about, but also do it in a way that allows your unique energy to flow without resistance.

If our energy is mapped out differently, then we should communicate differently. Each person has something unique to express and in their own way. By looking at the Human Design chart this way, I saw what and how our soul wants to communicate. A roadmap to your unique communication style and what will draw people to you. Some people will be good storytellers while others are good at explaining facts.

As a Manifesting Generator I loved creating a dialogue with my readers. I loved asking questions and allowing them to feel a part of the conversation. Going live without a script and trusting I'll know what to say was invigorating and filled my heart with a joy I rarely found in motherhood. I trusted my intuition to guide me and the results were incredible.

By clearing my Splenic channel, I created a highly engaged audience that loves what I do and wants to buy. Before, I struggled to be heard and blended into the masses even after doing a million "ideal client" studies. I'm still a work in progress and every day I have to remind myself to not overthink and surrender to the flow. But after less than a year, I can honestly say it has changed my life in profound ways. The more I connect to my inner knowing, the more impactful my words become all without me pushing or screaming to be heard.

THE TOOL

Would you love to learn how your Human Design type structures their message? *(This structure works best for online service providers)*

Each person communicates in a different way based on the way their energy moves through their body. Energy wants to flow resistance-free through the gates and channels you have defined in your chart. These are consistent energies for you, they're reliable and once you access them it feels like coming home. You feel comfortable speaking and know what to say and when to say it.

Are you ready?

Grab your chart and find your type. Each type has a different aura that is received differently by others. Not good or bad, just different. This aura helps guide you to how people perceive you when you first meet. Much like a first impression. If you've been studying Human Design for a while, you can likely guess what someone's type is just by interacting with them. It's your energy signature.

Projectors, For Projectors you have a penetrating aura, meaning you often see what others don't. You can sense someone's needs before they do. You're here to help guide people with your unique ability to "see" what needs to change. But because you see people so deeply, they need to be ready for you.

Have you tried to give a friend advice only to be shut down or ignored? It's likely the other person wasn't ready to receive your guidance. Manifestors and Manifesting Generators especially hate being told what to do. And often an unknowing Projector tries to tell other people they're doing things wrong and there's a better way if they would just listen to them! So many Projectors feel like they're shouting into a black hole online and no one is listening.

In your messaging your story needs to come first. Throw the "you" language out. What you feel called to share and help others with is likely something you've healed/changed/achieved in your own life. So, share how you did it! Share your unique way of seeing the problem and the solution that no one is talking about. You're here to help shift the paradigm.

With your unique way of seeing, you've also found a new way of solving a problem. Your system is what guides people to their desire. What does your system look and feel like? Give it a name and make it yours.

The most important piece for a Projector is to share your story and system of solving a problem from a place of complete knowing. Your audience is not there to validate your knowing and solution - that comes from within you. Create content to be visible and share your unique way of seeing and solving a problem.

Use this statement to talk about what you do.

I guide *(the person you love working with)* to *(desire your ideal client is seeking)* through my unique system *(name your system or share a little of why it's unique).*

Affirmation: My voice matters, I share my soul's message with complete confidence and my clients flock to me effortlessly.

Manifestors, where you at?

Your big bold aura is here to get the party started! You work in bursts of creativity and struggle when you're interrupted. You are a trail blazer, someone here to try new things and break barriers. Remember the guy that busted the four-minute mile? Then everybody was doing it. That's you.

Your messaging is all about the big vision and where you're taking people. What do you see is possible for yourself and others? Create train station stops along the trail that people can get on and off, but they're all leading to the same place, your big vision. What is the experience like on your train? We don't have to know how we're getting there. We only need to know that you're a confident engineer and know the way. Trust your wild hair ideas, you are not too big.

Use this statement to talk about what you do.

When *(your big idea happens)* we create *(people who embody your vision).*

Example: "When women are empowered to sell with authenticity, they're able to step into their role as CEO and build a business that's revolutionary."

Affirmation: It is safe to be me. My vision is my purpose and I step fully into that vision first so that I can guide others to it with ease.

Generators in the house?

You are one of the more populous types, but no less unique. You have an enveloping aura that when your sacral is turned on everyone wants to be around you. You're the steady friend that lights up a room. You're here to refine a repeatable process. What that is will be guided by your sacral and it's something that you lose track of time doing. A process that is honed and mastered over time.

What is a process you repeat with every client? How has it refined and become more potent with every pass? You are taking people from stuck to freedom through your repeatable process.

Keep your content conversational. Ask questions and draw your reader in like they're talking with their best friend.

Use this statement to talk about what you do.

I solve *(what problem)* through my process/method so that *(ideal client)* feels/can be/ do *(what result).*

Example:

I solve the struggle of "what's for dinner" through a simple system of meal planning which busy moms can do in just 30 minutes a week.

Affirmation: My process gets better with time and I honor my sacral passions. The world needs my expertise and I share my wisdom because it's what I love to do.

Reflectors, the 1% of the world!

You are the mirror to how those around you and the collective are doing. It can feel heavy and overwhelming at times to feel so much, but in time you will learn it is your greatest wisdom and blessing.

We want your insight on how we're doing. The world isn't always aware of its own needs and you are here to reflect back what we need. Your environment is so important to being a mirror. If your environment is clouded with negative energy, people, situations, the mirror is hazy. Fiercely protect your space and curate, live, and be in a place that inspires and supports you.

Create a community that values and appreciates your sense of what's needed. You should feel free to share whatever you're inspired by or desiring to speak about. What change do you want to see in the world? What deep desire do you have for people? Create your community around that.

Use this statement to talk about what you do.

I guide my community to *(a desire you have)* by sharing resources, inspiration, and guidance so that we can all live a more *(desired way)*.

Example:

I guide my community to see food as medicine by sharing resources, inspiration and guidance so that we can all live a more holistic and natural life.

Affirmation: I clear and ground my energy every day and know that what I feel is important but do not identify my worthiness with it. I share my passions freely and receive tenfold what I give.

Hands up **Manifesting Generators!**

My fellow multi-passionate brothers and sisters! We may take a while to find that "thing" that sustains us, but we have a hella good time trying all things along the way! Never let your meandering path sell you short. There is so much wisdom gained in doing things your way.

Respond to life and don't create ideas from your head. The correct path will light up like a Christmas tree when you release control of what the path looks like. Your sacral knows the way, but give yourself some breathing room before making big decisions. Whether you're an "Emotional Authority" or not, marinate on a decision for a day or two. Allow the idea to roll around in your head and live it out. How does it feel?

Your messaging is all about skipping steps, finding short cuts, and combining things you're passionate about. You don't have to combine every passion, but you likely skip steps to achieve something because of the way you combine or blend different tools or modalities. Share how you do that! And keep it conversation too, just like the Generators.

Use this statement to talk about what you do.

By blending *(two to three things you incorporate)* I help *(a broad audience)* to *(do what?)* so that *(they can have what they desire).*

Example:

By blending copywriting and Human Design I help spiritual entrepreneurs magnetize their ideal clients with their soul's message and get paid for their gifts and talents.

Affirmation: I love my multi-passionate heart. I give myself space to explore when I feel called. I pivot when I know it's time and share my way of doing things with confidence.

Did you love your type breakdown?

There's so much more that goes into creating your soul's message, things like your Throat Center gates, Incarnation Cross and Mercury gates. But this understanding is often the catalyst people need to create content and messaging that's unique to them and confidence to share their message.

If you'd like to learn more about each type and how to structure your message check out my resources page at cloudnine-marketing.com/resource

You'll find a free PDF and how to join my free Facebook community, Aligned Copy Posse.

You truly are a once-in-a-lifetime cosmic event and your soul has a message for the world that only you can give. Create your business message and brand voice around that energy and you'll love showing up in your business!

Love to you all!

Wouldn't it be magical if you always knew what to say and when to say in your business?

Rachael is your go to messaging mentor that blends Human Design and conversation copywriting to help spiritual entrepreneurs create their soul aligned message that attracts ideal clients all without shouting into a black hole.

She is the creator of the Copy By Design™ method that uses your unique energy blueprint to guide your message and copy so that you always know what to say and when to say it. Her method has allowed women to embrace their authenticity and confidently share their gifts. She's been featured on several podcast like The Part-time CEO, The Logical Manifestor, The Holistic Hoedown, and Purposefull Women.

Rachael is a fierce advocate for women using their voice for change. Whether that change is in your own home or half way across the world, every voice matters.

She works with clients 1:1 to craft their soul aligned message and has several entry level guides for writing with your Human Design.

Outside of her office you'll find her exploring the outdoors with her husband and two kids. They live in the heart of the Rockies on 2 arches of pure bliss.

To learn more, you're invited to visited cloudnine-marketing.com

CHAPTER 9

DISCOVER THE MAGIC WITHIN YOU

ALIGN YOUR UNIQUE SELF WITH WEALTH AND EASE

Sally Gamboa Parihar

MY STORY

I used to think attracting wealth was hard until I discovered all you need is to recognize your magic, have a little bit of fun, and you can be wealthy.

Wealth is the experience I get from healthy relationships, personal development, and my contribution to the world.

One day, I thought, *wow, I'm so blessed to be living my life with my soulmate. How many people get to meet and marry their soulmates?*

Although, It took two marriages and three young children before I met Bobby. This is a long and romantic story on its own.

We're now happily married together, and I'm pregnant with my fifth and final child. We are grateful to be living a flexible lifestyle where we mentor people online.

As you can imagine, with the children being homeschooled, we're busy. Fortunately, Bobby is very supportive, and he loves being a dad.

Before I met him, I was a single mom and decided to be an entrepreneur. I became passionate about inner work and spirituality.

On the other hand, Bobby was helping entrepreneurs align their names through Numerology.

This is one of the things we both can resonate with: we love conversations about spirituality and how we perceive life in that sense. We've become a power couple growing together while we raise our children and inspire others.

I remember it was a beautiful day; we were out on a boat with a couple of friends. Our maid of honor offered to take us out for an adventure around Vancouver Island. I could feel the air rushing through me and see where the water meets the mountain. We had amazing conversations, and all of a sudden, one of the questions was asked for everyone to answer, "what's your greatest fear?"

I waited until everybody shared their answers. They all shared something similar that made me feel like my answer would be the strangest one.

My original thought was *my greatest fear is not knowing my purpose and not living it out*. But when it was my turn, I said, "spiders!" Then I quickly turned it around and told them my original thought.

I can't remember how many times I've wondered about what I was living for. I was searching for my purpose until one day it found me.

One of Bobby's clients offered to do a Human Design reading for him. I remember we were in the car as he was telling me about his experience. I could hear the excitement in his voice.

"Oh, you're gonna love this! It's a combination of different things like Iching, Kabbalah, Chakras, Astrology, and quantum physics. It's logical." He said with confidence. He knows how I'm more logical than abstract, so he just knew that I'd love this. He said, "I'm going to interview her in my podcast." I said, "I'm excited! I'll be watching." I got curious, so I started to do my own research and pull up my own chart.

Found out my type, but I didn't know how to read my bodygraph. I was watching their interview as it was being recorded live. I was just fascinated as she explained how this system shows you how to make a decision.

I remember her saying, "Bobby, you have an open throat, and that just means you're flexible in that center." Bobby said, "That's cool; I talk for a living, that must mean something."

This made me more curious as to what a fixed throat meant. Bobby was curious too and wanted to learn more about me, so he got me a session with her.

I did more research before my session, so I had some ideas about my bodygraph beforehand. I was still very excited to hear what she had to say about me.

As I was sitting there listening to her reading her notes, she said, "you're here to guide others." When I heard this, I felt relieved because I used to wonder a lot about my purpose in life.

I noticed my body was relaxing, feeling relieved that I'm now certain about what I'm here for. She also made me feel validated when she mentioned, "you need to take some alone time and rest."

I had so much freedom that I had time to reflect on myself and recognize what I'm passionate about. When I met Bobby, one of the things that made me feel so blessed is how sweet he is when he said, "I want you to just be able to do whatever you want; I'll support you."

The thing is, I found out I was a mental projector. As a projector mom, a non-energy type who is not here to work but a natural learner and loves to study, you can just imagine the relief I felt after learning this about myself. I thought, *this must be one of the reasons why projectors are not supposed to have children*. Everyone is pretty much our child. I didn't know this until I got pregnant with my fifth.

But I'm blessed with my family. Bobby is a Generator. I have another Generator son, two Manifesting Generator children, and one Manifestor.

It was hard to assess my level of energy as there was always something that kept me busy. I felt I had to justify why I couldn't be there to take my other two children to school when I was pregnant and had another young child to take care of.

I'm blessed that my husband is relieved and still supportive after knowing my design and what I'm really here for. He was there helping me take care of the children. I felt guilty at times that I start to do more than I could just to feel like I was doing my role as a mother. And then I felt I was being seen as still not doing enough.

There were things expected of me as a mother. But I'm not like every mother or everyone else. As my husband calls me, "you're very ambitious," we both laughed. He wanted an ambitious woman but not someone who has many ideas that he can't keep up with.

I'm more active mentally than I am physically. I realized there's nothing wrong with that If I'm designed to have a strong mental awareness with a limited source of energy.

Most of what I do requires a lot of thinking and advising others. Working with energy can be just as exhausting as cooking, or doing dishes, or cleaning the house.

One of the things I enjoy doing is reading a book as I have my favorite morning cacao that my husband lovingly prepares for me. So I pick one of the Human Design books and sit in my favorite La-Z-Boy rocking chair in our lounge area.

Sometimes, my husband and I enjoy listening to the Human Design audios we bought. He learned a lot just from listening to them. This was when we decided to print out our charts and post them on our dining room wall. So whenever we're having a meal together, I refer to the charts and say a little something about each one of my family. My children learned quickly about their types. Even my four-year-old says, "I'm a Manifestor; I only eat hot food." We just laugh at how cute they are.

My children also ask me questions like, "what's my superpower?" and "can I give you energy?" I love teaching them when they come to me because there's no resistance this way.

Human Design is meant for children. But we have to get through the parents first so they can better guide their children. I find children are a lot easier to teach during their first seven years. There's no need to decondition them but to recognize them for who they truly are in the first place. It gives me joy when I encourage them to be their better version of their unique self.

Parenting was one of the challenging things my husband and I had to go through. We were not raised the same way, and that caused us to have different values and beliefs. As we continued to decondition ourselves, I've seen the difference this has made in terms of our relationship with each other. I noticed he's becoming more aware of how he responds to things. Before, he would get triggered easily. Now, I see him having more patience. Over time, parenting became easier for us.

Naturally, I recognized people for who they are. When I'm around someone, even when I just meet them for the first time, I notice that I can sense the right questions to ask.

One time, we had our new neighbor and a friend come to our place for my daughter's birthday party. My husband told me afterward, "you just seem to know how to get information from others; they just give it to you so easily and comfortably." I just smiled at him.

I notice things most people miss. I learned that I could also easily see how things are more efficient. Bobby and I have this daily mastermind where we assess where we're at in our life and share our insights on ways to improve them.

One time we were masterminding in the kitchen. While he was preparing cacao drinks for us, I came up to him and smiled. We usually make this joke and say to whoever is doing the dishes or any chores, "I'm not paying you to do that." We just laughed.

But jokes aside, I was suggesting during our mastermind, "you know, we can outsource some of the things we do and focus our energy more on the children and our passion." At first, he responded, "This is just temporary. Eventually, we will, but for now, while the children are young, I can do some of the responsibilities and get them involved."

I agreed and can understand his perspective. I know there are things that the children can do to help us, and at the same time, it teaches them responsibilities.

I told him, "the right people who will help us will come in divine timing." And it did. Now, we have people who help us with our gardening, cleaning, and downsizing.

Even the people who work with us, I get to know them through their design as it helps me recognize their true potential.

Now we have more time to focus on what we love to do. As I studied more about my family and the people in my life, I learned more about myself in the process. I recognized how unique I was, and it made me feel confident.

You know that feeling when you find something you lost for a long time but knew it was there somewhere? That was the same feeling I got when I found out my design.

It wasn't long before I started to show up with confidence. It was easy for me to accept myself and love what I truly am. But at the same time, I felt others didn't fully accept me.

I wanted to be recognized for what I'm excellent at and passionate about, especially by my husband, who I care about. I have mistaken his frustration with him not recognizing me. One time I felt I was overworking just to please him. I focused all day on the children and their needs and forgot to care for myself and my husband. I thought that made him happy, but in the end, I was tired and didn't have enough energy left for him or myself. This proves how self-care is important when starting our day.

I eventually realized I didn't have to feel bad for how others see me. As long as I knew my value, I didn't need to prove my worth. All I needed was to pursue what I love and share that with others. My success comes from guiding my children and others. I noticed when I feel successful, my husband is satisfied. In the end, how we feel is what matters.

When I started to show up as myself, that's when the right people started to recognize me for what I truly am. I started to receive different invitations. Some people who knew me introduced me to other networks. I was invited to do interviews and masterclasses and given opportunities to work with others, guide others, and even collaborate in writing this book with other authors.

I used to do many different things as hobbies which is fascinating because now these skills have become handy and helpful to have in my toolbox. I can just take what I need when I need it.

I studied Neurolinguistic Programming, which led me to become a Certified Practitioner of Human Interaction Technology. It has improved my communication skills which I use all the time.

I studied accounting and worked for a total of four years working for someone else until I had my own home-based business doing income tax for others. My husband and I have now incorporated our business, and I now get to manage our finances and file our corporate taxes.

I enjoyed dancing, and I still do it as a hobby and a way to connect with my husband and children. In addition, I learned Numerology from my husband and created his numerology app.

Everything I've learned has become very useful in my life. But when I discovered that I'm here to master one thing, I just knew Human Design was something I wanted to master. So next thing you know, I created my Facebook group and started to share everything I learned and loved about Human Design to help others discover their unique self.

Then I started to enjoy reading charts for others. Through this, I was able to guide them and learn more about myself in the process.

I'm glad that my husband and I have the same vision and passion for helping others come into alignment with who they truly are.

If there was one value I could teach my children, it would be how they can navigate through life by following their inner authority when making decisions.

My parents separated when I was growing up, and my mom worked overseas to support us. I was still fortunate and grateful to have my grandfather's sister, *"Lola,"* take care of me like her own daughter.

She's now in a better place. She lived a long life, and I believe she lived her purpose. She showed me what true unconditional love is by giving and caring without expectations.

I appreciate having Lola and my parents in my life because they were not there to make me work. It felt like they just knew and recognized me for what I am.

Knowing and embodying my design has made my life easier and wealthier. It also helped me understand, accept, and love myself as I accept the people around me. I feel more liberated. I love that I can now confidently be myself. I believe no one is broken; we're just different.

It's been a fun journey for me, and I hope it will be for you too.

THE TOOL

One of the things that helped us receive more in life was putting affirmation notes all over the house. Feel as you write down on sticky notes affirmations like, I am love, I am wealth, I am grateful for my family, and anything that feels aligned to you.

Place them on top of your mirror, by your switch lights, or by your bed where you can see them first thing in the morning. Depending on where you place them, make sure it says something about it. For example, on your fridge, it could say, "Thank you for our food that keeps us healthy." Gratitude works all the time.

If this is your first time hearing about Human Design, begin by observing and watching your life like a movie. This is how we can allow our mind to do what it's designed to do.

Feel into your environment and get rid of anything you no longer need, fix or upgrade anything you feel might be good to do, and buy something that will add positive energy into your house, like beautiful flowers, plants or even new furniture

When you notice you have to make a decision, feel into your body to see how it responds. Reflect on your life. How did you make decisions in the past? Feel free to write down your answers.

If you have children, I want you to experiment by asking them versus telling them to do something. See how that makes a difference.

Try changing your environment even by simply going out in your backyard. How does that feel in your body?

Notice how you are conditioned by your environment, including animals, plants, planets, your parents, family, teachers, and the people you surround yourselves with. How do you feel around different people?

Plants and animals have their unique design as well. There's beauty in all of us. There are one or more things that make you stand out if you recognize it. This is the magic that's different in each of us.

When you know your design, practice using your strategy and authority. If you let your body's intelligence and consciousness lead you, your life will flow easier and effortlessly.

Start surrounding yourself with people who make you feel good. When you are in the right environment, you'll start to attract the right people in your life.

This is not something you have to believe in but something you can experiment with. Have fun discovering your magic.

Remember, you are special and unique. Love yourself.

Sally Gamboa Parihar is a Spirit Guide, and a Teacher. Raising her family on Vancouver Island, she guides and mentors soul-driven entrepreneurs online to discover their purpose and unique self through Human Design.

Naturally, Sally is passionate about helping others recognize their value and align them to their true frequency. She also teaches everything she's learning about Human Design in her Facebook group. https://www.facebook.com/groups/discoveryouruniqueself

She's here to support the collective as she understands the importance of being in a community who support each other specifically in accepting and loving everyone as themselves.

As she masters Human Design, she currently helps others understand their own individual design, as well as relationships, family, and how to group a team to create the most balanced combination of energy.

Sally believes in her core values of personal development, healthy loving relationships, wellness, spirituality, educating children, and her contribution to humanity.

She's committed to differentiate in this world by living her design, guiding her children, and expressing her unique outer authority to those who recognize and invite her to share her gift and wisdom.

You can find out more about what she loves to offer through her website. www.sallygamboaparihar.co

CHAPTER 10

AUDACIOUSLY ALIGNED

STOP SHOULDING ON YOURSELF AND THRIVE

Jen Allen

MY STORY

Why can't I just be satisfied? I am good at this—no, I am great at this—plus the money is excellent, and my parents can brag about what a successful adult they raised.

That familiar feeling set in.

The one that nudges me after I have gone all in on something with my effort, heart, and soul: *There is more out there for you.*

Um, more than a multiple six-figure career that I have built from the ground up over the last five years?

Yep. Trust me, you no longer have the energy to serve and succeed here. Something has to change.

I should be able to stick it out.

My whole life I have jumped into a new activity, job, or exciting opportunity with both feet. I pick up new skills easily. I can figure out the blueprint for "success" wherever I land. I have the ability to deeply study the ins and outs of whatever interests me, find the resources I need, and learn how to connect with others in order to grow. I gain a measure of success at whatever I commit to and, after a period of time, I eventually get that feeling in my gut that says, "We are done here. It's time to move on."

I have been called brave and bold with every pivot, but it always feels scarier to stay than to forge forward in a fresh direction. I recognize the signs of burnout and pay attention to my increasing frustration and lack of energy to engage any longer. I am resilient to change. I know I will figure it out.

And yet, other people seemed to be able to power through. They appear to know what they want and can stick with it. They aren't embarrassed by their varied job history. They don't joke they are a "Jill of All Trades," while at the same time wondering if everyone thinks they are a quitter or expecting too much joy and satisfaction from their work.

"I just need to take the first quarter next year off to reevaluate my business," I explained to my husband mid-December of 2019. Exhausted, frustrated, and physically sick with an unrelenting head cold, I knew I'd hit a major wall. Thankfully, my husband subscribes to the "happy wife, happy life" philosophy, and was also well aware that my flame was burning lower and lower.

I was a REALTOR® and owned my own brokerage as a solopreneur. I hadn't had a true day off in five years and planned to refer business out for the first quarter of 2020. My goal was to figure out what I could adjust to stop feeling that pit of dread in my stomach whenever a new potential client contacted me. I had become "successful" in the eyes of my peers and earned an income I'd previously only dreamed of. And yet I found myself thinking, *money isn't everything.*

One of the first aspects I learned while studying my Human Design is that I'm a Manifesting Generator. My life is all about transformation and growth as I navigate what excites me and brings me joy. I'm meant to be multi-passionate and respond to what lights me up. I'm not here to follow the conventional path; I chart my own!

I picked up conditioning from society that I should select a career and settle down, but that is simply not who I am. I'm here to be a powerful creator and inspire others with my energy. However, at the end of 2019, my energy was non-existent. I was experiencing what is referred to as the "generator pause." This is a time we (often reluctantly) feel the intense urge to purposefully slow down to evaluate our current direction in life and reevaluate our next steps. *Is it time to shift my process or break off into an entirely new direction?* The pause can be the energetic reset necessary to keep shoveling for the gold at the next level or the catalyst to search for a new gold mine.

While taking this hiatus from real estate, I found myself reflecting on what my purpose is in this life. ***I should know my purpose***. I thought it was to help people with their real estate needs. Now, that no longer resonated with me. I was also a home stager and, in addition to staging my listings, I had been sharing the remodel of our home online for a couple years at this point. People loved my vision and style. Maybe design was what I should be doing?

Friends were asking if I would help them with design layouts and interior décor selections. I knew I was good at it and how much pulling together a space that supported me and my family lit me up. However, every time someone asked, I had that dang pit in my stomach. *Nope. I don't want to do that.*

My designs feel personal to me. They are my creative outlet, my play. I couldn't stand the thought of anyone pulling apart my creativity who wasn't able to see the complete vision. Even though my body clearly was saying "no," I was still relying on my mind to figure out what was next for me. Plus, I was desperately seeking my purpose so I could have something exciting to put my creative energy towards again.

I am good at this. People recognize this in me. They want to hire me. I am going to need some kind of work if I decide to leave real estate.

I registered a new company with the Colorado Secretary of State: Aligned Interiors Co. The name was intentionally a play on words. While everyone was asking me to help with the interiors of their homes, I couldn't stop thinking about an incredible tool and system for self-awareness I was studying called Human Design. I would get lost for hours (and still do!) as I went deeper and deeper into what the system taught me about myself and my relationships with others. I envisioned a future of impacting, inspiring, and empowering women with transformation of their *personal interior*, not that of their home.

This realization occurred as I became aware of my true purpose. There is nothing in your Human Design that will tell you exactly what job you are meant to have, but you do have a unique set of gifts and an energetic purpose you're here to fulfill. I learned that my purpose is to live my life in an authentic way that lights me up and inspires others to do the same. I ultimately am here to expand prosperity for others with my unique combination of gifts.

It has been enlightening to see how I've actually been living out my purpose over the years. As I mentioned before, I previously felt some shame about my colorful job history. Now I see how my skills were used to increase prosperity every place I worked. As long as I was satisfied with the job and felt valued, I was an incredible asset.

As a REALTOR®, I increased prosperity for families by assisting them with making wise financial decisions when purchasing and selling their properties so they could enjoy the greatest profit. Even in 2020, when I was no longer taking clients, I increased prosperity for my REALTOR® friends by referring them business. I now help others create prosperity by teaching them how they were created to attract opportunities, make decisions, improve relationships, and thrive!

In the midst of my attempt to figure out my purpose and clarify my next steps, the world came to a standstill. We were all directed to stay home, stay away from others, and cover our faces for health and safety. It was a shock to my system.

I've always had a pretty decent life. Yes, as an adult, I've faced numerous challenges and "everything happens for a reason" has carried me through more surprises and shocking events than I ever thought possible. I continue to persevere and grow with each upheaval, from economic downturns, to surprise pregnancies, to near-death experiences.

However, underneath the surface is an emotional storm subtly brewing at all times. I have experienced emotional highs and lows my entire life and had perfected my coping mechanism of numbing and stuffing down those emotions I was taught were bad or negative. You know, the "appropriate" and "acceptable" way to handle life as an adult professional. ***I should stop feeling this way.***

My traditional middle-class upbringing included a balance of activities, nature, travel, childhood friends, and parents who are still happily married. I first learned to numb my emotions with shots of Southern Comfort from the liquor cabinet at 12 years old. When I was in high school the melancholy, pain, and overwhelming feeling of being trapped was too much for me. One day I swallowed a handful of pills and chugged two beers, hoping I would fall asleep and fade away along with the depression. Imagine my frustration waking up 10 hours later with a terrible headache and twisted stomach, but still here to deal with the misery of life.

I decided that was a sign I was meant to be here and perhaps *not* talking about my feelings wasn't actually serving me. I told my mom what I had done, and she scheduled a visit with a therapist. I remember being fascinated by the pre-appointment evaluation as I was encouraged to think about myself in a different way while answering the many questions. *Oooh, this self-reflection business is interesting!*

I learned two things about myself during those therapy sessions:

1. I have higher expectations for myself than anyone else ever could.
2. My "condition" was labeled as manic depression.

More awareness! My extreme highs and lows had a name. Getting validation that I wasn't alone in this experience gave me reason to believe I could manage the lows if I could just catch them earlier. I also was determined to hang in there for the freedom I could sense on the horizon, also known as college.

I rarely talked about this experience with anyone until very recently because it was made clear to me that depression is not something nice, "normal" people discussed. I referred to my feelings as a spiral and I became excellent at catching myself as I began the downward decent, recognizing the spiral before I went too deep. The stuffing, numbing, and working through my emotions privately was working out for me. At least, I thought it was.

Of course, 2020 busted open the floodgates of emotional lows that I hadn't fully experienced in 25 years. That feeling of being trapped and unable to move through the emotions that I previously experienced as a teenager had become a constant battle. However, there was even more crushing pressure and less room to navigate, while at home with my children and husband all day, every day. Time alone in my own space, social gatherings, and working out at the gym had been key to moving through my emotions and they were all stripped away in a moment, with no end in sight.

I didn't want to be here anymore. The world was going to shit, and I was done with it all together. I would sob in the shower, all night long in bed, and on walks behind sunglasses, still trying to stuff and numb so no one worried about me. There were many days I would fantasize about how I could escape the deep pain I was feeling by leaving this world.

Then I made a life-changing discovery about the important role of my emotions. In Human Design, authority is how we are meant to make correct decisions for ourselves, and it turns out I am an Emotional Authority. These emotions come in the form of waves, ups and downs, that are unique to each person experiencing them. This is what I previously recognized and called "spirals." Learning the importance of honoring my emotions led me to finally stop numbing my lows with alcohol on December 15, 2020, at 42 years old. I decided it was time to take my personal power back and fully tune in to what my emotions were teaching me.

Just as important as discovering the role of my own emotions was learning that neither of my parents are Emotional Authority. They don't have these intense waves of emotions running through their bodies all day and night. In fact, my emotions probably made them quite uncomfortable and, therefore, I was never taught how to move through them in a healthy, productive way. Hence, the numbing and stuffing down plan I adopted early on.

It turns out about 50% of the population is like me—meant to get out of their head and into their emotions when it comes to knowing what is correct for them. I can see how many of those people, including my husband and boys, are riding these waves unaware of their importance in their lives. Part of what I share and teach others now is how there are no good or bad emotions, and that our feelings are here for us to work with and learn from.

I am learning to surf my own emotional waves and ride them with grace. One of my particular waves comes with extreme lows and melancholy, but that melancholy is also an important part of my depth and creativity. I appreciate the lows now as much as the highs, even if they do come at inopportune times. I understand now that these feelings serve me. I seek to be aligned with this inner authority given to me and hope to help others do the same.

THE TOOL

BECOMING AUDACIOUSLY ALIGNED

When I learned about my unique Human Design, I became aware of the "shoulds" I had given my power away to because of the conditioning I received from my parents, teachers, and society. This traditional "path to success and happiness" we are taught often runs counter to how we are energetically created to thrive.

You deserve to be authentically and unapologetically aligned with how you are meant to attract opportunities and make confident, correct decisions for yourself. Once you are aware of how you were created to navigate life using your unique blend of energy, gifts, and talents, you are on your way to audacious alignment.

Step 1: Recognize what energy is authentically yours, and what is being projected onto you through external conditioning or being absorbed and amplified by you when you are with others. What "shoulds" show up for you? Are you constantly overwhelmed and even paralyzed by all of the ideas you take into your head throughout the day? Do you feel under pressure to keep checking things off your list before you can actually relax? Are there certain people or places that make you feel most overwhelmed and under pressure?

Step 2: Give yourself grace and space to reflect on this newfound awareness. Be a non-judgmental witness to your life in the moment. *Oh, that is interesting, let's pull that thread a bit. Where does this "should" come from? What is my fear around not taking this action?* This takes practice and can be aided with meditation, journaling, and contemplation with movement (stretching, yoga, swimming, jogging). Experiment with what works for you!

Step 3: Decide what boundaries you need to establish within yourself, or with others, to allow for the practice of embodying your authentic self.

For example, if you become overwhelmed with the amount information and inspiration in your environment (and online!) experiment with boundaries around how much input you allow for. This can be temporarily hiding certain accounts on social media, giving yourself specific times in the day that are electronic-free, or even disconnecting from all media for a day, week, or month to get grounded in your own energy again.

Step 4: Dig deeper into understanding your specific of your Human Design and how your different aspects work together in a way that is unique to you and your life experience. There is much to learn about your incarnation cross, profile, channels, gates, lines, and primary health system aspects to support your alignment. This is ideally pursued after you experiment with the strategy of your energy type and your authority for a bit. However, some people (like me!) really enjoy diving deep initially and then zooming back out to integrate what they have learned. Please visit www.AlignedInteriorsCo.com/audacious where I begin the process of help you build understanding and awareness each aspect of your unique Human Design.

Step 5: Finally, give yourself permission to experiment without attachment to the outcome. Remember, in this practice you are simply an observer of your life. Your process will be unique to you, and you don't need to justify anything to yourself or anyone else. Stop giving into "I should" and start embracing "I absofuckinglutely want to." Get out of the never-ending thoughts swirling in your mind and start tuning in to the wisdom of your body. Be fully you. Live like you. Thrive like you.

There is so much peace and freedom in self-awareness and self-acceptance. Embrace your unique blend of energy and gifts to thrive authentically. Let go of the energy that was never yours to take on in the first place. Practice letting go of the expectations of others. Learn what is worth your time and energy to care about and how to release the rest.

Become more fully engaged in your purpose and on high alert for aligned opportunities life brings you. Learn how to create your own reality through taking radical responsibility, establishing energetic boundaries, and making more confident decisions (even if it feels like you don't have good options to choose between!) Your life, satisfaction, and peace are your responsibility alone. You can't abdicate them to anyone else. ***This is being audaciously aligned.***

Jen is the owner of Aligned Interiors Co., a personal and professional development company that teaches the Human Design System. She is a 1/3 Emotional Manifesting Generator, and her journey has been long and winding. Some notable parts include a Bachelor of Science in Hospitality and Tourism Management from Purdue University, an MBA with marketing emphasis from the University of Missouri – St. Louis, and numerous jobs in a variety of fields that lit her up at the time.

She witnessed first-hand the incredible impact of understanding and embodying how she was created to thrive using Human Design and becomes more audaciously aligned every day. Her greatest hope is that others experience this clarity and freedom for themselves.

Jen knows there are many books and online resources that can assist you with a self-study of your Human Design but believes the fastest way to audacious alignment is a foundational session with her as she focuses entirely on your energetics and how they play with each other. Visit www.alignedinteriorsco.com/audacious to access exclusive resources and special offers for "Stop Overworking and Start Overflowing" readers.

CHAPTER 11

RADIATING POWER

FROM EXHAUSTED TO ECSTATIC

Maggie Ostara, PhD, Certified Human Design
and Quantum Human Design Expert

I've been haunted by burnout for much of my adult life. Even though I naturally have a lot of energy, often more than those around me, I've found myself more than once horizontal and close to brain dead without truly knowing why.

Yes, burnout haunts or overtakes many of us. Maybe you?

Sleep deprivation, over-work, and not enough downtime all contribute to this epidemic. Yet I intuitively knew that something else played a key role, but I didn't know what it was. Until I discovered and learned to live in alignment with my Human Design.

When I made the commitment to using Human Design as an evolutionary tool, I discovered a new way of engaging with life through which I was able to shift from exhausted to ecstatic. Since I "got it," I know how to live so I have all the energy I want and need, creating an ecstatic buoyancy that I experience virtually every day.

I want to share with you pieces of my story, plus a potent practice you can use right now to begin radiating your sovereign power. You can also find additional resources at www.SovereigntybyDesign.com/sosoresources.

MY STORY

SEPTEMBER 2017

"Okay, what does that even mean, to 'wait to respond'?" I'm annoyed. I didn't understand what that meant the first time I'd heard it a few years before, and I didn't understand it now.

When I first heard that, according to my Human Design type (Generator), I'm designed to "wait to respond" and not to initiate, I dismissed the system as inaccurate. I'm an Aries Sun and I've always been good at getting things going. The idea that my strategy for engaging with life is to "wait to respond" did not resonate with me at all. This idea created so much cognitive dissonance that in my arrogance and ignorance I walked away from Human Design. But when I burned out *again*, I decided to take another look, a real look this time.

I'm sitting across from a Human Design expert who's doing his best to be patient. I get the feeling no one has ever pressed him so hard about what this means. It's important to me. I can't just hear this idea about one of the most significant aspects of my design, my strategy, and not get it. I have the feeling he's accustomed to transmitting information to clients and not having them ask a lot of questions, and certainly not pressing him the way I am.

Take a breath, Maggie, I tell myself. *Pause. Take a breath. See if you can take in what he's saying.*

"It's not that you can never initiate anything," he says. "It's more about how you enter into things. Once you've entered into something correctly, then you initiate inside of that. Does that make sense?" I can tell he's trying. But I've got a cotton wad in my head. Everything he says sounds muffled, like it's coming from the other side of a thick, closed door.

"You know what, Maggie," he says. "I think you just have to try it. I don't think anything I'm going to say now is going to mean any more to you than it already does. You just have to test it out and see for yourself." He smiles, warmly, as if from across a crevasse.

"Okay, well, how do I do that?" I'm doing my best to keep my tone even.

"Stop initiating and see what shows up."

"Just like that?"

"Just like that."

I felt bad that my annoyance and frustration had boiled over into my conversation with him. It certainly wasn't his fault that I felt so stirred up inside. What he was suggesting sounded like something I'd heard two decades before, and I didn't understand or like it then either. Blinders from my conditioning hid this gem from view, until I tore them off.

FEBRUARY 1999

I'm holding the Emperor card from the Thoth Tarot deck. I'm sitting across from Wendi, an elfin woman with penetrating brown eyes. We'd been doing shamanic work together for six months, and her guidance had helped me grow *a lot*.

On this day I feel challenged and uncomfortable. Eighteen months before, I'd started a new endeavor and I'd reached a significant level of success in that business, but it came at a very high price: exhaustion.

I could not and did not want to continue the way I'd been going. Every time I thought about working hard again, my belly knotted up.

My motto was: "if it's to be it's up to me" and I believed that for anything to happen, *I had to make it happen*. I knew how to work hard. You can't get a PhD without working hard. I did the work and created success, yet I was neither satisfied nor happy.

"I keep pulling the Emperor card," I say. "Why do I keep pulling this card?" I ask her.

"Take a good look at it," Wendi said. "What do you see?"

"It's red with two Aries rams. He's got a scepter and a crown, plus he's holding an orb of some kind. I imagine these are all symbols of power. What am I supposed to see?" By now I'm frustrated, bumping up against my inner limits.

"What else do you notice about him?" she asked.

"I don't know. He's sitting on his throne?"

"Exactly," she said, "he's *sitting* on his throne. *He's not doing anything.* He's radiating power and authority from his throne *without doing anything.* He's in his seat of power and he's confident in himself and his position."

"What does that have to do with me?" Now exacerbated, I wasn't getting it.

"He does not need to prove himself," she said. "He's completely *sovereign.* Yes, he's sovereign because he's the emperor but even more he's sovereign because of the *quality of his being.* You too, Maggie, have the opportunity to be sovereign in your life."

"What does that mean?" I ask. *"Being sovereign?"*

"He's sitting calmly, centered, confident, radiating power. Yes, the rams are there, yet they too are stationary. They're not running around making things happen the way we often think of Aries energy. Other figures in the tarot are engaged in some form of activity. But both the Emperor and the Empress are not. They sit in their seats of power attracting to them what they need and desire, confident it will be delivered to them."

She might as well have been speaking Russian.

"Yeah, okay, but they're *royalty,*" I say. "I don't see how that applies to me." Stubborn.

"Well, you keep pulling the Emperor card so there is clearly a message here for you," Wendi said. "In our work together, you've been clearing out of your energy field anything that is not yours. This is a vital step. You cannot be sovereign if you're carrying other people's emotions, patterns, old belief systems, or trauma. You cannot be sovereign if you're chasing other people's versions of success or happiness.

"You become sovereign when you are in charge of your own energy, your emotions, your beliefs, and your destiny. The Emperor card holds codes for you in developing your own sovereignty. You do not need to become him, but you do have much to learn from him."

This was the first time I had heard someone use the term *sovereign* and *sovereignty* in relation to me and as something I could cultivate in my own life. The frequency and tonality of the words captivated me immediately, and I've been exploring what they mean in my life and those of my clients ever since.

OCTOBER 2017

The Emperor isn't doing anything, I remember Wendi saying. *He's just sitting on his throne, radiating power.* I pull out the card again and wonder, *is he waiting to respond? He's not initiating. He's just sitting there and things come to him. I can try to do that.*

Even though 20 years had passed, and I'd worked with sovereignty in many ways personally and professionally, I'd never absorbed the piece Wendi was trying to transmit to me about sitting and radiating and having what you want come to you. I'd practiced Law of Attraction, getting into the vibration of what I wanted, with considerable success. But I'd never stopped initiating and making things happen. Being in action was what I knew.

Remembering the Emperor, I make a pact with myself: *For two months I will not start anything. I'm going to see what happens. I'm going to wait and see what shows up.*

My conditioning about having to make things happen was so all encompassing I literally could not see how anything would get done it if I didn't do it. This wasn't conscious or purposeful, but that belief was still running my life. I'd been living inside a version of myself that supported my achievements but also led me to burning out.

As soon as I make this pact, I run smack into a disbelieving voice inside asking snidely: *Right, how is that supposed to work?* My belly tightens up, my breathing shallow. *I don't know*, I think. *But I'm ready to find out.*

What I couldn't see, and what Human Design gave me, was *the specific practice of response* that taught me how to dance with the Flow of Life. My biggest challenge was trusting that the Flow of Life would bring me things to respond to—*and the right things!* While the world is full of opportunities, they had to be the right ones for what I was wanting.

Once I stopped initiating and started paying attention, I discovered very quickly that I had plenty to respond to! I began to see emails, social media posts, books I was reading, courses I was taking, things clients said to me, conversations I was having, as providing me with ideas and opportunities to which I could respond. Responding wasn't about doing nothing. It was about engaging with the world with divine intelligence leading the way.

The first big thing that came was a request to help a friend with a project he'd been dreaming of for years but didn't have the skillset to create on his own. He had connections and knew how to interview people, but he had no idea how to turn that into an online conference—and I did. I felt a hearty "yes" in response to his request and off we went developing this project for several months. It was quite lucrative and fun for both of us! Although I spent plenty of time on this project, I had all the energy I needed to do it, and I didn't fry myself. I was ecstatic!

RADIATING POWER

Something very interesting began to happen. My energetic posture shifted from being forward and outward directed to being settled inside myself. It was like I came home to myself instead of always pursuing something.

Wendi had said the Emperor card has codes for developing my sovereignty. *He's sitting on his throne, radiating power, attracting to him what he wants and needs.* She didn't have the language of Human Design, yet she was describing a way of being that's beneficial to all Human Design types, especially Generators, Manifesting Generators, and Projectors (about 90% of us).

I wondered if I purposefully practiced *radiating power*, could I influence what the Flow of Life brought to me? Intriguing, right?

I tapped into my practice of kundalini yoga, an ancient and potent wisdom tradition focused on energetic mastery, and added to it my intention of receiving guidance from the Flow of Life and becoming magnetic to what I desired. Sitting in my seat of power, doing my breathwork (I'll share this with you below), trusting spirit, I gave thanks for receiving what I wanted and wondered by what pathway it would unfold in my life.

You've probably heard the phrase: *you create your own reality*, and I believe that's true. Yet we don't do it alone! That part often gets left out the picture. It's more accurate to say *you co-create your reality with the Flow of Life.*

As I began to trust the Flow of Life, I relaxed into being guided and supported. My energy expenditure went way down as response taught me how to tap into and ride the deeper flow of energy always moving through our planet and our lives, individually and collectively.

I fine-tuned my awareness for what I had energy for and what I didn't and committed to only doing what I had energy for. In the past I would use my will power to push myself when I didn't have energy, exhausting myself. I thought that was just how life is. I discovered that when I had energy for something, I also was tapping into the energetic support of the Flow of Life, so I used a lot less of my personal energy and was fueled by cosmic energy.

Radiating power cultivated my sovereignty by building the strength of my nervous system as well as my energy field. As my radiance grew, so too did my command of my life, a cornerstone of Feminine Sovereignty as I teach it.

This has led me to being more focused, more productive, more easily prosperous, and much happier, all sustainably and with a lot less effort. Radiating power, receiving support from the Flow of Life, and tuning into being guided have fostered my sovereignty and moved me from exhausted to ecstatic.

THE TOOL

RADIATING SOVEREIGN POWER WITH THE MASTER BREATH

Every Human Design type is designed to dance with the Flow of Life in a specific way. I've shared with you how, as a Pure Generator, I'm designed to do this. If you'd like to go deeper into this, or find out about the other Human Design types, you can access my video series and gorgeous eBook that covers this subject by going to the resources page I've created for you at https://SovereigntybyDesign.com/sosoresources. You'll also find additional materials on avoiding and healing from burnout, plus more on Feminine Sovereignty.

This *Radiating Sovereign Power* practice helps all Human Design types build their energetic integrity, radiance, and potency, and release outdated beliefs, stuck emotions, and stagnant energy. Whatever your type, I invite you to try this practice and imagine yourself in your seat of power, radiating, and attracting to yourself opportunities, resources, and direction from Source. Let me know how it goes!

This practice employs the master breath from the yogic wisdom traditions. I've found this practice enormously beneficial and use it regularly. I'm providing written instructions here, and you can also follow along with me in a video I created for you. You'll find it on the resources page.

INSTRUCTIONS

Move and stretch your body to open up your joints and warm your muscles. Rotate your hips and do some spinal flexion to loosen up. This makes sitting much more comfortable.

Sit in any position, either cross legged on the floor or a cushion or in a chair. Close your eyes and bring your attention inward. Begin by scanning your body and taking a snapshot of how you feel. Do you need to shift anything to be more comfortable? Do that now.

Set your intention. What do you want to bring into your life? What do you want to release that's been holding you back?

Place your hand on your belly just below your navel. Our practice will activate the energy of this power center. Open your mouth, stick out your tongue and pant like a dog. Can you feel the way your belly moves in and out when you do that? Now close your mouth and accentuate the inward pulse on the exhale, then release and lightly inhale through the nose. This does not need to be fast or super intense. It's more of a gentle yet firm pulse of the belly inward on the exhale and release on the inhale. Experiment and find a rhythm that works for you. This is the master breath, also known as "Breath of Fire."

Once you've got the hang of it, let's add a mudra or hand position. Bring your palms together in front of your heart in prayer position. Lightly press the palms together and press your thumbs into your breastbone. Close your eyes, focus on your belly, and do the master breath for three minutes. Setting a timer will let you fully relax and drop into the practice.

When the three minutes are up, inhale fully and hold your breath for as long as your comfortably can. Then release the breath and your hands, placing them on your thighs with the palms up. Keep your eyes closed and stay very still. Notice how you feel now, energy expanding all around you. Enjoy this!

Bring your awareness into your heart center. Breathe gently into your heart feeling your belly and rib cage expand. Tune in to the light in the center of your chest, the radiance of your heart. Allow the light to grow with every breath as you imagine yourself radiating outward from your core. Use the master breath here if you choose.

Fuel your heart with uplifting, positively expectant emotions as you imagine experiencing your intentions as manifest now. Feel yourself supported by the Earth underneath you, and open to receive the light of your soul into your heart even more. Stay here as long as you like!

You may want to write in your journal any insights or "a-ha" that came in during your practice. Don't think about this; simply allow the deeper wisdom of your soul to speak to and through you.

NOTE: You may practice the master breath for longer than three minutes. I've done this for up to 31 minutes with different mudras every few minutes. I would recommend one of these increments: 3, 7, 9, 11, 22 or 31 minutes. I provide you with more guidance on this on the resources page.

A recovering academic, **Maggie Ostara, PhD** left her prestigious job as the Director of Women's and Gender Studies at Columbia University when she realized she's not built to work for anyone else. (Now she knows that's part of her Human Design!)

Since then, Dr. Ostara has become a Certified Human Design and Quantum Human Design Specialist (Level 4), a Certified Clarity Breathwork Practitioner, a Certified Radiant Body Yoga Teacher, and a highly sought-after teacher/mentor. She teaches high-achieving women how to develop their feminine sovereignty, to activate their Human Design super powers, and to unleash themselves from society's prescription of success in favor of their own.

She's created the 8 Pillars of Feminine Sovereignty and the Six Feminine Sovereign Archetypes, plus over 20 educational programs focused on spiritual growth and building soul-inspired businesses that positively impact the world. Take the quiz: *What's Your Feminine Sovereign Archetype?* at SovereignQuiz.com to find out more.

With two decades of experience supporting 20,000+ students and hundreds of clients through her online programs and conferences, Dr. Ostara teaches how to avoid overwhelm and burnout, make reliable decisions, create a bigger impact with less effort, and transform inner liabilities into powerful assets and allies.

She lives in a small town in Northern California with her black feline familiar and her NB 20-something year old. Find out more about her work with Human Design at SovereigntybyDesign.com. Get your free companion resources at SovereigntybyDesign.com/sosoresources.

CHAPTER 12

PARENTING WITH EMOTIONAL AWARENESS

TAPPING INTO YOUR INNER CALM

Kristy Martin

MY STORY

I got pregnant with my first child at the age of 21. I thought it was a fairly big accomplishment that I had made it to that age, considering that where I grew up had the highest teen pregnancy rate in the nation. I beat the statistics but I was still a young, and completely unprepared, mother.

I was still developing my own sense of self and where I fit into the world. I was still learning how to navigate life, my career, finances, self-esteem, being in a marriage, and my emotional landscape. Strong displays of emotion were extremely uncomfortable for me and I avoided any conflict like the plague.

I had another baby at the age of 23, then at 26, 27, and 28 (yes, there are five of them!). At the same time, I was working as a nurse in my local emergency room and I was a master at compartmentalizing my emotions.

It was the only way to survive there. But unprocessed emotions are a recipe for disaster later on.

I often feel as if I have grown up alongside my children. While raising them I have experienced extreme weight loss, depression, addiction, and more. And through it all, one thing was clear. I had little control over my emotions when things got chaotic. And things got chaotic often. So, my solution was to use numbing behaviors and activities.

Fast forward to the fall of 2019. I was excited to head into a new school year because I took many things off my plate and was ready to give more attention to my family and growing my business. What I didn't realize was that although lightening my schedule a little was a step in the right direction, it wasn't going to be enough to bring me the calm and patience to my parenting I so desperately needed and wanted.

With five boys, school pick-up days were hectic. We had four different dismissal times at three different schools plus a 30-minute car ride to get home. Combine my lack of emotional regulation, theirs, and oppositional behaviors, and things could get explosive.

I pulled up to the school pick-up line and put the car in park. I wanted to greet my tiny humans with a smile and show them how excited I was to see them but there was an underlying pulse of anxiety. A thought was buried deep in the back of my mind: *How chaotic and overwhelming will the car ride be today?*

The bell rings and the first wave of kids starts pouring out of the gates. After a few moments, I see two of my boys running to the car, giggling profusely and shoving each other along the way. My body tenses because this is a trigger for me. Somewhere along the way, I developed a need to control my environment, to keep things calm, peaceful, and conflict-free.

They open the door, still laughing and pushing each other, and they fall into the car. Literally fall, one right on top of the other, a tangle of arms, legs, backpacks, lunch pails, and water bottles. Parents behind us are impatiently waiting for us to move while I desperately whisper-yell, "knock it off! Get in the car correctly so we can go!"

A teacher locks eyes with me sympathetically and says, "have a great rest of your day!" "We will!" I reply with a forced smile while my eyes flashed, *help me!* I pulled away and we went to the back parking lot to wait for the next school dismissal.

Human Design had not yet entered my world. I wouldn't be introduced to it until a few months later. And what I learned blew my mind and helped me better understand the dynamic between myself, my children, and how we were all influencing each other emotionally.

There are nine centers in Human Design (these are the shapes in the center of your chart). Each center corresponds to a different life force energy and shows how you process that information. If the center is colored in, that means it is defined and you will usually experience that energy in a consistent manner. If the center is white, that means it is undefined and is where you take in energy from the world around you and amplify it.

One of these centers is called the emotional solar plexus center and it holds the energy of our emotions and feelings. Mine is undefined, so I take in the emotional energy of others and it builds. Oftentimes, I would say, "I don't know where these intense feelings came from, they just hit me!"

Back to the parking lot. My undefined self is with my two boys who have defined solar plexuses. I'm pulling in their emotional energy and it's manifesting in me as anxiety, irritation, and impatience. They don't have much effect on each other. As one gets more amped up, the other remains pretty even keel until he gets annoyed with his brother. Meanwhile, I'm stewing in these intense feelings, the pressure is building, and I'm trying to keep it together.

The next school bell rings and after a few minutes, my next boy comes running out to the car. He also has an undefined solar plexus and a very low frustration tolerance. After a few minutes, he's usually grumbling at his brothers, "Can't you be quiet? You're so annoying!"

At the next stop, my oldest hops in the car. He has an undefined solar plexus as well. "How was your day?" I ask him. "Fine," he replies as his brother starts making farting noises and cackling. I sigh in frustration again, taking the behavior personally. *Why do they always do this to me? Can't they see how frustrated I am?*

We pull up to the final stop and the last kid gets in. He has a defined solar plexus and the chaos ruffles him the least. He usually has a long-winded story or off-the-wall question for me, but I'm like a pressure cooker at this point. And when he says, "Mom?" I end up snapping back at him, "What?"

"Geez, never mind," he says. I instantly feel bad. It's not his fault his mom is frazzled; it's not any of theirs. It's my responsibility to manage my own emotions. Emotional awareness begins with me.

We start our trek home and I take a deep breath. Things are quiet and I think, *it's all going to be okay*. After a few minutes, I hear someone quietly say, "Dude, seriously, stop it or I'm going to punch you." I let out a heavy sigh and say, "Whatever you're doing, you need to stop." A minute later, I hear a thwack and then, "Mom!"

A goldfish cracker comes flying through the air and hits me in the side of the face. "Okay, that's enough!" I bellow. I grab the wheel, yank it over to the side of the road, and screech to a halt, kicking up a huge cloud of dust. I can't hold it anymore and I start sobbing.

Someone sighs and rolls their eyes next to me. Someone else is still yelling. "Enough!" I scream. "Everyone quiet now!" My throat now feeling a little raw, I launch into my lecturing about how we are supposed to treat each other, about how we properly ride in the car, about how we should handle things next time. That last one could go for me too.

In the end, we made it home. But I knew something had to change. And it had to start with me. When the pandemic slowed the world down in March 2020, I suddenly found myself with the desire to begin exploring more holistic wellness options. I began with learning Reiki, which I discovered was a wonderful self-healing and stress-reduction tool.

Next, I learned about tapping (which I will be sharing more about a little further on), an effective way to help regulate my parasympathetic nervous system and instantly bring calm to my mind and my body. I was even able to use it to help my children with their anxiety and stress. I decided to become a practitioner so that I could also teach others.

I now have tools like Reiki, tapping, breathwork, and meditation that help bring me back to the present, help calm my body's response, and help me in demonstrating healthy emotional management to my children. Does that mean I've never lost my temper again? Not at all! But I notice that the less I practice self-care and stress-reduction for myself, the harder it is for me to manage my emotions and show up with compassion.

And now when these situations happen, like on a recent road trip to San Francisco, I feel far better equipped to control my own emotions and handle emotional outbursts with better ease. I don't scream and cry or lose my cool nearly as much and they feel more supported. And it is such an empowering feeling.

Tapping is one of my favorite tools to use and is what I want to introduce you to in the next section. I've used tapping at home, in the car, on an airplane, in the store, and use it any time I need a reset in my energy or emotions. It's incredibly versatile and safe for anyone to use.

THE TOOL

Emotional Freedom Technique (EFT tapping) is a self-help technique that combines cognitive-behavioral psychotherapy with acupressure. It was created by Gary Craig and Roger Callahan in the 1980s and has been gaining popularity around the world. By stimulating acupressure points, they were able to help people deal with stress, fear, pain, and phobias.

Tapping is an excellent tool to use for regulating the nervous system and reducing anxiety. It is done by tapping your fingers on certain energy meridians, or points on the body, which are believed to correspond with different emotions and issues. The tapping stimulates acupressure points in this area and sends a calming signal to the amygdala which is responsible for sending out a signal in times of stress, which triggers our "fight or flight" response.

While you are tapping, you are also talking through the issue. The first few rounds that you do should be focused on giving voice to your problem and getting out what you need to say about it. The last few rounds are about turning things around, focusing on positive affirmations, and stating how you are now choosing to feel.

I recommend tapping on only one issue at a time and repeating the rounds as many times as you need to reduce or eliminate the intensity of the negative feeling. Start by identifying your issue. This will be the focal point of your tapping session. Next, rate the intensity level of your emotional or physical discomfort on a scale of 1-10, with 10 being the worst.

Then, choose a set-up phrase. Come up with a sentence that acknowledges the problem you're trying to overcome and release. Then this is followed by a statement of self-acceptance. For example, "Even though I am experiencing a lot of frustration with my kids, I still deeply love and accept myself."

Here are the tapping points you will use, in order;

- The karate chop point—on the outside of the hand on the pinky finger side (this point is only used when you first begin)
- Above the inner eyebrow
- The outer side of the eye
- Under the eye
- Under the nose, above the top lip
- The middle of the chin
- Under the collarbone
- Under the arm—approximately 3-4 inches below the armpit
- The top of the head

For a video demonstration of the points and this tapping exercise, please visit www.theselfprojectstudio.com/book-resources.

You can follow along with this script or create your own. Tapping works best when it is specific to your situation, thoughts, and feelings so please feel free to replace words and phrases to be specific to your situation. You can even make up your own scripts as you become more comfortable.

Let's start by taking a deep breath and then begin to tap the karate chop point while speaking your setup phrase 2-3 times. "Even though I'm feeling this frustration and anger with my kids, I still deeply love and accept myself. Even though I feel so angry and I want to yell, I still completely love and accept myself."

Tap the inner eyebrow: "I am feeling so overwhelmed right now."

Tap the side of the eye: "This anger feels so big."

Tap under the eye: "I can feel the pressure rising in my body."

Tap under the nose: "I can feel I am about to blow my top."

Tap the chin: "I always feel so frustrated on these car rides home" (or substitute for your situation).

Tap under the collarbone: "Because things or behaviors are happening that trigger me."

Tap under the arm: "And everything just feels out of control."

Tap the top of the head: "I really want to scream and yell and cry."

Repeat the above, moving through the points again (excluding the karate chop point) for 3-4 rounds. Then you will move on to the releasing stage and making statements of acceptance and affirmation.

Tap the inner eyebrow: "I am choosing to calm down."

Tap the side of the eye: "I am choosing to let these overwhelming emotions pass through my body."

Tap under the eye: "It's okay for me to release the anger and frustration."

Tap under the nose: "I am choosing to feel safe and calm now."

Tap the chin: "Letting all of this tension melt away from my body."

Tap under the collarbone: "Feeling the pressure release and calm flowing into the body."

Tap under the arm: "My whole body is relaxing now."

Tap the top of the head: "I am choosing calm now."

Repeat the above, moving through the points again (excluding the karate chop point) for three to four rounds. Then, take a deep breath and slowly let it out. At this point, you will want to return to the rating scale to reevaluate the intensity level of your feeling or emotion from one to ten. Repeat the tapping sequence until you are a three or less on the scale.

You can use this technique as many times as you like, for anything you can think of! My favorite part of this tool is that it is always with you. It puts the power back in your hands. The power to heal, the power to thrive, and the power to be the parent you want to be.

Kristy Martin is the founder of The Self Project Studio and she is on a mission to help other moms who feel like they lost themselves and their passion for life. She guides them through rediscovering who they are and helps them navigate through life and parenting difficulties with more empowerment and joy.

She is a certified Life coach, Master Reiki Practitioner, EFT Tapping Practitioner, and Breathwork Facilitator. She uses all of these techniques to help her clients find their inner calm, confidence, acceptance, and empowerment.

After she left her career as an emergency room nurse to be a stay-at-home-mom, Kristy found she was missing that fire that came from helping others. She learned all she could about holistic wellness, not only for her own healing journey but also to share with others. She has also battled with ADHD, disordered eating, skin picking, and alcoholism and this has made her into a passionate advocate for these disorders.

Personal growth and self-awareness have been a huge part of Kristy's growth and healing journey. She launched her podcast, The Self Project Podcast, in May 2020 and has produced over 100 episodes with incredible guests on healing, wellness, and other issues that affect women. You can listen at www.theselfproject.com/podcast.

Kristy currently offers a monthly membership group that guides you through self-discovery, healing, nervous system regulation, building emotional resilience, navigating motherhood, and reducing stress and anxiety. She also offers one-to-one coaching sessions and Human Design chart readings for yourself or your whole family.

In Human Design speak, Kristy is a 2/5 sacral Manifesting Generator. Her life purpose is to follow her joy and new experiences and to enthusiastically share her findings with others. It's perfectly normal for her to be juggling multiple things at once and to abandon projects as quickly as she starts them. Her innocence motivation has her always looking at things through an idealistic lens and makes her want to keep her family and friends laughing frequently. Human Design helped bring her this exact self-understanding and self-acceptance that she has always wanted.

Kristy lives near the Sequoia National Forest with her husband, their five boys, and two dogs. You can often find her on social media, trying out her acting and videography skills or lost in Canva, creating beautifully unique graphics. She also loves expanding her writing skills and you can find more of her work on her blog at www.theselfprojectstudio.com/blog.

CHAPTER 13

DISCOVERING A NEW STORY

FROM TRAUMA TO EASE

Robin Winn, MFT

MY STORY

Have you ever had those niggling feelings that something wasn't right:

That you didn't belong on earth? That you didn't have a purpose?

Or that you were a mistake?

From a young age, these questions plagued me.

I'm five years old, lying in my bed staring at the ceiling, wondering how I can escape. I don't belong here. Someone must have made a mistake. I think about putting a plastic bag over my head. My parents have told me that kids have died from playing with plastic bags. I like that thought. It gives me a glimmer of hope. It makes me feel safe. Until I realize I can't. I curl up, putting my head under the covers. I know I'm bad. If I died, I would go to Hell.

I was plopped into a family of big people. Seven of them by the time I came along—two parents and five older brothers. They had big voices and big personalities. I was lost in that crowd. My voice was a whisper.

My dad was in the military, so we moved every three years until I was nine when he retired to a small town in Northern California. Outside our new home, I would climb the fence of the dog pen and sit perched on the chimney ledge. That was my safe space. That's where I could write poems and daydream. That's where I could exist.

Most of my early life I spent trying to figure out who I was and what I was here to do. I was clueless. I knew I was different. And that I didn't fit in. I was desperately trying to make sense of what seemed like a phenomenal disaster.

I did make heroic efforts. I worked hard to look, be, and act "normal." I developed an acute awareness, a watchful eye. *What did people wear? What kinds of things were okay to say?* More often than not, I would mess up.

I remember in 7th grade, I showed my mom a poem I'd written about feeling lonely. She read it, and then in an exasperated tone, asked:

"Robin, where did you get that from?"

Okay, so no deep poems about feeling alone and wanting connection allowed.

The retreat to the inner recesses of my being began young and increased as time passed. By the time I was in my twenties, I was no longer hiding on the chimney ledge above the dog pen but was seeking refuge in rebel territory. It was the late 70s and early 80s in Berkeley. I became lovers with a Catholic nun and hung with *very* progressive priests.

I had a sniffer for what was taboo and rushed towards it, looking for my people. I found a group of wild, lesbian witches who introduced me to ritual, astrology, tarot, and psychics. We trance danced and made dolls with fetishes in their chakras. In a lunar yoga class, drinking flower water, I met my (now) wife.

At twenty-five, I was facedown, in my underwear on a bodywork table, when Marion Rosen demonstrated on me. Nestled between soft white cotton sheets, her silky hands traversed my body. Their gentleness disarmed me. Her hands were listening to me. I was being seen and touched by a wave of kindness. Then she spoke. Her words to my classmates exposed me far more than my naked body: "Robin may look like she has a perfect body, but I wonder what is hiding beneath this smooth exterior."

And boom! Pandora's Box flew open, revealing my inner mess.

Imagine that twenty years have passed. It's 2004. I'm now 45. With a persevering passion, I have done everything I could to find peace. And to a large degree, I've succeeded. I've taken the deep dive. Unearthed what I was unable to bare—faced the pain. I've established a functioning ego through therapy. I've discovered relief from suffering through The Work of Byron Katie. I have the tools to meet whatever pain arises.

I have found a dynamic resting place.

My wife, Yarrow, and I are living an idyllic life on North Dream Farm Road, overlooking Tomales Bay in Inverness. We have a circle of like-hearted friends and a rich life. I'm a successful somatic psycho/spiritual therapist devoted to helping others navigate their suffering. I make art, teach qigong, lead Speaking Circles, study The Diamond Work and immerse myself in Tibetan Buddhism.

Then I meet Human Design.

You know the saying that *you don't know what you need until it shows up?*

With all the wealth of understanding and the massive toolbox I'd acquired, I was unprepared for the turn my life would take with the introduction of Human Design.

At the time of my first reading, Yarrow and I had been together twenty-one years. We'd done a ton of therapy both individually and as a couple. We'd studied with extraordinary teachers. We'd been through tough times together and found our way through. We'd shared the journey and the awakening in that journey.

So when I learned that I was a Generator and she was a Projector, and that Projectors weren't designed to work in the same way that Generators were, my brain spun around a few times.

Duh! No wonder!

For all the work we'd done, there was a place we couldn't resolve. There was a judgment we couldn't get past:

She thought I was a workaholic, and I thought she was a lazy bum.

I couldn't understand why she wasn't compelled to work. It baffled me.

With the distinction between Generators and Projectors clearly delineated, I stopped seeing her as deficient. I stopped trying to fix what I perceived was broken.

I was able to see what I loved most about her was that very quality of being that she so deeply embodied. I recognized the well of support I received from her commitment to, and celebration of, non-activity. She, likewise, opened to my activity as a necessary and positive force, a supportive force.

This understanding of difference was the beginning of a practice of getting to know one another in ever-deepening ways that continues to this day.

I had a few other takeaways from that reading, but they didn't set me on a path. I wasn't compelled to delve into Human Design. It felt too hard to comprehend. The complexity of the system was beyond my reach.

Fast forward nine years.

It's 2013. I'm visiting my friend Jane, and as I sit on her couch, I see a red book on her coffee table. It jumps out at me. In a second, I have opened its cover and am mainlining it. There is a stream of energy coming from the book into me. It's Karen Curry's (now Karen Curry Parker's) book—fresh off the press: *Understanding Human Design*. I deliriously imbibe its contents.

The information lands and reorganizes me. It all makes sense. Instantaneously, I become a Human Design devotee.

Earlier in this chapter, I spoke about not knowing what the heck I was doing here on earth. How alienated and isolated I felt. How disconnected I felt. I recalled my long journey of discovery, with years of bodywork and therapy, deep dives into spiritual practices, and finally coming to peace with life through Byron Katie's work.

Human Design made sense out of all that crazy disorder. It gave me a context to understand who I was, why I had such a challenging childhood. It explained why I was driven to help others find their way back to themselves.

Over the next eight years, as I dive into the waters of Human Design, two things happen. The first has to do with my pilgrimage with and into my Human Design chart. This journey brought an awareness that enabled me to make sense of my life story. The second involves a transformation in my work life.

Hang with me for a moment while I share what my Human Design chart revealed in relation to my story.

During my first thirty years, I was designed to learn by bumping into life and discovering what doesn't work. Those first thirty years were indeed a doozy! Combine that with my Sun, the biggest energy in my chart, emanating the energy of Difficulty at the Beginning, or Innovation. I am rightfully designed to have difficulty in the beginning!

As I write this, my heart aches for that girl who had to traverse that challenging terrain. I recognize that those difficulties weren't wrong or bad. They were simply part of my puzzle piece. But there's more.

This powerful individual Sun energy brings a deep knowing from the future accompanied by a natural melancholy from not fitting in. The new information coming through is not always readily welcomed or accepted. It takes time for the new to take root. Case in point: I gave everyone in my family Neti pots for Christmas back in 1981—they probably use them now, but back then? No. Of course I didn't feel like I belonged. I was from the future!

Add to that the fact that I had an Open Head, Open Ajna, Open Throat, Open Identity, and Open Will Centers. This made me vulnerable to merging with other people and left me grappling with what I thought, who I was, and what I valued. It was naturally challenging for me to be seen and heard. It was practically inevitable that I would question my value.

As I recognized these fundamental conundrums in my chart, I eased up on myself. While I had come to peace with who I was, I still felt shame and embarrassment about those early suicidal feelings that plagued me. The chart gave me a context for why I felt the way I did.

I learned through my chart that my purpose involves seeing what's possible for humanity and helping people move forward in new and innovative ways. This gave me a ground—a rudder. It gave me permission to be my wild innovative self.

I also discovered that struggle is my spiritual path. I'm designed to struggle and awaken through struggle! That explained a lot. I could stop making myself wrong for my journey of struggle. I could simply appreciate those struggles that make me uniquely positioned to help others with their struggles. Wow! My job is to discern the worthy struggles and see new ways through.

In the same way that understanding the difference between my wife as Projector and me as a Generator became a life-long practice, understanding my quantum, multi-dimensional self through my bodygraph became a practice, an ever-deepening exploration.

This new information reframed my story and shifted my perspective on my past. It gave a context for trauma and brought a new level of ease.

Alongside my personal revelatory awareness, Human Design was infiltrating my work as a psychotherapist. It impacted how I understood and worked with people in surprising and unexpected ways. I had been given the golden key. When I ran charts for clients who I had worked with for years, I suddenly had a whole new context and understanding of what was going on.

No wonder my Projector client with seven open centers, including the Throat and Identity center, felt unseen and unsupported by her parents. Suddenly, we could begin to see the trauma story for what it was—an aspect of the chart. My client's experience—much like my own—shifted from a story of being victimized by people and circumstances to being empowered.

As I sat with my clients, I kept their charts on the side table, referring to them often. Our work transformed as their chart became a grounding point, an anchor for them to understand their challenges and strengths. They opened to a new level of ease as they began to align with themselves.

It came to the point where I wouldn't take a client if they weren't open to having me run and work with their chart. It just didn't make sense to work without this extraordinary tool. Eventually, I shifted my work from psychotherapy to Human Design coaching. My passion for Human Design led me to write books that made Human Design easily available to coaches and psychotherapists. Ultimately I began training professionals to use Human Design to bring more ease and success to their work.

The impact of Human Design on me and my work with clients and students points to the power of this technology to transform our lives.

Human Design brings the light of compassion to difference. It enables us to accept ourselves and one another. It expands our understanding of who we are. It gives each person their rightful place on earth, with respect and honor for who they are. This is no small matter. In fact, it has great ramifications for the future of our world, especially at this pivotal time.

THE TOOL

First things first:

If you haven't already, download your chart here: https://clientsandhumandesign.com/free-chart/

(Note, you will need your birth time, date, and place.)

With your chart in front of you, begin by smiling at your chart, sending a wave of love towards this rendition of yourself.

Can you approach your chart with curiosity and wonder?

Can you decide to embrace your design and open yourself to receive the teachings it has for you?

Call on the light of awareness to support you.

Take a few minutes to contemplate the foundations of Human Design:

- Stop thinking you should be different than you are.
- Start recognizing and being yourself.
- Stop attacking/rejecting yourself.
- Start loving/accepting yourself

Acknowledge that you matter.

See yourself as a unique, multidimensional-quantum being who is an essential part of the human puzzle.

Now that you've entered into a relationship with your chart based on recognizing the possibility of who you are, let's deepen your understanding of yourself by looking more closely at your centers, especially your open centers.

If you're not familiar with the centers or have all your centers defined, go here: https://clientsandhumandesign.com/stop-overworking/.

These open centers are the place where we don't have consistent access to ourselves. It's where we merge with others. It's where the ego grabs hold of *anything* to feel *something*. These are often called our pain points because they're where we can be conditioned to believe we're other than who we are.

They are also where we connect to the mystery of life, the unknown. They are where we gather wisdom.

I think of them as God Portals. The place where we connect with the All of Life. Each one is a spiritual path to embrace, explore and open into.

Look at your chart and see which of your centers are white.

Know that where your centers are white, you're taking in all of humanity through them.

For a moment, stand in awe and wonder as you look at your open centers.

This is your non-physical self. The vast emptiness of you. This aspect of you is equally important as who you take yourself to be in your definition!

Now recognize that each of these open centers requires your awareness. Here you have the huge job of filtering what comes towards you. Can you be awake and stay in inquiry? Basically, you will be asking yourself: *Is this me? Or does this belong to someone else?*

Each of the Centers has a theme or a particular energy that reflects what kind of energy you'll have to navigate.

For example, the Head Center takes in and amplifies thoughts and inspirations. You will be asking yourself: *Is this my thought? Or someone else's?*

Take time now with each of your open centers.

Sit in stillness with them.

One at a time, contemplate the directives below for each center.

See what comes.

Journal your revelations.

What do you discover?

Take on the teachings of each open center as a practice.

Activate awareness of them in your daily life.

IF YOU HAVE AN:

Open Head:

Stop trying to come up with answers to everyone's questions.

Start choosing which questions to answer that are interesting to you.

Stop identifying with your thoughts.

Start witnessing your thoughts as a way to stabilize your mind.

Pause. Contemplate. Journal. Activate Awareness.

Open Ajna:

Stop trying to be certain.

Start resting in not knowing.

Pause. Contemplate. Journal. Activate Awareness.

Open Throat:

Stop trying to be heard.

Start waiting to be asked or acknowledged before you speak.

Stop blurting out your thoughts.

Start being discerning with your voice.

Pause. Contemplate. Journal. Activate Awareness.

Open G:

Stop trying to figure out who you are and what direction to go in.

Start allowing yourself to be as you are: changeable and multi-directional.

Stop trying to get love.

Start knowing there is nothing you can do to get love or lose love. You *are* love itself.

Pause. Contemplate. Journal. Activate Awareness.

Open Will:

Stop trying to prove who you are.

Start being curious about what you value.

Stop questioning your value.

Start recognizing you are value itself. There's nothing you can do to gain or lose value.

Pause. Contemplate. Journal. Activate Awareness.

Open Sacral:

Stop trying to be a doer.

Start honoring and respecting your energy.

Pause. Contemplate. Journal. Activate Awareness.

Open Emotional Solar Plexus:

Stop identifying with everyone's feelings!

Start discerning what feelings are yours and whose feelings you're amplifying.

Pause. Contemplate. Journal. Activate Awareness.

Open Root:

Stop trying to relieve the pressure you feel.

Start befriending the constant pressure you live under and discern what's yours to do.

Pause. Contemplate. Journal. Activate Awareness.

Open Spleen:

Stop holding on to things that no longer serve you.

Start trusting it's safe to let go.

Stop taking on everyone's fears.

Start discerning which fears you're merging with vs. which fears are yours.

Pause. Contemplate. Journal. Activate Awareness.

For further support, download my book for free: *Understanding the Centers in Human Design: The Facilitator's Guide to Transforming Pain into Possibility*

https://www.clientsandhumandesign.com/free-book

Robin Winn, LMFT, is the bestselling author of *Understanding Your Clients through Human Design: The Breakthrough Technology;* and *Understanding the Centers in Human Design: The Facilitator's Guide to Transforming Pain into Possibility.*

Robin is an innovator who is here to expand horizons and help people realize their innate potential.

With a background in Rosen Method Bodywork, Anat Baniel Method NeuroMovement, qigong, Speaking Circles, Diamond Logos, Tibetan Buddhism, and The Work of Byron Katie, Robin brings a rich and deep perspective to life.

After working for twenty-five years as a psychotherapist, Robin was introduced to the Human Design portal. Not only did understanding Human Design dramatically transform her work with clients, but it also opened a new depth of appreciation and compassion in her marriage.

Robin says: "Human Design is alive in me, an ever-deepening recognition of who I am. It is a potent reflective medicine that continuously grounds and supports me and the people I work with, to navigate the journey of being human, embodying and embracing our differences and stepping into our magnificent Selves."

Passionate about the power of Human Design to transform lives, Robin devotes her time to training coaches and therapists to elevate their work with Human Design. She believes Human Design holds a key to finding a new way forward for humanity.

Robin is a writer, speaker, transformational coach, founder, and the director of *Foundations of Human Design Certification Training for Professionals.*

She lives on Maui with her wife, Yarrow, and their mysterious cat, Kali Ma.

CHAPTER 14

PIVOT TO PASSION AND PURPOSE

HOW TO BUILD TRUST AND REALIZE YOUR FULL POTENTIAL

Catherine Skreiner

MY STORY

For years I'd had a niggling feeling, a voice, nudging me from time to time, saying *there's more out there for you.*

You can't keep doing what you're doing, hoping another job will make you happy. What are you doing with your life if all this pushing and prioritizing work isn't making you happy?

The thought of finding my 'passion' felt so cliche that I scoffed and thought, *that's really nice but let's get real, that only happens in the movies, not to people 'like me.'*

How wrong I was.

When I received my first Human Design reading I experienced that indescribable feeling of being very seen and understood by a complete stranger who only had my time, date, and location of birth to create such magical accuracy. It gave me a much needed boost and a jolt of confidence that who I was was enough for the first time ever.

At the time, I was deep into my digital marketing business, serving clients in the areas of performance media, digital strategy, and analytics. It was a career I had for over 14 years, and while I was certainly challenged by the ever changing social media landscape, I couldn't ignore the persistent feeling that things needed to change and that this feeling had been there for as long as I could remember.

Doing a good job for my clients brought me satisfaction, recognition and respect, but did it make me happy? No, not a chance. Realizing this was one of my biggest wake up calls.

For ages I didn't know what it felt like to feel 'lit up.' It always felt so oddly out of reach, or something that only other people experienced. Twenty or so years in the same career will probably do that to you right? Plus, throw in a busy family life with two school-age children and it's easy to think that feeling burnt out and a little uninspired is the new normal.

This sense of dissatisfaction is not unfamiliar as we traverse the years of our career. We chase dreams of having 'a calling' and finding our purpose but never quite find the right fit. I spent so much time thinking that finding your passion was something that happened to other people, it felt fictional.

It feels so apt that 2020 was the year I finally woke up and actually started listening to my inner signals. And when I started listening, I realized I simply didn't get excited about my business, no matter what the measure of success was.

2020 is a year our generation will remember forevermore. The impact of Covid-19 has been felt far and wide, and at the time of writing, still ongoing. During this time, despite a healthy client roster as a digital marketer, the upheaval of the pandemic brought so much into clear focus: not least that I had long mistaken the pursuit of being outstanding in my work for passion.

Through a series of serendipitous events, and one particularly life-changing breathwork workshop, I made the decision to pivot and pursue my passion, a career in Human Design.

It was mid 2020 when a friend invited me to join her at a breathwork workshop. This wasn't going to just be an hour of breathing, this was a transformational, immersive half-day experience. I knew very little about it, not to mention who was running it, but I just knew it was something I needed to do.

I got excited and booked a ticket. The breathwork workshop was truly amazing, for so many reasons. I processed and moved a lot of painful energy and felt a long awaited sense of peace. When a level two workshop was announced for the following month I signed up without hesitation.

Here's what was happening in my Human Design as I made this decision:

As a Sacral Manifesting Generator, my sacral center shows me what lights me up and gives me a clear 'yes' or 'no' answer. However, my splenic center will very often tag along with an intuitive hit just for good measure. It feels like an inner knowing that something is correct for me, even though I often cannot explain why.

In my Human Design I have a channel connecting my spleen to my sacral center. This channel is the 27-50, The Channel of Preservation which is centered around a nurturing instinct that brings great satisfaction. Allow me to put it into context.

The 27-50 Channel has a great emphasis on being driven to take care of everyone and work for the preservation of humanity. It's like having an invisible contract with the world to put everyone else's needs above your own. As a mother, wife, and a business owner I felt this deeply, and I was exhausted by constantly giving.

The fact I was drawn to such a deeply nurturing opportunity that didn't quite make sense to me at the time, was one of the first signs my soul was pushing my mind out of the driver's seat and itching to take over.

Around the same time I had begun my search for the perfect mentor in Human Design and I'd found what I believed to be the correct opportunity for me. I visited my mentor's website time and time again over the course of the next few weeks feeling more and more excited each time. I hadn't known what I was looking for, but yet I'd found it.

Now with most spiritual experiences there are no guarantees, and I didn't know exactly what I was seeking clarity on until I was there. The question I was wanting guidance on was: *Am I meant to pursue a new career in Human Design?*

The breathwork workshop was held in a huge old warehouse, hipster cool at its best and I felt strangely out of place, but also so at home and very welcome in the space I now shared with over 100 total strangers.

We were cleared with sage as we walked in and I found a spot to roll out my yoga mat and get set up. The nerves started to kick in and I located my friend in the crowd which made me feel a little more comfortable. In hindsight I'm happy that I wasn't able to be situated right next to my friend, from my first workshop I knew things tend to get pretty emotional in these workshops.

I went back to my mat and started to prepare for the session by journaling on all the feelings that were swirling around in my head. I knew a little of what I was in for and this time the nervousness was more a feeling of excitement. Excitement for the possibility of what I might find, experience, and the clarity I might discover on the other side.

I can only describe the answer I received as feeling like every cell in my body was screaming at me *Yes!* Everything felt fizzy, stirred up, effervescent. It was the most resounding 'yes' my body has ever given me, and perhaps the most important decision I've allowed my body to make instead of my mind.

I walked out of that workshop feeling the best I had in years. Decades of clouded thinking and feeling stuck melted away. I was so very clear in my decision and it felt bold and exhilarating.

But how exactly did I find myself at such a crossroads? Let's go back a little, because it took me a long time to figure out my 'why,' and I don't mind saying that it wasn't until I was 43. I'm 44 at the time of writing. Here's some of what I have spent the better part of three decades stewing over:

- I couldn't make a 5, 10, or 20 year plan = fail;
- I could never articulate my strengths and values = fail;
- I didn't know where I was headed in my career and felt like I had no desire to climb the corporate ladder = fail *and* I felt unambitious.

Human Design brought me back home to me, and in my eyes, that's the gift of a lifetime. It allowed me to recognize and transmute the challenges of my past. I could see with clarity where challenges I experienced early on in life had become ingrained energetic blocks that played out, over and over.

I felt understood and like I'd discovered a language I could now apply to how I've always felt, what I've always known within myself, but never knew quite how to articulate. What immediately stood out to me was that:

- I ignored the signals from my sacral time and time again. I had 'no time' for the things I used to enjoy and I spent my days doing work that drained my energy instead of recharging me, which was contributing to significant sacral burnout;
- I swapped working in corporate for working for myself in the pursuit of freedom and flexibility, yet I found myself suffocated by a business model that wasn't energetically supportive and centered entirely around trading time for money;
- I avoided confrontation like the plague and found myself seeking approval and validation from people who didn't have my best interests at heart;
- I didn't recognize my strengths. In fact, I could barely articulate what they were. It felt as if they'd been buried somewhere deep beneath my facade of busyness and perfectionism.

In our world of hustle culture, especially in the entrepreneurial space, leaning back and trusting your body instead of your mind is radical. But it's that radical self trust that will bring you home to your soul. Because she's waiting for you.

When you move from burnout and scarcity to purpose and prosperity you can expect peace, satisfaction, a feeling of success or perhaps a beautiful sense of surprise. There is an ease to your day, a beautiful flow where things are good, perhaps even great, consistently. Over time, you come to know this ease and flow as being your new normal.

There is a sense of stillness, a knowing that you can trust the guidance you've ignored for so long. The guidance from your soul, through your physical body.

THE TOOL

Reconnecting with your body and its wisdom is essential for understanding your soul purpose. It's time to get grounded and familiar with the signals our body sends us. Signals that we've often ignored or shut down, many times through a sheer lack of awareness due to the pressure we feel day in and day.

It feels like we simply don't have the luxury of reflection or much needed introspection. But, to truly tune in, we first need to slow down. If you have a lot on your plate and a busy schedule, making time for this will no doubt feel challenging.

'Keeping busy' was one of the driving forces that kept me stuck in a cycle of overwork and dissatisfaction for so many years. Allow me to share some of my favorite methods for connecting with, and grounding my body.

EXPLORE ANY PRACTICE THAT BRINGS YOU BACK TO YOUR BODY AND GROUNDS YOU AND THEN CONSIDER THE FOLLOWING STRATEGIES:

Try breathwork, guided meditation, or walking/being in nature. Give yourself the opportunity to connect with your body, with your own energy in an un-rushed state. Be patient, it has taken you years to get to this point. Unraveling and recognizing your conditioning is not an overnight process.

Notice how it feels when you are feeling good. Do you feel satisfied, at peace, successful, or surprised?

Notice how it feels when you feel stressed, overwhelmed, and unhappy. Is it anger, frustration, bitterness, or disappointment that arises? Make a note of how often you feel this way.

What percentage of time do you spend doing things that don't light you up? Be brutally honest here!

Consider your family life. Where are you spending time on things that don't light you up?

Consider your career or business life. Does it drain or energize you? Do you have a yearning to pursue a new direction or study a new discipline?

What is holding you back? What patterns or beliefs (conditioning) come up when you think about taking steps in this direction?

What do you do for fun, joy, and play?

Do you take time to be silly and playful with your kids?

Do you allow yourself time to be curious, learn, or rest without guilt?

Do you allow yourself to experience new things without expectation and judgement?

Do you celebrate your successes and achievements before moving onto the next goal?

What do you love to do? How often do you have time to do these things? If your hobbies have fallen by the wayside, think back to what you used to love as a child. If this exercise leaves you feeling a little defeated, don't be discouraged!

If you struggle to create a list of things you love to do, and find that feelings of anger, frustration or bitterness are present more often than not, you're not alone. These are the signals your body is sending for a reason, the communication is real, and there are very real actions you can take to get back into alignment and start overflowing!

SIGNATURE MOMENTS

I love the practice of embracing signature moments, a practice I learned from my mentor, Eden Carpenter.

A signature moments practice is a little like a gratitude practice, an opportunity for you to connect with your energy type's signature theme. Your signature theme is a key sign you are thriving in your alignment and it's the by-product of correctly living your energy type's strategy.

GENERATORS AND MANIFESTING GENERATORS—YOUR TASK IS TO LIGHT YOUR SACRAL FIRE.

You're designed to enjoy everything in life so add in more opportunities for play, pleasure, and joy in your day to day. This might look like keeping your home looking beautiful, curating each space you love to spend time in to make it feel even more satisfying. Wear the clothes that you love, don't hide them away for a 'special occasion' if they make you feel amazing! Don't be ashamed of what you love or be afraid to love and be excited by your life.

MANIFESTORS—YOUR TASK IS TO CREATE A PLACE OF NO RESISTANCE.

You're designed to feel at peace and this comes from honoring your vision and pursuing your dreams from a space of calm and tranquility. Where in your day are you able to create space to feel peaceful and nurture your connection to spirit/source? It might be music, meditation, journaling or simply enjoying a hot cup of tea and a few chapters of your favorite book.

PROJECTORS—YOUR TASK IS TO RECOGNIZE YOURSELF, YOUR VALUE, YOUR TALENTS AND POWER.

You are designed to feel success and this signature theme is rooted in the theme of recognition. Make a list of all your achievements and accomplishments so that you can connect to this high vibrational energy of success. Go on, brag a little. It's time you recognized just how amazing you are!

REFLECTORS—YOUR TASK IS TO SET UP MOMENTS OF SURPRISE AND DELIGHT.

You are designed to use your sampling aura to experience great wonder. Practice getting into the energy of anticipation and allowing something to be even better than expected. It can be as simple as that first cup of coffee in the morning being much more magical than expected. Cleaning or rearranging your home or favorite space can result in a lovely surprise and can be very impactful as your environment is so important to you.

WHERE ARE YOU EXPERIENCING THE MOST CONDITIONING?

The centers in your bodygraph that you need to pay particular attention to are your undefined centers. These are the centers in your bodygraph that will be white and they are an area in your energetic blueprint where you are more susceptible to conditioning and the non-self energy of these centers. For me, these rang very true when presented with the following questions;

- Undefined Head Center: Am I trying to answer everybody else's questions?

- Undefined Ajna Center: Am I trying to convince everyone that I am certain?
- Undefined Throat Center: Am I trying to attract attention?
- Undefined G (Identity) Center: Am I looking for love and direction?
- Undefined Ego (Heart) Center: Do I think I have something to prove?
- Undefined Emotional Solar Plexus: Am I avoiding confrontation and truth?
- Undefined Sacral Center: Do I know when enough is enough?
- Undefined Splenic Center: Am I holding onto what isn't good for me?
- Undefined Root Center: Am I in a hurry to get things done so I can be free of pressure?

Every single decision we make takes one of two paths: moving us closer or further away from our true purpose and authentic nature. It's these series of decisions that make or break us and when we learn to follow our personal authority in our decision making it will guide us to the correct path; be it in relationships or our career.

Most of us are moving through this life on autopilot, making decisions based on 'shoulds' from our conditioning and allowing our overwhelmed and under-pressure minds make the big calls instead of tuning into our inner wisdom.

We feel frustrated, angry, and bitter when things don't go our way, but also feel like we don't know where to start with getting things back on track and discovering what it is our soul truly desires.

If you are new to Human Design I recommend you have a reading with someone you trust who will give you an empowering experience and practical suggestions that can meet you where you are currently at.

You were designed to fulfill a specific purpose in this life, and have been given a blueprint to help you navigate and maximize your precious lifetime on this earth. Human Design is the path back to your true and most authentic self. Enjoy the journey back to you!

Catherine Skreiner is an energetic business strategist and Human Design guide who has worked with hundreds of individuals, business owners, and leaders alike to help them understand how to work with the Human Design system in their personal and professional lives.

She fuses her 14+ years in digital marketing and experience in large and small businesses, combining it with the Human Design system and Gene Keys, to help clients achieve success and drive impact through the integration and embodiment of their unique energetic gifts.

Catherine knows first hand how it feels to be out of alignment with your unique energetic blueprint and now helps her clients create more aligned businesses through Human Design.

She works with clients to understand how they can approach sales, navigate high pressure decision making, and foster a culture of joy and happiness in their businesses. Her work centers around helping business owners and leaders to deprogram from generic leadership advice and discover their own style, customized for their energetics.

Catherine is a 3/5 Sacral Manifesting Generator and a mum to two school-aged children, both of whom are 2/4 Manifesting Generators. Together with her kids and husband, a 6/2 Self Projected Projector, they live in Perth, Australia.

https://www.catskreiner.com/book

https://instagram.com/cat.skreiner

CHAPTER 15

NAVIGATING YOUR ENERGETIC CURRENTS

A PATH TO PROSPERITY

Alana Heim, CPA/PFS, CFP®, Certified Human Design Specialist

"The mountains are calling and I must go."

- John Muir

MY STORY

Five years ago, I answered that call and trekked up the path to reach the mighty peak of Mount Rose. Alone. As I sat on top of the world, I felt deeply connected to all that is. Sovereignty led me to that moment of deep connection with nature, the elements, and being in the space closest to Source energy. I connected to my inner dual essence; my deep resolve to achieve, and my playful, lax side. I sprawled out on the jagged warm stones, happy to make friends with ladybugs and chipmunks. I connected with myself, a woman exuding defiance and inner knowing that the breathtaking magnificence surrounding me was as expansive as my very own being.

At 10,776 feet, I realized I was on my path to prosperity. I felt deeply liberated within and without. I'd journeyed five miles up, gaining nearly 2,000 feet in elevation, to rest my achy, naked feet in the dirt. To feel the cool air tickle my arms and make the hairs stand up. To connect to the sun placing delicate, warm kisses upon my skin. I smiled, knowing I had reached a new level of freedom. I was no longer clinging to ways I was "supposed" to live life. I was navigating life *my way* because of my choice to fully align with my Human Design.

I hiked the Mount Rose Summit trail numerous times before, always with friends or family. However, this journey was different; I trekked it solo. I chose to embark unaccompanied as part of an experiment to more deeply *inner-stand* myself and my Human Design. I was ready to navigate the energetic currents within my chart with more purpose and vigor.

As a Projector, I'm one of three Human Design Types that has the sacral center, the most powerful motor, undefined in my chart. That means I receive inconsistent energy from the world around me. The power of the sacral is felt as life force, work force, and sexual energy. Nearly 70% of the population wields this energy consistently.

Known as Generators and Manifesting Generators, these individuals wake with a life force energy that is similar to having a full pot of coffee that must be consumed by the end of each day. From even one whiff of coffee, they ride the stamina of a racehorse. Generators love to work. When it is aligned work, they do it all day, every day, without a thought of vacation.

As a Projector, I don't have that Generator energy. My energy flows completely opposite. The more I work, the more I long for a vacation. When I rest and play, I'm aligned to offer my own perfect work. Work that includes offering guidance and brilliance to those who recognize my ability to support them. Slowing down opens me to receive invitations to share my wisdom, love, and gifts.

Without consistent sacral energy, I knew hiking the mountain alone would pose a new challenge. It could be a long, tiring journey to the top. Yet I saw it as an opportunity to experiment with one of two motors in my chart, my defined will center.

During previous hikes, I had the luxury of being surrounded by Generators. It was such a gift to simply be in their presence and amplify their life force energy. It was easy to reach the mountain top with them by my side. Sometimes we hiked to see how quickly we could get to the top. Other times, it was about how fast we could go up and back to the car. It was intriguing to witness my companions rushing through our rest at the top. I wanted to savor the accomplishment. For them, the been-there-done-that box was checked, and it was time to go.

I appreciated the opportunity to create a goal to rest at the top. I knew my defined will center would get me there. It expects a reward. Its sustainable energy wants to work hard, rest hard. Once the will commits to a goal, it says what it means, and means what it says. End of story. Obviously, I made it to the top, because my will center commanded that outcome. *Wink, wink.* Even without a defined sacral center, I conquered that mountain. Triumphant, my will and I rested together like God on the seventh day, because "we" earned it. For over an hour and a half, I relished in the glory of my achievement.

Reflecting on the journey, I see the moments where my "head energy" doubted we could do it. *Let's just take a quick break. Let's rest here for a bit.* Yet when the taste of salt hit my tongue from sweat dripping down my face, my will pushed me harder. *You can do this. You've done it before.* When a steep increase in elevation caused my quads and calves to agonize and burn, my thoughts screamed louder, *Just stop. This hurts.* My will kept me on track. *Just. Keep. Going.* I felt conflicted. My will said *go* and my head said *no*. The split in my chart was at odds. On this day, my body won. It felt liberating.

When it came to making decisions, my head used to win all the time. When I let that happen, I often doubted myself and my ability to make good choices. Eventually, I learned to operate from the other motor in my chart; the emotional solar plexus. Doing this required giving myself plenty of time to *feel* or *experience* my emotions, rather than letting my mind "tell me" I felt them.

When I decided to hike Mount Rose, it was not a mental decision. It came from the *feelings* in my solar plexus paired with the *deep resolve* of my will. I knew my emotions needed time to process. My decisions can't be made on a whim, regardless of what my head tells me.

This trip was the catalyst to helping me understand the difference between being in my mind versus my body. I knew I needed to learn how to connect to the emotional side of my body. I was really good at suppressing my emotions. However, feelings are meant to be felt. It's really hard to feel them if they are locked away. I was ready to change that. By choosing to align more deeply with my Human Design, I created the space for the universe to test me.

Back-to-back death experiences of a life-long friend and my 17-year-old cat, erupted dormant volcanoes within me. Years' worth of emotional energy burst out of me like fire and ash. The heat of tears radiated down my face, leaving an infinite stain of pain and sadness. My blurred eyes were bloodshot, puffy, and red, day after day. My throat felt raw and hoarse. All of the force I held in the depths of my body was released, leaving the remnants of emotional obsidian in its wake.

My treasure chest of emotions, buried deep beneath layers of crust, was unearthed. The emotions within were now free to be shared, seen, heard, and felt. Death was the key to unlocking the chest—my chest—to reveal that my heart is whole and full of love.

Now, whenever I face anything evoking emotion, I feel it. I cry tears reflecting joy, sadness, or disappointment. I'm able to fully experience silly kid movies, impactful speeches, and unexpected events that send me reeling. Sometimes I get so frustrated that I feel like I'm in a room with no exit. Once I process the emotion, I become so clear and calm that I can see the doorway to possibilities I couldn't access before.

In Human Design, I'm known as a 1/3 profile. I'm designed to learn through investigation, then experimentation. The line one is foundational and introspective, needing information and stability. I'm very inquisitive and creative, with a desire to be bold and expressive. It's important to courageously dive deep into investigating, so I can feel safe and secure. If more information is needed, I go research. This alleviates so much anxiety for me. When I embrace my creative, bold side, I exude an inner sense of security and self-empowerment.

The other part of my learning style identifies as a line three. I love experimenting and enjoying dynamic experiences. It's about change and movement. Once I fulfilled my need to investigate the mountain, it was time to experiment. Every hiking journey created new experiences. Participating with different individuals and groups created new adventures. Each hike reached the same goal, just in a different way. For my lone hike, the experiment was about adapting the journey so I could navigate my own energies, and connect with myself and Source. To be on my own and still achieve the goal.

My solo Mount Rose journey was a transformational gift allowing me to dive deeper into self-exploration. Typically, I know I always have something to get done (undefined root), with less time than I think (undefined spleen), with more work than I should take on (undefined sacral), with more to say (undefined throat), while aimlessly flowing with whatever direction hits me (undefined identity). My private hike taught me to transmute those perceived weaknesses into strengths. I had something to achieve, and I did it with an abundance of time to hike and rest. I spoke less to the outer world and more to my inner world. I followed the trail to the top with power and purpose.

Throughout this story, I've given examples of how I weaved various aspects of my Human Design together. There's no one part of the chart that is most important. *It's all of it.* Every aspect of the Human Design chart affects your path to prosperity. If you are not familiar with some of the terms, that's okay. You're invited to return to the story, as needed, to integrate the Human Design seeds I have planted. I revealed my type as a Projector with an undefined sacral center. I shared examples of the force of my will center, and how I make emotional decisions with my solar plexus center. I spoke about mental energies and the split in my chart. Lastly, I discussed my learning style as a 1/3 profile.

For me, prosperity is being sovereign and having the freedom to live the life that I choose. The mountain taught me I can climb alone and still be supported. I can stand atop that sacred space and feel the magnificence of *my being.*

I AM…healthy, whole, perfect, prosperous, and complete. The power of *I am…*who I'm designed to *be.*

My life has exploded with prosperity because I chose to align with my Human Design. I am a healthy two-motors Projector. I love myself, value myself, honor my energy, and teach others to do the same. My defined will gives me the ability to find a balance between serving myself, my family, and the world around me. It's why I am a thriving Projector. I work more freely as it fits my life. I enjoy following my Projector strategy, sharing my gifts in an aligned-wait-for-timing-and-recognition-kind-of-way.

Your path to prosperity is about remembering who *you* are. When you know yourself, the prosperity you want appears in all areas of your life: purpose, career, relationships, family, health, wealth, and spirituality. Prosperity shows up as freedom, sovereignty, sustainability, and any of the good, fun material stuff you are ready to receive when you connect to the Source love-light within *you*.

It is crucial to know the prosperity mountains you face. Many of them originate from within you. Some appear outside of you via others telling you to do it *their* way. However, their prosperity path is not the one you are on.

Human Design is a gift that supports you in climbing any mountain, internal and external. It isn't a cookie-cutter tool. Neither is prosperity. Both require unique, individual, integrative approaches. When you *innerstand* who you are, you navigate the currents of your natural prosperity flow with calm and ease. Prosperity is yours to proclaim because it is not about what you have. It is about *who you are!*

THE TOOL

My clients are people just like you who want to create sustainable prosperity. I guide them to align who they are with what they want. I became a Certified Human Design Specialist to support my clients in deeply knowing themselves. I weave the chart into prosperity consulting sessions so clients can integrate who they are into their life, their choices, and their actions. The chart helps me see their patterns that can be resolved. This creates the space for planting and nurturing new prosperity consciousness.

I created the Prosperity Compass to support you with expanding your prosperity consciousness. This five-step process follows a tribal compass model, starting in the East, and moving clockwise to end in the North. The steps guide you to:

- Step one - Envision your wealth: determine your vision and values.
- Step two - Energize your wealth: discover who you truly are through Human Design.

- Step three - Self healing: heal the wounds of your past and strengthen your resilience.
- Step four - Wealth healing: develop your relationship with money.
- Step five - Nurture your wealth: establish a wealth building foundation to create more value in your life and in the world.

You are invited to participate in an exercise of the Prosperity Compass below. Additionally, you can gain further support at https://www.prosperityalignment.com/book-resources.

What you need: Paper, pen, any dollar bill, and a mirror or phone.

What to keep in mind: The full Prosperity Compass journey takes between 6-12 months to work through, and continues to evolve throughout your life. Allow this exercise to get you started with where you are right now. Take time to acknowledge your gifts, and release all judgment. Be gentle and loving with yourself.

Step one: *Envision your wealth* is about defining what wealth is to you. It is where you get clear on your vision, clarify your values, and begin saving for your dreams. I highly recommend you read and implement *Profit First* by Mike Michalowicz.

Exercise:

Breathing is key during this exercise, so let's begin with a deep breath. Notice how you breathe in and out. For the remainder of this exercise, please keep your mouth closed. You can tuck your lips inward, and gently bite down to hold them shut. The intention is to allow nose breathing to connect you to your inspiration. You'll also become aware of any tension that builds during the exercise, causing you to open your mouth.

1. Grab the dollar bill and place it between your palms. Close your eyes and feel the energy of you with the money.
    a. What do you notice?
    b. What thoughts come to mind?
    c. How do you feel?
    d. What emotional energies appear?
    e. Write down all that is revealed to you.

2. Connect to your vision of prosperity. Pick one or all areas to include in your vision - purpose, career, relationships, family, health, wealth, and/or spirituality.
    a. What does prosperity look like?
    b. What does it feel like?
    c. Are you already on your path to prosperity? If not, what's in the way?
    d. Take a deep breath and look at the bill. Ask it how it's here to support you on your path to prosperity.
    e. Does money play a role in your prosperity?
    f. Do you welcome money onto your path?
    g. Is money important in your vision? Why or why not?
    h. Jot down the awareness that comes forth.
3. Look at the bill again. Grab the mirror (or your phone with the camera on selfie mode). Take a deep breath and look at yourself.
    a. Who do you see?
    b. What prosperity do you see within you?
    c. What are your strengths?
    d. If you could see money as ***M***y ***O***wn ***N***atural ***E***nergy ***Y***ield, how would this affect your path to prosperity?
    e. How would money like to play with you?
    f. Capture all of your realizations.
4. Witness your body's responses to these questions.
    a. How does your body feel?
    b. Is there tightness or constriction anywhere?
    c. Do you feel lighter or freer?
    d. What physical reactions grew louder? i.e., pains, emotions, racing pulse, tight chest
    e. Are you still breathing through your nose?

f. At any point, did you open your mouth?

g. Write down your observations, and feel them too.

This exercise is designed for you to remember the gifts of prosperity already sourced within you. During the exercise, you should have connected to money, prosperity, and you - your image, energies, and physical reactions. The deeper purpose was to expand your prosperity consciousness.

It is time to boldly proclaim who you are, and what you want, so you create sustainable prosperity in your life, and in the world. Prosperity consciousness has to evolve on the planet, and it starts with you.

Alana Heim, CPA/PFS, CFP® (sounds like Anaheim) is the owner and soul essence of Prosperity Alignment, Inc. She guides you to create sustainable prosperity by aligning who you are with what you want. Alana serves in a unique role of being a 5D Prosperity Facilitator. She has a background in financial planning and technical strategies. She pairs this conventional experience with out-of-the-box thinking, Human Design expertise, neo-shamanic remote energy healing, sound channeler, Quantum Alignment System™ training, and intuitive wisdom. She helps you to transform your relationships with self and money. Alana is a two-time best-selling contributing author to *Abundance By Design: Discover Your Unique Code for Health, Wealth and Happiness with Human Design* and *What's Money Got to Do With It?*

Everything is energy. More importantly, *energy* is everything. Alana helps individuals, couples, and entrepreneurs navigate the energetic currents beneath their business, life, and money, so they naturally flow in the river of infinite prosperity. She is on a mission to apply her Atlantean healing powers to expand prosperity consciousness, so humanity gets it right, and reaches new earth on the organic matrix timeline.

Alana, a 1/3 Emotional Projector, lives in Reno, Nevada with her Projector husband and their three children, a Projector daughter, and a set of girl-boy Generator twins. When the mountain calls, you know where to find Alana.

Ready for more prosperity? You are invited to connect with Alana at www.ProsperityAlignment.com.

Additional Resources:
https://www.prosperityalignment.com/book-resources

CHAPTER 16

A DANCE WITH HUMAN DESIGN

FINDING YOUR WAY TO YOUR TRUE SELF THROUGH SELF AWARENESS

Rev. Bamboo Ilana, L.Ac., MS

"The soul has been given its own ears
to hear things the mind does not understand."

- Rumi

MY STORY

Mine is a story of an ultimate humbling, improbable survival, a few fairy-tale miracles, and then learning tools for living peacefully with the both/and paradox of my "not-self" and my "true self."

By the time we come to this part of the story, I already explored, studied, practiced, and/or immersed myself in many systems and modalities.

As we raise the curtain, the year is 2016, and I'm a member in a Life Purpose Mastery year-long program with *Scientific Hand Analysis* as the fundamental tool we learned for developing one's business. It is based on the data and information from fingerprints and markings in the hand. As it turns out, one's life purpose, life lesson, and basic operating system for life can be determined by our fingerprints. It's a very nifty tool.

At the start of the program, the coach gave each of us a copy of The *Definitive Book of Human Design* by Lynda Bunnell and Ra Uru Hu. And while I loved *Scientific Hand Analysis*, it was Human Design that gave me the practical, objective tools that would later save my life.

Later came about three years later when, following a lumpectomy on my leg, the lab detected cancer cells, and the doctors delivered the sentence of cancer. Anal cancer, to be exact. *It made perfect sense to me. I've held on to all this sh*t my whole life, and now I had to let it go!*

By the time I had to deal with the cancer, I had changed so much; I wasn't the same person I was from years earlier. From this, I sourced the instant recognition that to heal, I would need to let go of all the resistance, fear, pain and everything else I held onto my whole life. And not only did I need to let go of so much, but I also needed to allow myself to receive the support I needed from others.

From the beginning, every one of my oncologists encouraged me to choose chemotherapy and radiation, which I flatly refused. Instead, I chose natural healing treatments. There were nutritional supplements and energetic, emotional and spiritual work. I used various modalities and did time-consuming procedures. I used spiritual tools, meditation, imagery and so much more.

The journey took me deep into myself. It set me up to face the real issue, Trust and Surrender. I was to learn more deeply about receiving, and allowing more gratitude, joy, and love into my life, even as I let go of my persistent defensiveness.

I had a tremendous amount of support along the way from friends far from where I was living. An essential portion of the support provided sustained energetic, emotional balancing, which allowed me to experience greater awareness and open to the ultimate transformation in many ways.

With my time and focus occupied with all these modalities, my business in the San Francisco Bay Area suffered and eventually folded.

My healing processes took me to Southern California for treatments, but finances became an issue with the loss of my business practice. I was invited to join the clinic in exchange for treatments, and I accepted.

What ensued was a long string of consecutive bad experiences with housing. Without sufficient finances to secure a place of my own, I bounced from situation to situation, at times homeless, struggling to keep a roof over my head. This was a difficult time.

The cancer brought me to my knees and forced surrender, humility, and the softening of my life-long habitual hardness. Oh, and recognition of others and their suffering, and greater compassion for self and others.

I experienced many epiphanies that changed me dramatically.

One of the notable miracles brought me to a home in Ventura that backed up to a business on Main Street. Garbage trucks came by early in the morning, at least four days a week, an incredibly irritating interruption of my inner practices. Then one of the granddaughters moved in with a very big Great Pyrenes puppy who was unruly, untrained and got into everything, including destroying some of my things. So my life, instead of focusing on healing, became an ongoing series of irritations.

Then I realized that the irritation on the outside reflected the irritation I felt on the inside. So that night, I started doing the *Ho'Oponopono* chant/meditation, continuing as I woke up through the night, and in the morning, all of the irritation was gone, completely gone. I couldn't even touch inside of myself where the irritation had been.

That was amazing, but even bigger was the dawning of an awareness of how much I isolated myself and rejected the world, neglecting to appreciate life or what people did for me. I rejected all of it. And that had to stop, now.

One of my Human Design chart lines describes Simon the Stilyte sitting upon a spire, meditating and escaping from the world. That morning I saw how this was my style, everywhere and all the time. It was a default, knee-jerk reaction. My healing happened when I could choose when and how I took my space.

DOUBT

The inner conflict that blocked my healing was doubt that I could heal vs accepting the validity of the doctors' prognosis. The emotional clearing of this doubt involved learning acceptance and releasing what no longer served.

Another epiphany occurred after the last scan in June of 2020. The tumor had grown a lot and was threatening my life. I had no choice but to accept chemotherapy and radiation or die.

What the hell happened in my body to bring me to this place?

What was I missing?

I knew what it was.

For some reason, things got confused when I checked in at Kaiser to begin chemotherapy and radiation. It allowed me to go back to my meditation. In the period when I was supposed to be seeing the oncologist, I was busy meditating. This thought came into my head: *What if everything I thought and believed was wrong? Could it be possible the chemo and radiation were life-giving rather than a death sentence?* I thought, *I can go with this idea.*

Something immediately shifted in me that altered the course of treatment. Before, I was so afraid of chemo and radiation I would have killed myself from the fear.

Instead, the next scan was clear of cancer and the tumor. I was so blown away by these results. I didn't realize how heavy the weight of death was that loomed over me. But now I could have a life again. How could I not be grateful for my life?

Was there one specific incident that turned things around? Something to brings these pieces together?

Can you be your best true self when you are your not-self?

What does it mean to be your true self?

Follow your "strategy" and "authority," make decisions correctly, and then allow all to happen. Be the passenger in the body watching, being amused.

Imagine making decisions without any yes-buts; no second-guessing. Imagine being able to let it flow, feelings of ease, confidence, joy, pleasure, and laughter mixed with melancholy, sadness, want, desire, hopefulness, guilt, etc., all the emotions and possible feelings a human experiences in a lifetime. Then imagine that they all disappear like clouds in the sky. Everything comes and goes in its own way and timing, and *you* are good with it all.

Does this scare you, or do you think it might be nice to have that ease?

Do you wonder why you do what you do and how you do it? Or do you come up with stories about why, how, and what you do based on what your mind tells you?

The biggest/greatest impediment to being your true self is your mind.

Your mind is great for doing research, gathering information, and collecting data. When you can separate the mind from decision-making, you will feel a lot more relaxed and comfortable with your life. To make that separation, you need to see what your mind is doing and how it's doing it.

Your mind runs old tapes that question anything and everything that might take you into unfamiliar territory. It wants to keep you safe and will use any means possible. The easiest way to control you is to make you feel bad about yourself. Most people do a great job of allowing the mind to torture them with negative self-talk, doubt, and questioning you when you appear to be stepping out of line.

I invite you to reflect on your life's journey and pick out what resonates for you. If it triggers a thought or feeling, great. If you can identify with my inner journey in your life, great. I pray that you find something here that serves you well. I have spent a great portion of my life with my inner dialogue, and it's best if you can find your true voice to help guide you to your true self. It is your life and your experiment.

THE TOOL

TOOLS FOR SELF AWARENESS

GROUND RULES

- Be willing
- Be curious
- Be non-judgmental toward yourself
- Recognize that the essence of you is perfectly wonderful and good

SELF-AWARENESS GUIDELINES

- Life Happens. How well can you be aware of your thoughts and behavior as you live your life?
- Do you make time for self-reflection?
- Can you sit and meditate and allow your awareness to inform you of what is important to notice?

In meditation, as taught by Pema Chödrön, Adyshanti, and countless other spiritual teachers, when a thought comes to your conscious awareness, allowing it to be and going back to your focus without attachment to the distraction is the practice. It's about thinking about something and then going back to where you were without engaging.

Realize any mind chatter that denigrates or diminishes you is not you. These are voices you've heard from outside of your mind "should-ing" you. Dismiss these. *Be gone (See Poofing exercise below).*

Living your "strategy" and "authority," as taught in Human Design, is about reducing the resistance that makes life more difficult. As a result, life gets easier even when it's a challenge. As you let go of the attachments to your resistance, you're able to cope with greater ease, comfort, confidence, more joy, and less stress.

If and when you decide to experiment with your Human Design and are willing to follow your strategy and authority, when you commit to noticing and being aware of what you do and say and how you respond to any and every thing, changes happen.

There's a ground-level acknowledgment of who you are: You are a unique, magnificent individual, unlike anyone else, with a unique perspective and purpose/essence. You're here to express that as your true self.

The mind is wily, clever, and determined to control you and your life. We can call it ego if you like, but it's still the same.

The mind attempts to protect you from yourself, but in fact, causes more harm by beating you up and controlling your decision-making process. The more you give in to the mind and allow it to make your decisions, the more suffering you experience.

According to your Human Design, adhering to your inner authority allows you to fire the mind from decision-making and relegate it to the data and information gathering department where it belongs.

The number one tool to assist you in your life's journey no matter what path you choose, bar none, is self-awareness.

A GROUNDING EXERCISE

1. Find yourself in a comfortable position.
2. Take several gentle breaths and exhale with ease. You can take some big breaths too if you like, bringing yourself into the present moment/present.
3. Conjure up a grounding cord for yourself. It can be any substance, color, diameter, thickness.
4. Send this cord from your tailbone down to the center of the earth (about 4000 miles down) where you can connect with Gaia, the Earth spirit. You can say hello to her if you like. She is there and responds. I generally ask her if she wants a blessing and give it to her.
5. Ask her to send grounding up to the tailbone, and no further up, in your body.
    a. Notice a difference.
    b. Send everything in your body that is not yours down the cord. Anxiety, worry, stress? Down the cord it goes. It all vaporizes and is recycled safely.

c. Use grounding to keep you stable in the world when you feel knocked about. Some people feel safer when grounded.

The point of grounding is to help you be present in the moment. Whenever tension and anxiety make breathing difficult, spend time grounding while working on your breathing.

TOOL FOR SELF EXPLORATION—YOUR MIND

Now that you're grounded, what's next?

You can watch what you do and say. You can explore how you interact with others.

Have you checked out the patterns of your mind and how it controls your life?

The mind runs tapes from the past in an attempt to keep you safe. This exercise may give you a heads up and perhaps a way to gain control over your mind.

Have you ever considered mapping out the patterns of your mind? Can you identify the fundamental patterns that your mind uses to get you to comply with its control?

YOUR MIND THEMES

1. Write down the stories you tell yourself regularly.

2. What triggers these thoughts?

"CHANGE THE CHANNEL" TOOL

The mind is very wily. It loves being in charge of your life, and it will use any means possible to convince you that it's right and correct. Rational and logical thinking has been the top dog for decision-making. The problem is, the mind doesn't function in present time. It relies on past experiences to determine what is safe for you now. The mind also gives you access to thoughts that don't even belong to you.

THE PROPER FUNCTION OF THE MIND IS TO GATHER DATA, RESEARCH, AND INFORMATION. THAT'S IT.

How can you control the mind or direct it to its proper function?

Changing the channel gives you control of your mind, temporarily shifting focus from one thing to another, helping to get you to a better place in yourself. Over time, it increases awareness of your mental process and allows you to choose where you want your mind to focus.

Our mind takes us down rabbit holes of repeating self-destructive or counterproductive thought-forms. If we want to stop them or find a more comfortable place in our head, it helps to practice changing channels.

If you're watching TV or listening to an audio presentation and it turns out to be something entirely different that you aren't up to dealing with, what do you do?

You can think about changing channels as you would think about changing the view of what you are looking at.

Do you look out of this window or that window? Do you need to have a specific view that you turn to, or can it be more arbitrary?

Changing a channel means that you're aware of your mind's focus at this very moment. As a result, you're willing to shift it from one thing to another.

Do you suffer through a program you don't want, or do you do something about it?

Can you hit a button or turn the dial to find something more appealing?

Changing channels is a way to become more aware, taking charge of what your mind is yammering to you about. It allows you to shift your emotional and mental state to something more useful immediately and in the long run.

Can you catch yourself when your mind starts running off down the spiral of despair, unworthiness, fear, or whatever that yanks your chain?

THE PROCESS

You may want to establish the channel you're planning to change to before starting this exercise. It can be a beautiful scene, adventure, or whatever works for you that would take you to a better place. **Find something easily accessible and that works for you when you're in the depths of fear or experiencing something negative.** It can be a default channel you always go to or something that comes up in the moment. Experiment with your new channel surfing.

- Sit and notice your mind. What is it telling or showing you? Does this serve you in a positive way, or does it hurt you?
- Declare to yourself that you're changing the channel and focus your attention on shifting to your new channel. If you like it, great, otherwise keep switching channels until you're comfortable.
- When you get to a better place, breathe as slowly and deeply as you are able. Let your breath be comfortable and easy.
- And Breathe. And Breathe. And Breathe some more.
- Let your body feel your mind and your breath relaxing.
- And say thank you to yourself.

POOF!

And it's GONE!

Another similar technique I've used for years is something I call *Poofing:*

1,2,3, POOF! And it's gone.

It works like a charm for me. It cuts out all the muck in the middle and shifts the attention immediately.

Any thought that isn't right, just POOF it away!

Count: 1,2,3 POOF!

Let me know how it works for you.

For more exercises to address stickier and more challenging issues, contact me.

Bamboo Ilana is a Licensed Acupuncturist, Myofascial Therapist, and Spiritual and Life Guide. She is also the creator and founder of FasciaTouch™, a multifaceted program resolving chronic pain through treating the whole person.

The aim of her work is to guide her clients' healing away from masking their pain, but toward its roots, with tools and techniques that address the physical, mental, emotional, spiritual, and energetic components underlying their pain conditions. She also developed a non-exercise program that gently reduces pain, inviting the body to open, allowing for greater freedom of movement.

Bamboo has worked in the healthcare field since 1985. Following a life-changing experience with cancer and prompted by the state of the world today, she is now shifting the focus of her healing work.

While still loving the hands-on aspect of Myofascial work and the massive transformations her clients achieve from it, Bamboo now focuses on guiding clients to live their true self by living their Human Design. Her personal experience with this system was a critical factor in cancer survival.

In these times of great uncertainty, anger, and hatred, Bamboo honors how the Human Design System can help to know with deeper certainty one's own personal truth rather than relying on messages coming from the outside. The result is an improvement in decision-making ability, clarity, peace of mind, confidence, and most importantly, compassion and love for self and others. All this helps her clients weather the storms of today's life, bringing joy even during difficult circumstances.

Besides the physical support Bamboo offers, her clients also need to be able to reduce the fear they hold in their bodies, which causes more damage than anything else. She brings the combination of her gifts, talents, skills and experience as the foundation for a well-rounded holistic approach to healing.

A link to more of the story: www.bambooilana.com/story

Join me for Human Design discussion at:
www.facebook.com/groups/PersonalTransformationwHumanDesign

CHAPTER 17

DANCING IN THE DARK

BRIDGING THE GAP BETWEEN FEAR AND FLOW

Ashley Ashida Dixon

MY STORY

Be honest with me. I can't be the only one who has stood in the shower with tears and half-washed hair and dripping all over my face, freaking out and thinking: *I won't survive this. There's no money. I'm a burden on everyone I know. There are so many ways I don't measure up, and I let people down. I'm irresponsible, and I just cannot get it together. I'm not okay. Will I survive this?*

Give or take the half-washed hair part.

Now I'll be honest with you. That shower scene exists in a not-so-distant past. And while not on the same scale at all, it reminds me of when I was a kid. But not only did I question my survival, I thought I was dying, literally.

AFRAID TO DIE

This moment is ingrained in my memory. I was watching a TV show, alone and in the dark. A woman was diagnosed with cancer, and I remember seeing its effect on her life, family, and friends. I felt a wave wash down my body. I immediately took on all the fear. I believed her reality to be mine as well, inevitably. I had no physical symptoms, yet at ten years old, I was convinced that my life was over.

I couldn't imagine graduating high school, getting a job, or having an apartment of my own. If I managed to sleep, I'd wake up with tears at the thought that there was just no future to be had for myself. I remember thinking, *why have dreams or goals if I won't live to see them?* I was concerned about causing grief for my family. I was bombarded with worries about opening up to my parents about the harsh news. *Is my being "sick" going to make them feel like bad parents? I don't want to worry or burden them; they have so much going on already.*

Sure the thought of dying was scary for me, but not as much as speaking up and confronting that fear. The idea of getting a confirming diagnosis scared me even more.

I kept it all a secret, and one fear spiraled into many. I avoided the doctor. I didn't speak up when I was feeling ill. I dodged triggering conversations about my health and the critical health concerns for others in my family. For example, I remember watching my grandfather getting sick and passing away while I actively avoided him the whole time. It wasn't easy to do because he lived in my house. And while I loved him, my deep fears kept me far from sharing that love with him in his final days.

This carried on for the next sixteen years. I was living in morbid fear.

Simultaneously I was presented with an opportunity that would change my life. And I believe it's what kept me alive and able to thrive in my own way while not having it all figured out. It was also my first taste of what felt like to *flow*.

I was provided the opportunity to study dance.

DANCING FOR MY LIFE

It was in third grade where some random woman interrupted our math lesson to address the class. *Thank goodness.*

She asked, "Who would like to dance?" I raised my hand right away. The woman handed me a pamphlet to audition for an arts program at a different school.

I took the information home with me and said to my mother, "I want to dance, but what if I don't like it? I've never been on a bus before, and I'm scared to go to a new school."

She smiled at me and said, "You can try it out, and if you don't like it, you can always go back to where you are now."

I was nervous, but I also really wanted to do it, and with the love and support of my family, I tried it, I loved it, and I got good at it.

It would be the middle of the night, and my parents, asleep. The moonlight coming through the sliding glass door casts a shadow on the floor where I sit alone, in my living room. The air is still, and it's quiet except for the music lightly streaming out of my super cool boombox. My CD of choice is the television score to *The X-Files*, my very favorite show, with its famous tagline: *The Truth Is Out There*, which says a lot about me.

And the music from this show isn't at all like the stuff you hear on the radio. There's no conventional beat or rhythm. You won't find a chorus or a melody. It's a disorganized organization of sounds that are sometimes harmonious and beautiful, and other times, chaotic and dissonant. You know, artsy stuff.

I *loved* dancing to this music. I would close my eyes and allow my body to respond to the vibrations, to the frequency. I'd have a song on repeat. While becoming familiar with it, I'd also discover new sounds and patterns. I would observe my body responding in ways that continuously surprised me. A loud clanging of bells would have my head moving from side to side with fury, and in an instant, a sad violin would softly send me to the ground with my arms floating up to the sky. *No amount of thinking would have produced such flow.* It was an improvisational dance with the creator. The present moment and I were one.

It was in those moments I felt free!

I danced almost every school day for the next ten years. I was hesitant to dream yet, some of my wildest dreams came true. It was the very beginning of an exciting and rewarding dance career that took me all over the world and even jumping out of a plane willingly! All of this resulting from a *hell yes* sacral decision I made when I was nine years old.

Dancing opened up doors for me and within me. It took me so many years to realize that my classes were a consistent spiritual practice. Every day

I would tap into my body through improvisational movement. That process allowed me to transcend my worried mind and move me toward the next best decision for myself.

One of those decisions was to open up about my fears to someone I felt safe with. After sixteen years of hiding my deep heartache and pain, my shoulders felt light. I hopped. I skipped. I jumped. I heard that sassy background music going on wherever I walked as if I was in a rom-com. It was a new level of freedom, and I had only scratched the surface.

Once I got vulnerable and expressed my truth, I accepted my humanness and took bolder steps towards my growth. I faced my fear of the doctor and enlisted all the help of spiritual and emotional support.

I realized how exhausting it was to keep myself bottled up or hold myself to perfectionism and societal standards. I got a taste of unconditional love, and I did not want to return to the previous conditions.

*****

Learning about my Human Design has helped me understand the way energy swirls inside me, around me, and through me. As I look at my 10-year-old self, I'm able to understand her better. I'm able to love her and appreciate her courage and power.

And I may find myself in the shower again, crying with overwhelm, questioning my existence and my ability to survive. So I allow myself to be in that shower.

Am I a good mom? Is my son okay? There's so much I want to do for my family; can I do it all? I need more support, but I feel like I have nothing to give in return. Can I really make money to support my family without betraying myself?

And then I question where those questions are coming from. *I've been here before. I think I know what's happening. That sounds like a conditioned open heart.*

Same person. Same bodygraph. A new level of understanding.

*****

Acceptance is what bridges the gap between fear and flow.

When you can be present and accept *what is*, you can stop doing and start *flow*ing. Your body will indicate the correct flow for you.

THE TOOL

DANCING IN THE DARK
A 3-STEP
TO *DANCE IN THE DARK* IS TO:

- bravely explore the present—a tool to shift perspective
- exist amongst the unknown—mindset tool
- embrace the process as is, in co-creation with all that is—grounding tool

STEP 1: BRAVELY EXPLORE THE PRESENT.

Understand the dark for what it is.

I believe the word "dark" has a bad rap as it's usually associated with negativity. The truth is, we can associate negativity with anything. So let's start seeing stuff for what it is. Darkness can provide safety, like the womb, a home for creation and growth. The dirt can be a moisture-rich, safe environment for a plant to break out of its shell. Its growth is a movement (or dance) upward toward the light and it blooms into a more realized expression of itself, all while rooted in the dirt.

To *dance in the dark* is to bravely explore the present, lovingly exist amongst the unknown, and embrace the process *as is*, in co-creation with all that is.

Reality doesn't cease to exist in the dark. The truth isn't being reflected upon by the light on the outside. We can tune into our consistent energy, our individual truth, from within (reference the defined centers in your Human Design chart).

STEP 2: EXIST AMONGST THE UNKNOWN.

Know that confusion is a temporary state.

Let me ask you this. What would happen *inside you* if the lights were to shut off unexpectedly? What's the first thing you would be compelled to think or do? I'm not a fan of hypotheticals but roll with me on this one. Take a second to close your eyes and imagine.

What came up for you?

I'll tell you what came up for me! *Oh, shit, what the f*** just happened? I can't see anything. What if I bump into this table that I know is there, but I can't see it. Why is this happening to ME right now? I have all this stuff to do today? What is going on?*

I can imagine that whatever thoughts arise in response to this question could easily be different depending on who you're with or what you ate for lunch that day. Do you *really* know what you would do? *This is why I'm not into hypotheticals.* We may probably find ourselves scrambling to find the solution right away within those states of uncertainty. We can look into our undefined/open centers in our Human Design to bring more light to this.

The point here is to understand that we cannot rush the natural process of creation. A temporary state of confusion is simply a new way of life coming into maturity. We wanna eat that cake before it's out of the oven, but it's still in the process of cooking!

Confusion feels a lot like that, huh? Hot and not ready yet.

STEP 3: EMBRACE THE PROCESS *AS IS*.

Move around, make a home, and experience yourself in this state.

Close your eyes.

Breathe deeply into the now.

Open your eyes.

Take a look around.

What do you know to be true?

Where does your body naturally want to go without interference from your mind?

How do you experience your authority from your Human Design chart?

Be an observer of yourself with unconditional love. No judgment. This moment is new, and you can do what you can do.

Does your body want to lie down? Maybe sitting down is better for you? Need some water? Basic needs aren't so basic; they're essential.

In moments of sudden discomfort or confusion, I have found that my body likes to lay flat on the floor and sink down into the ground. With each exhale, I allow the earth to hold more and more of my weight. The heavier I get the lighter I feel. I only want what is mine, and I release what is not.

You can find what works best for you in this life by daring to do things differently. Let your inner-knowing be your guide. Let the music of the unknown move toward yourself even if the direction isn't clear to you. Any movement toward your true self is the right move.

Ashley Ashida Dixon is a mother, Human Design Analyst, Intuitive Guide, speaker, and artist with over 20 years of experience as an entertainment professional. She has toured the world with Katy Perry and The Backstreet Boys, taken the stage for stand-up, improv, and traditional theater, and is now a prolific content creator. Ashley uses her skills as a performing artist to engage with and curate large community followings on multiple live-streaming platforms. As a speaker, Ashley uses her knowledge of Human Design to inspire and educate creatives of all types. Throughout her work, Ashley champions cultivating diversity, creating social impact, and celebrating individuality.

Ashley is the founder of Decondition Daily to provide resources and support for those on a lovingly relentless path of autonomy and self-advocacy amid adversity, fear, and constant change. Those on a path of healing and liberation while not having it all figured out. It's time to decondition from the status quo and create lives that don't revolve around the systems and structures that don't serve us. How do we do it? Step by step, moment to moment, daily.

Get to know Ashley by visiting @AshleyAshida on all platforms including:

Instagram https://www.instagram.com/Ashleyashida

Tik Tok https://vm.tiktok.com/ZMew9Brpg/

Clubhouse https://www.clubhouse.com/@ashleyashida

Facebook https://www.facebook.com/AshleyAshida/

CHAPTER 18

ADDICTED TO BURNOUT

THE LESSON THAT ROCKED MY WORLD

Connie Kanella Aramento, Intuitive and Self-Awareness Coach

MY STORY

When I was a little girl, I would get lost in my thoughts, dreaming of the day that I would have my own talk show, be that fierce leader changing the world in a big way. Every time I watched Oprah with my mom at 4 pm right after school, I imagined myself being her, feeling loved, appreciated, valued, and inspiring. I always called myself the Greek Oprah sinking into that feeling of being an influencer and expert. I was like, *yup, that's going to be me someday, no doubt, making a lot of money and then giving it back to the world and those in need, that someone who will always be remembered for her contributions.* I would often have to snap myself out of La La Land because I wished it was already happening.

Patience was not in my vocabulary. Being the youngest of three, and the only girl to immigrant parents from Greece, my family came here with one suitcase in 1972. They were both from the same village in the Peloponnese region, and their marriage was arranged. My mom didn't even have her dad walk her down the aisle at 16 because he was working on the railroads in New York doing what he needed to do to give them a better life in the United States.

When my parents arrived for their fresh start, they had to jump right in without knowing the language and culture to survive. It's a typical immigration story, minus the boat, with the entire family living together in one house, helping each other out. The woman did everything when it came to the home, and the man worked for his family. My mom eventually became a seamstress, and my dad was a painter, and they, unfortunately, had to do things without the support or help of parents soon after they arrived. They learned quickly that you have to work hard to make it regardless of how tired you felt. For them, failure was not an option.

As the third kid, I witnessed how hard everyone worked and felt like that was the only way to be successful in life. Play was okay, often criticized, but work was what got you what you need in life, *so they said*. Every day was a routine and felt mundane. When my parents came home from work, my mom would be stressed and tired preparing for dinner, and my dad would nap for an hour and then ask for his cognac. After school, my brothers and I played with our friends for a little while and came home for Greek dinner by 6:30 pm. Aside from math homework that I often struggled with, my evening duties included setting and cleaning the dinner table and listening to a full hour of business conversations between my parents, uncles, and brothers without anyone ever asking how I or my day was. I felt so frustrated and alone at times as if I didn't matter. I was often reminded I was the girl, not the boy, and there were specific things I could and couldn't do. I felt as if no one really cared because as long as I was doing what I needed to do, told what to do, and did it, then all was good. My mom had little patience. She was focused on taking care of everyone and dealing with my dad, who was sick a lot. And then me, because I always had headaches, stomach issues, and even mono for three years.

It wasn't until after the restaurant businesses opened up that things started to shift for my family, especially with money. As I turned 13, I was forced to work every weekend, constantly being reminded by customers that I was too young to work. I would always reply with, "no, I am not; I want to work here," as if I was a trained robot. I swear I was the richest 13-year-old out there.

At that time, fifty bucks a day was a big deal, and I was always reminded, "the more you work, the more money you make." I eventually got addicted to it and felt like I missed out not being a kid hanging out with my friends on the weekends. I was named *untouchable* by the boys at school because my mom kept me working on the weekends so I wouldn't have a boyfriend. She knew I was safe in the restaurant, which, ironically, I named "the jail."

As time went on, the jail became my home school away from home. It taught me about life; I met all different types of people, from drug addicts to the rich. I felt like I was in charge; people knew who I was. I was like a local celebrity treating people to free eggs over easy and bacon at 4 am. Deep down, though, I was missing out on the fun due to my family's expectations. Eventually, I grew to love it because of the power I felt within myself while I was there, and I didn't want to let anyone down.

This was my world and my identity until I decided to do what my parents never wanted me to do, move away. I remember the day in 1999 when I moved into college in Rochester, New York, as a first-generation college student, and knew it would be the end of living at home and the beginning of figuring out who I really was. I knew that to truly discover my purpose in the world, *I needed to leave home behind and venture out on my own to create my life, my way*. I needed to make this sacrifice.

I didn't know that the lesson of hard work and money would have me facing the 'burnout and broke' lesson instead, and that I would have to rewrite my whole way of living life to free myself from this burden. I thought I was dreaming of it all, but instead, I was actually talking to a doctor in real life.

Doctor: "All of the tests came back normal; there's nothing wrong with you."

Me: "But there has to be. I can't move, my body hurts, my headaches have been going on for months, and my spine is stiff. How could I possibly be in so much pain? This isn't normal."

Doctor: "You have to go on medication; this is all anxiety. Take some time away from work, and get some rest; you are stressed and burnt out."

No one ever told me that being an adult would be this complicated. It was the day after Thanksgiving in 2016. I called my mom, asking her to come to help me because I just came home from the hospital and needed her. I was given some crazy cocktail that had me seeing visions of ex-boyfriends to get rid of the 90-day pain extravaganza in my head. I thought I was seriously tripping or crossing over and thought, this is it.

When my mom arrived after her long drive, she looked at me as I was sitting in tears, curled up on the couch, and said, "Connie you are your father; you have anxiety like him." I thought, hell no, and denied it all because my whole life, I swore I wouldn't be sick like my dad because I didn't want to suffer. I couldn't understand logically how I got here. I had two little kids under the age of five, and my husband, who, with every stare I got, made me feel like *I was a failure*. I kept thinking, *how could this have happened to me? Where did I go wrong?*

I spent the next four months getting every test done, trying to find something wrong with me, and also feeling like a zombie taking everything from Prozac to Lorazepam and having therapy. Not feeling good was a pattern I was familiar with as a kid, and it increased when I left for college, but I would keep going. I would not feel well for a while. I went to doctors, and they didn't find anything. You would think I would be ecstatic, but instead, it created more confusion in my mind.

During those four months, there were days I couldn't get out of bed and felt helpless. My husband didn't know how to deal with me, and became a single parent doing the best he could while I focused on getting better. It was all emotionally draining, and I truly didn't want to go back to work, but we needed to pay our bills. I had to rise from this all-time low.

As I sat home trying to figure it all out, I realized how I got there. In 2011, I had my daughter, and my uncle passed away six months after due to cancer. He was 54 and like a second dad to me. He was the hardest worker I knew. During those dinner conversations as a kid and in "the jail," he taught me the most about life. The one thing he always said was, "follow your own path and always believe in yourself no matter what." When he passed, I lost faith in myself, and I also lost a promotion I knew I deserved. I was also grieving and dealing with postpartum depression too.

I chose to stay in a job because of the financial bonus I received to train my new boss. I was bitter they chose this guy, knowing I was qualified for the role, and in return, I worked harder to prove my worth. I was reminded again that "*hard work pays off*" and "*this is how I will be successful.*" My bitterness got the best of me, though, as I took on more projects to feel recognized, valued, and ultimately loved. Unfortunately, I was burning the candle at both ends, and my body began to react. I kept trying to convince my husband and my family I could make enough money on my own as an entrepreneur and leave the hell hole, eventually. Boy, was I wrong, and that day after Thanksgiving in 2016, I began to replay all of my childhood rules in my mind saying, *so many people in this world work this way, why can't I?* I realized I wasn't meant to.

While I was out on medical leave, I found mindfulness meditation and connected with a former business and spiritual mentor. As I was talking with her about what happened, she shared with me my Human Design chart and that as a 1/3 Splenic Projector, I was here to advise and guide others and be of service in the now. She also shared with me that I am not meant to work a 40 hour work week, and that burnout is very common because I do not have a defined sacral.

We talked about the importance of needing to be invited to the big things in life, such as career and relationships, and that constant working was going against the way I am designed. "Bitterness is how Projectors often feel when they are not in their design," she said, and I thought *I found the code I've been missing, but who the heck am I now?*

THE TOOL

I soon realized that my whole life, I was surrounded by Generators and Manifesting Generators. Now I know why I often felt misunderstood as a kid, and why I needed so many naps. One of the most amazing gifts of this discovery was connecting with my beautiful talents and the need to be recognized through invitations. At first, I resisted this because I saw it as completely shifting who I thought I was, which shocked my ego. Being told that I have lived my whole life against my actual design left me with the same feeling I felt when I went off to my first day of college, nervous and lost. I suddenly understood how I got to burnout, why anxiety was showing up, and that my bitterness got the best of me. I wasn't true to myself, so as a result, I started over. If you find yourself in this space, here's what you can do:

1. Surrender, ask for help and release the guilt. Get the rest that you need and focus on daily meditation, specifically body scanning. Focus on your breath with feet on the ground in a comfortable position sitting, and begin by connecting to your body. Start with your feet, noticing what is there without judgment, only awareness. If you feel something, just notice it and say "release" to any pain or sensation that feels uncomfortable for you. Move your way up through your ankles, calves, knees, thighs, hips, belly, chest, hands, arms, back, neck, face, eyes, head. Repeat this daily.
2. Buy a journal, and start writing. Ask yourself, "how do I feel today? "What am I thinking about today, and how do I want to feel?" Identify how your intuition is showing up for you, where your thoughts get in the way, and identify your ego voice. If you notice a thought of negativity, shift to feel how you feel and connect with your desired feelings.
3. Take advantage of holistic healing tools such as craniosacral and myofascial release therapy, or sound and energy work. Find a mentor, spiritual teacher, or practitioner in your area that can help you release the trauma or wound that showed up as physical or emotional pain for you.
4. Communicate clear boundaries with your family and friends sharing your needs in this moment, and open yourself up to being vulnerable. This is healing.
5. Tap into your creativity. What are your passions? What makes you get up in the morning and makes you lose your sense of time? Do that.
6. Evaluate your system. The environment that you are in, your job, does it work for you, or are you working for it? If not, what would support you feeling healthy? What might that look like? Go for it.
7. Have a support network including a doctor you trust and even a functional medicine doctor, spiritual teacher, and therapist. Focus on your health and wellbeing from the mind, body, and soul. You need all three. Trust the process.

This is a great starting point to your healing journey. I discovered that the message of work hard to earn money made me broke and sick, literally. What I saw as a kid was how others made their earnings, and I followed their design, not mine. As time has gone on, I have learned the power of patience, stillness, routine, and that hard work is not the only way to abundance and prosperity. My daily mantra is "I am enough, and I am seen." When my body speaks, I listen and give it a break instead of feeling bitter. Now I can say that my addiction to burnout to achieve success has been transformed into being addicted to rest and invitations. I no longer look at my body with frustration but with curiosity and love, and now I get to feel like that Greek Oprah as host of my own podcast.

To learn more about my story and the tools that I used to heal my health challenges and anxiety blended with Human Design, visit https://soulsyncwellness.com/resources-2/.

Connie Kanella Aramento is an intuitive and self-awareness coach, and the CEO of Soul Sync Wellness, LLC for the past 12 years. Her personal mission is to bridge the gap between leadership and wellbeing through spiritual growth and personal empowerment. She believes that we all have a path and have to connect back to our soul for it to lead us. She specializes in helping women finding their inner gem by getting out of their head and into their heart, and is especially connected with those who are overworked and burnt out. As a licensed Gallup Strengths coach she works with individuals, teams, and organizations to create communities of collaboration and innovation through communication. Connie has coached more than 2000 people, inclusive of her 17 years in Higher Education, presented countless workshops focused on life success, leadership, positive psychology, mindfulness, among many others. She has served as a keynote speaker at conferences and has led large-scale transformational leadership and wellness programs. She is the author of many workbooks, including the Soul Sync Core Workbook, teacher and guide of her Feel to Heal online courses, and the host of Humans on a Mission podcast on Empower Radio. Connie offers intuitive readings, coaching, courses, and welcomes you to the Soulvolution virtual community to learn more about how to evolve at the soul level. She holds certification as an Integrative Nutrition Coach, B.A. in International Studies, and M.S. in Educational Leadership. Outside of her career, she loves her two kids, Sophia and Michaelangelo, and resides with them, her husband John and cavapoo, Gizmo, in Holden, MA.

CHAPTER 19

FINANCIAL FREEDOM

BECOME AWARE OF YOUR BLOCKS AND EXPERIENCE WEALTH

Janette Gallardo

"Money is life energy that we exchange and use as a result of the service we provide to the universe."

– Deepak Chopra

First and foremost, I want to thank you for grabbing a copy of this book and for your interest in using Human Design to become aware of your blocks. Before we dive in, I want you to close your eyes and take a deep breath. Acknowledge your surroundings and allow yourself to connect to your breath. Whether you are a newbie to this or a Human Design junkie, I want you to know that I see you. You are an extraordinary human being! Let Human Design become the vehicle to give yourself permission to own your unique traits and let go of anything not serving you. Experimenting with Human Design is a fun way to get to the core of who you are. You get to question the tool, find what resonates, and experiment with how things show up for you. Financial freedom through the lens of Human Design is a holistic program that brings blocks to the surface so you can transform the way you engage with your thoughts, habits, and the world around you. The results will allow you to be in alignment with yourself so you can live a prosperous life.

MY STORY

Human Design is a tool that transformed all aspects of my life. It allowed me to create awareness around my unique traits and provided a deeper understanding of who I am at the core. It permitted me to stop questioning why I am different and own my natural way of being. By understanding my design, I changed how I manage my finances because I understood myself more. Everything is connected, but we are so used to only treating the symptoms. We get so fixated on money, but rarely do we take the time to get to the core of the issue. Working on your blocks and honoring your design can give you the answers you have been searching for. Not getting to the core of those blocks is the barrier to true prosperity.

Feeling unfulfilled at my job was a constant struggle, not to mention, my head would entertain every thought that crossed my mind. *I'm not getting any younger and don't want to wake when I'm sixty doing the same job, but why do I feel stuck and unable to move forward?* Leaving my job was not an option. *How would I make a living and support my lifestyle?* I would ask myself this when the thought of quitting crossed my mind. Coworkers would refer to me as the "money lady" as I looked over the company's budget and tracked departments' spending. *My relationship with money was healthy,* I used to tell myself. I would blow at least $1,500 in any given month on the soft-as-butter jacket, the crafted Italian shoes, and the timeless coats. My spending patterns came from having a split in my design, as this gave me the illusion that something was missing. In addition, I was not honoring my emotions as I wouldn't allow myself to feel them. My mind was running the show, and I compensated myself with material things for working in an environment that didn't align with my natural way of being.

Working on my design allowed me to identify blocks which helped me leave my six-figure job. I learned I could see other people's gifts, but

I can't see my own. It made sense as I thought everybody felt comfortable working on their finances. Exploring methodologies and questioning them is part of who I am. It would aggravate my boss when I would ask why we were doing things a certain way; I would get "because we have been doing it this way for years." People at work carried projections in how they perceived me; I felt pressured to meet their expectations. I learned that people projecting on me is part of my design; this allowed me to not engage with their projections. In addition, being around the correct people is crucial as the wrong people can drain me, which can be detrimental to my health. Starting my own business allowed me to identify projects, people, and conversations that energize me. I stopped following the work hard, play hard mentality, started tuning in to my body, pursued my way of being without resistance, and made decisions based on my design.

I envisioned having the confidence of others to put myself out there. *Even if I was self-assured, I didn't have anything to say*, I would tell myself. Words wouldn't formulate; it felt like I had a block on my throat. *What is wrong with me? Why can't I speak up?* I felt insecure about speaking my truth and giving life to my voice. Punishing myself for not speaking up during meetings was my go-to, but even when I would talk, I would punish myself for not liking my voice. After presenting projections for the year, I told a coworker, "I hate the sound of my voice; everybody does, right?" I got an odd look in return which made me wonder if I was the only one who didn't like their voice.

The anxiety to give life to my voice came from deep conditioning from my upbringing. Growing up, my aunt would give me a hard time with my voice. "Stop sounding like you are whining and start speaking clearly," she would tell me after mimicking me. Over time I lost my voice. When sharing my insight, my palms would get sweaty, my heart rate would increase, and I felt butterflies in my stomach, and these feelings would get in the way when trying to formulate thoughts into words. I identified this block through Human Design, and after working on this, I now feel confident speaking with clients while walking them through their financial journey.

Understanding other people's designs and how this can positively or negatively impact others has been a life-changing experience. When I met my husband, I was intrigued by his drive and clear goals. He has a clear and consistent direction which I found magnetic, as I am the opposite.

Early in our relationship, he shared he wanted a weekend cabin in the woods with plenty of land so we could enjoy a hike in nature with our dog and have a woodworking shop. I, on the other hand, need flexibility and major purchases felt restricting. *What if I want to take off to Europe next month or travel the world for a year?* My fear of committing to big purchases came from fear of the unknown combined with my need for flexibility. My husband's sense of direction and ability to see the big picture allowed me to let go of my fear of the unknown and step into buying a house and a weekend cabin in the woods. Creating awareness of who we are at the core will impact our relationship with money and our relationships in general, especially the one we have with ourselves.

Human Design made me realize that I can welcome wealth into my life once I live in alignment with my design. When you get aligned with who you are, the fears, the blocks, and the negative self-talk go away. You then feel supported at the core and understand you will succeed at whatever you decide to do. Not because you have found your purpose but because you have found yourself, and that is true freedom.

THE TOOL

Human Design is your blueprint which maps out your unique characteristics and how to best engage with the world around you. The centers are the geometric shapes located inside the bodygraph. Each center has a special attribute and can reveal potential blocks, as centers can become deeply conditioned by your upbringing and environment. A quick way to identify blocks is through centers where you may be acting from a place of not-self (conditioning from your environment). Most of us operate from a place of not-self, which becomes part of our habits, and it's hard to identify who we're here to be. As you start questioning your habits and identify blocks, you begin to live life by your design. Ultimately, decision-making comes from following your natural way of being without resistance.

Before we begin, I want you to take a deep breath and place your right hand over your heart, and repeat, I am unique and will honor and love who I am. For this exercise, you will need your bodygraph, which will help you identify your potential blocks. To get your free bodygraph and centers guide, visit https://www.vittasolutions.com/hdresources. I will walk you through a set of questions, write down the ones that resonate, and feel free to go deeper. You will need those answers for the following money mindset exercises.

The head is our inspiration center. Most of the time, we let our minds engage with every thought that comes to mind. The key is to get into the habit of entertaining the ideas that matter. Now let me ask you this, do you get anxious when thinking about your finances, or do you find yourself overthinking in general? Do you become easily overwhelmed with your finances? In what other areas of your life is your mind creating mental pressure that can turn into anxiety or self-doubt? Discern blocks: am I engaging with meaningless thoughts?

The ajna allows us to process thoughts and creates certainty. When we engage with meaningless thoughts and try to figure them out, this can cloud our vision and confidence. Do you find yourself obsessing about finances? Do you try to convince others that you are finance literate? Do you find yourself trying to convince others that you are intelligent or confident? Discern blocks: am I trying to be convincing? If so, where is this coming from?

The throat gives voice to our centers, and it's the primary focus of the entire bodygraph. It can be under tremendous pressure to speak; the key is to know when to talk and what to share. Do you feel insecure about talking about finances or talking in general? Do you find yourself talking excessively about money (how good or bad your money situation is)? Do you give voice to every thought? Do you try to attract attention with your words? Discern blocks: am I contributing to the conversation?

The self (G) center is your compass for direction. Do you need flexibility in the direction you are going? Do you feel paralyzed with making significant purchases because you feel you won't have the freedom to change your direction? Do you get worried about the direction of your finances? Discern blocks: am I looking for direction? Can I permit myself to explore different alternatives with my finances without getting paralyzed?

The heart center houses your willpower, self-esteem, and self-worth. Do you put pressure on others to keep promises? Are you unable to keep promises? Do you have low self-esteem around your finances? Does someone take care of your finances? Discern blocks: what am I trying to prove to myself or others? Why am I allowing others to take care of my finances?

The sacral is your life force center. Do you feel frustrated and not financially accomplished? Do you work to the point of exhaustion to make money? Discern blocks: am I doing things I am not passionate about? Why?

The spleen is your intuition center. Do your mind and other people overwhelm you over financial matters? Do you hold to every penny and constantly think of how to spend less money? Discern blocks: am I holding on to people or things that do not serve me?

The solar plexus is the center of your emotions. Do you make impulsive purchases, or are you a shopaholic? Do you avoid money conversations? Discern blocks: am I avoiding meaningful conversations? Am I emotionally shopping?

The root is the alignment center. Do you put others under financial stress? Do you find yourself taking on the financial stress of others? Discern blocks: am I creating unnecessary stress for myself or others?

Human Design is a robust tool. Only focusing on one area of your bodygraph will not give you the whole picture; I highly recommend getting a full reading to experience the advantages of this tool.

MONEY MINDSET EXERCISES

Once you have identified your blocks, you can move into the money mindset technique to help you reveal your stories or beliefs around money, which can help with the de-conditioning process. Have the blocks you identified from the previous exercise handy. Find a quiet place where you can relax. Start by taking a deep breath (count to five), then hold your breath (count to five) and release your breath (count to five). Do this three times. Imagine stepping into your childhood home. Walk to your favorite place in the house and take a seat.

Ask yourself the following question:

- What are the core money beliefs that are running my life?

Close your eyes, take a deep breath, and imagine the first money block on your list. Allow yourself to bring everything that comes to mind, even if it doesn't seem to be related to money initially. Trust me, everything is connected, and identifying everything that shows up is critical.

Ask yourself the following questions, then take your time and listen to the answers from within:

- Where did I come up with this belief or story? Take a few minutes to go deep and allow the answers to come to you.
- Is this my belief, or did I adopt this belief from someone? Allow the image of the person from whom you inherited this belief to show up.
- Is this a belief that brings abundance into my life? Take a deep breath and allow the answer to sink in.

Open your eyes and write down everything that came up for you during this exercise. Don't question it; write it down.

- Take a moment to reframe this belief.
- Write down how this belief has shaped your life and how it has helped you in your journey.
- Rewrite this belief by creating a new belief that aligns with the life you aim to live.
- Write down the new belief and replace the old belief every time it shows up.

We are in charge of our reality, but we first need to look our past in the eye and give a new meaning to the story, which allows us to take responsibility for the future we want. Choosing interpretations that move our lives forward will enable us to welcome the unknown and trust that the outcome is better than planned. I want to clarify that this process takes time, and it's not something you can master overnight. The key is consistency and to practice every day when those old stories hit your mind's headline.

MONEY TECHNIQUE EXERCISES

We have been working on money mindset, so now you get to take action. The most important place to start is getting intimate with your finances; this will give you clarity and confidence. The more confident you feel about your finances, the better decisions you will make. If you currently do not feel confident about your finances, it doesn't mean you are stuck or you can't change things. Change won't happen overnight, but if you are consistent, you will gain financial confidence in the long run.

Here is an exercise that will get you started to take control of your finances. I know what I'm about to ask you will not sound appealing, but trust me, it will get easier over time.

1. Log into your bank account and print out the last two months of your bank statements.
2. Categorize expenses into "wants" and "needs" and create a list of all the "wants."
3. Calculate the total amount for each bucket and calculate the percentage ("wants" divided by total spending)
4. Be conscious while making future purchases and determine if they are "wants" or "needs" (and remind yourself of the "wants" percentage when considering giving in)
5. Have a financial plan with short- and long-term goals
   - Short-term goals can be paying off credit cards, saving money for upcoming events.
   - Long-term goals can be paying off loans, saving for retirement, investing in property.

1. Repeat Steps one through five the following month
2. Track your spending and compare it to your plan
3. Reduce your wants by 50% for the coming months
4. Increase your savings by 25% for the coming months
5. Increase your investments by 25% for the coming months

Money creates a false sense of security, and money is not the problem. Our blocks around money are the issue. Money is not bad; money is just energy, and we can use money to create the life we desire and impact the world. You can make changes in your finances; the key is to become self-aware of your blocks to experience true financial freedom. We are all a work in progress, and our most significant contribution to the world is to keep on working on ourselves. Financial freedom is living life inflow and in alignment with our highest self and with others, so we can welcome wealth into our lives. Let our minds be conscious and our hearts be open as we thrive to prosper together. This is my wish to you, my wish to us!

Janette Gallardo has 20 years of experience in business finance. She has worked at the headquarters of private and publicly traded companies and managed up to $25 billion in revenue. She gained international experience while working at the headquarters of ABN AMRO Bank in Amsterdam as a Strategic Planning Analyst. Her finance experience is in Strategic Planning, Budgeting, Forecasting, Cost Analysis, Pricing Analysis, Financial Modeling, and Mergers & Acquisitions. In addition, she is a Human Design Guide and utilizes Human Design to create awareness around blocks while working with clients on their finances. Her calling is to impact others positively. Her mission is to get people to change their relationship with their finances; as she likes to say, she "Humanizes finances for conscious individuals." She has channel 16-48 (a design of talent) activated, taking her into the rabbit hole of exploring and mastering finance, Human Design, and mindset modalities. When Janette is not working, you will find her hiking with her husband and two German Shorthaired Pointers. She loves to travel, learn about other cultures, and has lived in the Netherlands, France, Mexico, and the United States. She is passionate about wellness and self-growth and has found a love for yoga, meditation, and mindfulness. To learn more, visit www.vittasolutions.com.

CHAPTER 20

LEARNING TO LET GO

THRIVING IN THE WORLD AS AN EMPATH

Amber Clements, Certified Human Design Specialist & Transformation Coach

MY STORY

My head was spinning. I barely had a moment to catch my breath. I could hear everyone so loudly, but not a single person spoke. The pressure of anger, disappointment, worry, and frustration reverberated through every part of me. I wished there was an off switch. I couldn't stand it any longer. I felt so selfish. I had to do something!

Only one hour had passed since the 13 of us were squeezed into a minivan on a nine-hour drive back to Bangkok. Our ferry had broken down, and the only way I could get my 12 tourists back to the capital city was in this 10-seater minivan.

As the tour leader, I sat in the front of the van next to the driver while the others crammed into the back. Earlier, over the phone, my manager forcefully instructed, "You must take the front seat and get the tourists back to the hotel as quickly as possible!"

As the tour group sat in silence on that trip, I felt their responses. One man silently threw daggers at me through the back of my seat. He thought he should be sitting where I was. Some worried about the safety of the journey. Others judged my competence because I couldn't find an appropriately sized van in the brief hour I had to find alternative transportation.

But no one spoke. Instead, they sat mutely in their thoughts and feelings, making it impossible for me to relax. I could feel and hear everything they weren't saying in every part of my being. I couldn't turn it off.

They were the longest nine hours of my life.

My name is Amber, and yes, you guessed it, I'm an empath!

What is an empath?

The Oxford Dictionary of English defines an empath as *(chiefly in science fiction) a person with the paranormal ability to perceive the mental or emotional state of another individual.*

Paranormal abilities aside, I've always sensed other people's energetic 'stuff,' as I like to call it, and my heightened sensitivities made it difficult for me to feel like I was thriving.

My life experiences are muddled with pain, confusion, sadness, depression, and all the other internal responses that come from not understanding how to cope with my sensitivities and the influence of others.

As a child, I was deeply tuned into the emotional energy of my parents who danced with the idea of divorce for most of my life before seeing it through when I was 17.

I always felt at the mercy of others, constantly on alert to how they were thinking and feeling and never wanting to upset anyone. To keep their negative feelings or thoughts at bay, I continually sacrificed my needs for theirs.

I recall on my sixth birthday, my mother coming home with two ice creams. Without thought, she grabbed one chocolate and one vanilla. "Amber, as the oldest, you can have the first choice," my mother announced, holding out both ice creams.

I loved chocolate, so I naturally reached out to grab the chocolate ice cream only to feel my younger sister's disappointment about being left with the vanilla one. My body clenched. *I so wanted the chocolate one!* But I couldn't fight my senses and instead reached for the vanilla ice cream. My sister's face beamed with joy. "Yummo," she sang as she enthusiastically grabbed the chocolate ice cream and ran off to enjoy it.

There was no thank you for giving up what I wanted. Both my mother and my sister went on their way blissfully unaware of my small sacrifice.

My childhood is littered with these experiences, which, one after another, took me away from myself and my own needs.

The problem was that the moment I chose my own needs over others, I felt terrible. It somehow felt selfish to allow myself to feel joy while I was sensing someone else's discomfort. My mantra was, "I'm sorry." I was forever apologizing for everything. If I had a dollar for every time someone told me to stop apologizing, I'd be a wealthy woman.

So, I became a 'yes' person, a 'let's do whatever you feel like doing' kind of gal. I did everything in my power not to upset others and chose instead to do things that made other people happy. I often sacrificed myself for the benefit of others. I was the class clown taking the blame for something, so others didn't have to.

One morning a friend sent me an email titled 'Your Human Design.' I brushed it over. *My human what?! Probably some crazy spam out to waste my time.*

I flicked past it.

The following evening, I was bored of watching reruns on Netflix. *Surely I hadn't watched everything?* I picked up my laptop and scrolled past the email again.

This time I paused on it long enough to skim the body of the email. 'The new astrology,' it read. 'Blah blah blah. . .Your personal report is attached and it's all about you.'

About me? Well, how can I go past that?

Curiously, I opened the attached report. "You are a rare Human Design reflector type. Reflectors make up only 1% of the population," it stated in the opening sentence.

It continued, "You are born with the ability to experience empathy in every sense of the word."

WHAT?!

I spent the next three hours like a keyboard warrior on Dr. Google. *What is a Human Design Reflector?*

The more I read, the more tears poured down my cheeks. *Where did this Ra Uru Hu person come from, the originator of this information? And how did he know me so well?*

For a moment, I suspiciously looked around the room for cameras. *Was I under surveillance? Had he been watching me?* I felt exposed as though someone dove into the depths of my soul, unlocking my internal secrets.

My life started to make so much sense. I stood up tall in the lounge room and bleated out loud, "My name is Amber, and I am an Empath!" My dog half-cocked his head wondering what all the noise was about before laying it down again, unimpressed.

It dawned on me how many of my life choices were influenced by others. I was 30-something, unmarried, and still chasing the American dream.

"Once you settle down and start a family, you'll find true happiness," at least one of my friends or acquaintances said every month for as long as I can remember.

I had three degrees, was highly skilled, and still climbing the corporate ladder because, "You haven't made it unless you've made it to the top," I heard the media, colleagues, and Facebook ads telling me year after year. "You need more. More. *More!*" came the bombardment of voices around me.

I even once said with pride, "I don't get out of bed for less than $1,000 a day" to anyone who'd listen. If this was a marker for success, I needed to let everyone know I was making it.

The problem was, I no longer loved the type of work I did. It felt contrived. My life didn't feel like my own. I was living in the third person.

"Oh Amber, you've got it made," a friend blurted to me at a BBQ one Sunday. "How do I become just like you?"

I was a fraudster. I didn't feel like I'd made anything at all. I certainly wasn't feeling joyful or internally thriving.

I was assimilating.

I turned up to work in my Dolce and Gabbana suit and spent at least 40-hours each week actively contributing to this career aspiration.

But every morning on my walk to work, I thought to myself. *Is this it? Is this living? Is this making it?* Something had to change.

I was tangled up in so many other people's thoughts, feelings, pressures, and fears that I barely had room to be myself, whatever that was.

Reading that Human Design report and about my natural empathic qualities was my hallelujah.

I studied everything I could about it, eventually certifying as a Human Design specialist. This newfound insight gave me life-changing knowledge.

Armed with this information, it was time to make some personal changes; it was time for me to let go.

I started with work.

"No," I said boldly, my stomach twisting in knots.

"I understand your view, but I don't agree with it!" I brashly informed a senior executive. "I have a decade of experience that tells me otherwise, and I will not succumb to agreeing because you want me to."

The executive glared at me, forcefully stating, "Well, I'm taking this to the top. You've done your dash now, Amber." She shoved her chair back and stomped to the other side of the room.

I left that office unapologetic. I wasn't going to play the game any longer. *I would NOT succumb to doing what everyone expected me to do.* I'd witnessed and experienced in-house bullying one too many times. I felt her thoughts and feelings, but I was not going to lose myself to them.

A week later, my superior stated coldly, "We need to determine if you're the right fit for this job. Your position is in review."

My boss's jaw dropped when I replied, "Actually, I also need some time to determine whether this place is ethically the right fit for me."

A few days later, I resigned. I walked out the door and never returned to that type of environment. I no longer needed to prove myself or try to emulate what others considered 'successful.'

From there, I cleared out many other areas of my life. I cleared out so much I suddenly felt empty.

What do I do with myself now? I spent the next few months seeking other things to do.

Who the hell am I? I couldn't work this out at first. *What do I like doing or even want to do?* The questions kept coming.

One morning, I woke, and for the first time, I didn't feel compelled to get up and 'do' something. Instead, I sat in my gorgeous, neglected backyard and took it all in.

The emptying helped me notice the flow of life outside of myself. I watched a flock of noisy miner birds in my yard each take a turn to dip into my pool. The birds watched as their companions dove one by one toward the surface of the water just enough to wet their beak and belly. They then dried off in the bare branches of the frangipani trees surrounding the pool.

I felt so present. These birds had probably been visiting my yard for years, yet this was the first time I'd ever noticed them.

What else hadn't I noticed? What other magical pieces of the world had I missed out on because I was too busy following others according to their thoughts, feelings, and beliefs?

In this time of stillness, I let each day dictate my activities.

One morning I woke to see the sun singing through the winter sky calling me outside. I spent that day basking in the sunlight, out and about in my natural surroundings.

Another morning I woke to feel an urge to write. In the absence of doing what was expected of me by others and away from their influence, I felt this internal yearning to put pen to paper. I spent the day typing out a memoir that almost turned into a book.

I learned to go with the flow instead of doing all the things I felt I should be doing. Life was an adventure again; each next day a little unknown. I allowed myself to literally go with the flow with whatever presented itself to me internally or externally.

"You're doing what?" a friend bleated some months later when I told her that I'd quit my job and was now practicing Human Design. "But you had such an amazing career! This must be paying a lot, though. Right?" I shook my head.

She couldn't understand my choices. A look of pity shot across her face. "Don't worry," I assured her. "I'm really happy. Really, really happy."

She was still confused but equally overwhelmed by my reassurance. "Yeah," she nodded. Then after a while, repeated, "Yeah, I can see that."

My ability to tune in to what everyone else was thinking and feeling didn't reduce. In some ways, it was stronger than ever. What was different was my ability to notice it while not succumbing to it. My natural skills and preferences began to emerge again. Some of these I'd lost as a child, such as writing. With this gift restored, I wrote my first book and had it published. I found joy in just being me. I no longer needed to chase anything in the pursuit of happiness.

I now work in a way that honors my energy and allows me to go with my flow. I am loved unconditionally for the first time by someone I'm still tuned into, but with whom I have healthy boundaries that protect me from his 'stuff.' Having healthy and happy people in my life also means I'm not constantly caught up in their negative thoughts and emotions.

From this place, I thrive.

Exploring my empathic triggers has helped me understand myself and how other people affect me. I've learned how to let go of other people's 'stuff.' I now use my empath superpowers to stay connected to others without losing myself.

Today I'm thriving as an empath. I wonder, *are you?*

THE TOOL

To get an idea of your empathic attributes, ask yourself these questions.

1. Do you take on other people's thoughts and beliefs?
2. Do you feel other people's emotional energy?
3. Do you sense the heart of someone underneath their external behavior?
4. Do you sense other people's pain or fear?
5. Do you feel pressure from other people even if they haven't spoken about it?

Did you answer yes to any of the above questions?

If so, you are empathic. The more questions you answered with yes, the more empathic qualities you have.

Once you have a clear understanding of what makes you empathic, you can begin the process of releasing whatever you're holding onto that doesn't belong to you. In Human Design terminology, we call this conditioning.

Conditioning refers to the 'stuff' we adopt from other people, such as their thoughts, beliefs, fears, and so forth. As a result, we become conditioned to act or think in a way that isn't natural for us.

For example, if you pick up on other people's thoughts, you may hold onto their beliefs about yourself and the world. If you feel other people's pressure, you may forgo your natural internal process and instead live according to the pressure you pick up from others.

Once you understand how you hold onto other people's 'stuff,' it's time to let it go and clear it out. This includes everything you need to do to offload the trauma and negative impacts caused internally by being empathic and truly clearing out the energetic junk you've collected through your life.

This can be an extremely cathartic process because it's about letting go of anything that's no longer serving you.

Many different techniques can help you release what isn't yours. One simple technique is grounding. This shifts other people's 'stuff' out of your body.

LET'S TRY IT NOW.

First, take yourself outside.

Take off your shoes and plant your bare feet on the ground. Make sure the ground is natural, meaning it's grass, dirt, sand, or some other natural part of the earth.

Ensure your feet are placed firmly on the ground, so they are connected with the land.

Take a deep breath in and let all the 'stuff' you've picked up from other people dissipate through your body and into the earth. Let mother nature help you let go.

Close your eyes and imagine the thoughts, feelings, or whatever else you've been empathically collecting from others be sucked out of you into the ground.

Breathe.

Enjoy the feeling of the ground under your feet and be thankful for the opportunity to connect with it.

This is a simple and easy process that you can do anytime. It doesn't take much, but it can help you let go and reconnect with yourself. Do it as often as you can during the day. Sneaking outside for five or ten minutes is not only great for releasing this energy back into the earth, but it also reinvigorates the soul and your connection with mother nature.

When you release everything that isn't yours, you make space for something even greater: more room more you!

When you're not consumed and impacted by other people's 'stuff' you can use your empathic powers for the greater good of all. Empathy allows us to remember that we're all connected. It prevents us from becoming self-absorbed and uncaring of others.

When you embrace the compassion that your empathy provides, you increase your capacity for connection and understanding. Just don't lose yourself in the process. A world without empathy would be a very sad and lonely place indeed.

Know your value and your self-worth, and love yourself for everything that makes you who you are, including your sensitivities. Don't be the victim of your empathy but rather use these superpowers for the betterment of all *and* for yourself.

The world will be a better place when there's an abundance of thriving empaths. When we harness our ability to be tuned in and connected, we demonstrate how to be both concerned for the wellbeing of others and be self-empowered at the same time.

To learn which parts of the Human Design chart make you empathic and other techniques you can use to release and restore yourself, visit my resources page at https://amberclements.com/resources

Amber Clements is a rare Human Design Reflector and author of the book *The Human Design Reflector: Barometer of the World.* Born in England and raised in Australia, she grew up with adventurous parents seeking a better life.

Amber is a Transformation Coach and qualified Change Manager who works with you to make lasting personal change. Her passion is to help you shine from the inside out.

For a decade, Amber worked as an organizational change expert, helping organizations navigate their way through transformation. Her own transformation journey allowed her to transition, so she now works with individuals on a personal level. She has finally found her happy place and uses her empathic and intuitive skills to offer people a safe space to show up just as they are.

As a certified Human Design Specialist, Amber draws on her Human Design expertise to help you first understand yourself. As a certified practitioner in Biofield Tuning and Quantum Alignment, she then uses these therapies to help you let go of what needs to be released and restored to unleash the vitality, happiness, and abundance that is naturally within you.

Amber's two great passions are travel and education. She's traveled to over 60 countries and lived and worked across three continents. She holds a collection of degrees and combines her deep practical knowledge with 25 years of teaching experience to help you through your transformation journey.

When not traveling or working, Amber loves to hang out in her beautiful garden and spend time playing her medicine drum. She does her best to savior her moments of solitude but equally loves to connect with people from all over the world.

Learn more about your unique Human Design chart and the types of transformation programs Amber has on offer at https://amberclements.com

CHAPTER 21

WHAT IF NOTHING'S WRONG?

RELEASE THE PRESSURE OF PERFECTION BY LEVERAGING YOUR UNIQUE DESIGN

Lauren Armstrong

MY STORY

We spend so much of our lives trying.

Trying to be good kids.

Then good students.

Good employees.

Good bosses.

Good based on other people's definitions and expectations of what 'good' actually means. But what if trying, in general, were flawed? What if trying, simply meant "T.R.Y." - tirelessly resisting yourself?

I found myself trying for years. Trying to fit into the mold of what I thought was expected of me.

I tried to get good grades in school.

Tried to get a good job out of college. Naturally it was the job that paid the most.

But with all of that trying, I found myself in a place where I 'made it' on paper while spending my lunch break crying in my car. I made six figures, had a 401(k) and a pension in the oil and gas industry by age 22, but I wasn't making any sort of impact and found myself having a daily existential crisis.

This can't be my life, this is not my purpose, is this really it?

I truly believe that everyone is put here on earth with something they're meant to do and I knew that working as a cog in the wheel of an oil and gas corporation was not my purpose in this lifetime.

Which led to the guilt-shame spiral of *I'm so lucky to be in this position, I know how many people would kill to be in my shoes. How dare I want more?*

So I did what any sane person would do and I started a side hustle trying to do something I wanted to do with my life.

I wanted to do something that was fulfilling and successful, that allowed me to be an equal contributor to our household while also bringing meaning to people's lives and making an impact. Something that felt like a worthy cause to spend my life on.

And I thought in order to do that I needed to be someone I wasn't.

So I tried that.

After work and on the weekends, I tried to build a business, exhausted trying to do both and doing neither well. I realized I had a choice to make. I could either go all in on making my business work or I could stay and try and make corporate work.

The day I made this decision is a day I remember vividly. A coworker, Gary, stopped by my 'cube' and we were talking about his retirement. He had moved to Houston for one three-year assignment 25 years ago from California and he was looking forward to retirement in three years' time when he could move back home and his life would actually begin at the age of 65.

When he left, my thoughts started racing.

Could I do this for the next forty years?

Could I celebrate birthdays in the 'energy hub' at least once a month?

Could I work through weekends for the next forty years to get a leg up?

Could I spend hours of my life in meetings that could have been quickly solved with an email?

Could I share my opinions and be told that 'that isn't the way we do things around here'?

Could I be on someone else's schedule determining how and where I spent my life?

I couldn't, and how could someone possibly do that to themselves for so long when they didn't love it? It was then that I looked around at my coworkers, at my director above me, and the VP above them and realized that was not the life I wanted to live. They were overworked, they weren't spending time with their families, and they were unhappy in this company's version of success. There had to be something more and if I didn't escape my golden handcuffs, I would be exactly like Gary in 40 years. My life was worth more to me than that.

Once I made the decision that I needed to leave my corporate career I enrolled in all of the courses and certification programs I thought I needed to make my business successful. It was only logical that of course someone outside of me had the answer on how to do this thing. If I just started operating the way successful business people did, and I took their courses and applied the same strategy it would be a matter of time until I, too, was successful.

Why not? That was the way I operated my entire life up until this point. Understand the expectations, achieve them. Parents, teachers, bosses—I knew the game.

So why then, was I working more in my business than I did in my corporate career while making next to nothing and following the advice of super successful entrepreneurs?

Enter Human Design.

It was after another failed launch that I stumbled upon Human Design while scrolling my social media feeds. I learned that there were over two billion configurations of "Human Design" and your unique combination showed you how you were wired to interact with the world around you.

Always interested in learning more about myself, I read a little about my 'type' and felt like someone had ripped a page out of my diary, sharing my desires, my fears and what ways of being would likely not work for someone with my energy makeup. I felt seen and understood in a way I never experienced before.

Every single marketing and sales strategy I was trying fit within that list of things that likely wouldn't work for my energy type.

The thoughts that had been running in the background:

Maybe I'm not cut out for this.

I should have never left corporate—I'm going to have to get a job.

I'm going to have to admit to failing at this.

I'm not as smart as I thought I was.

All of the work, all of the guilt I had about giving up the corporate job and the shame about this business of mine not working out as quickly as I thought it would, seemed to relax, just a little.

These strategies weren't working for me, because they weren't meant for me. I could do something about that. I could change that. I wasn't broken.

Every action I was taking in my business was coming from a place of what I thought I 'should' do. They came from a place of believing that someone other than me knew what was right. I was paying these 'experts' for their strategies. I was paying them because I didn't trust myself, because I told myself I didn't know how to run a business, but all they were sharing was what worked for them. And those experts had a very different energetic makeup than I did.

When their way didn't work, I blamed myself. I never asked *what if this way isn't for me?*

The perfectionist tendencies I was cultivating my entire life to check the boxes and achieve societal expectations led me to believe I needed to follow someone else's formula for success, when in reality I had my own formula mapped out in *my* Human Design all along.

I was making myself wrong and trying to fix myself, trying to fit into the box of business expectations, rather than recognizing that maybe it wasn't a lack of willpower, or conviction, intelligence or execution, but rather that the strategy was not meant for me.

Our brains are literally wired to tell us we're wrong, show us where we may be in danger and help us fix it. Neuroscientists call it the "negativity bias" and from an evolutionary standpoint it's great, but when we are trying to create a life that we don't have evidence is possible, we may find that it's ruling the show. It leaves us doubting ourselves, our capabilities and believing that we are not enough as we are.

Human Design shows us what is truly us and what is simply a negativity bias from our minds. We get to shift into flow and ease rather than continuing to resist and 'fix' ourselves. Our energetic blueprint shows us where we can stop trying so hard and notice what's a distraction telling us to seek for answers outside of ourselves rather than coming back to the truth within, that nothing is inherently wrong with us. There is nothing to fix.

When we align our ways of being and actions in the world with how we are wired to show up, building our business becomes so much easier. I started experimenting with the ways of being that were laid out in my design in my business on a Wednesday. I shifted how I was talking about my offers, what I had available that would be more in line with my design, and the energy I was bringing to my audience and clients. I took basic business principles and applied *my* Human Design to shift them to fit my design. I had four coaching spots available in my practice, and by Monday I sold them out, after months of trying strategies that did not serve me by those 'experts'.

There was such a noticeable difference in the way I was showing up in the world that I had friends and mastermind colleagues asking me what I was doing differently. What I found so fascinating about the experiment was that what 'worked' was doing what came so naturally to me and what I was resisting for so long. I had all these beliefs around what business should be, that it had to be done a certain way, it had to be hard. What came naturally to me couldn't work in business, it wasn't how everyone else did it and they were successful.

But it turns out that is exactly what did work for me: recognizing where I was being distracted by negativity bias, who I was at my core without all the expectations, and the work I wanted to bring into the world. That is the beauty of Human Design: when we stop trying so hard working against ourselves, we realize that nothing's wrong.

THE TOOL

"Everything is energy and that's all there is to it.
Match the frequency of the reality you want
and you cannot help but get that reality.
It can be no other way."

- Albert Einstein

Humans are vibrational beings, made up of energy just like everything else and our feelings each have a vibrational frequency. You may notice that when you're trying really hard or your mind is being taken over by the negativity bias, you may feel the feelings of doubt or worry.

But when you find yourself in flow, doing work you love to do, you may feel the feelings of passion or belief, hopefulness or happiness.

This concept is illustrated and explained beautifully by the emotional guidance scale. It's explained by Abraham Hicks in the book *Ask and It Is Given*. But I heard about it for the first time in Gaby Bernstein's Book, *Super Attractor.*

It's a scale of our feelings and emotions, in sequence from our highest vibrational feelings to our lowest.

Here's the emotional guidance scale from highest vibrational feeling to lowest:

1. Joy/Appreciation/Empowered/Freedom/Love
2. Passion
3. Enthusiasm/Eagerness/Happiness
4. Positive Expectation/Belief
5. Optimism
6. Hopefulness
7. Contentment
8. Boredom

9. Pessimism
10. Frustration/Irritation/Impatience
11. Overwhelm
12. Disappointment
13. Doubt
14. Worry
15. Blame
16. Discouragement
17. Anger
18. Revenge
19. Hatred/Rage
20. Jealousy
21. Insecurity/Guilt/Unworthiness
22. Fear/Grief/Depression/Despair/Powerlessness

If you're wondering what on earth this has to do with your business or even your Human Design let's tie them together, shall we?

When we are in alignment with our Human Design, we are feeling those top three feelings.

When you are feeling those things, your vibration is higher, therefore opportunities that come to you will be in tune with that frequency. This is based on the Law of Attraction and the Law of Vibration as summed up by the quote that opens this section.

The frequency of success, satisfaction, peace, and delight are natural when we follow our Human Design, specifically our type, strategy and authority which you can learn more about in the resource guide for this chapter.

When we don't follow our Human Design, we tend to be out of alignment: frustrated, bitter, disappointed, and angry.

Those feels are shown in number 10 down. When we are in that state, we attract things in our lives and businesses that are at that lower frequency. This is a universal law, like gravity.

The quickest way up the scale is through aligning with our Human Design or practicing gratitude, helping us see how much we have in our lives to be grateful for, especially in moments when we feel like we don't have much to be grateful for.

I hear from a lot of successful entrepreneurs about being 'in alignment' and 'managing your state' and that our frequency comes first. These are the energies and frequencies that they're talking about.

So let's start here. Because everything is energy.

Which number between 1 and 22 are you feeling now around your life, purpose, or business?

Now without judgement, notice that feeling and where it is in your body. Can you sit and feel that vibration? What color is it? What shape? You don't have to have all of the answers, but notice what this feeling really feels like in your body rather than in your mind. When you've gotten a good grasp on it, let's move on.

What number do you desire to be feeling? Sometimes if we are pretty low on the ladder it can be hard to jump all the way up to the top, so look a couple of numbers up if that feels better than a large jump up the rungs.

What does that desired feeling feel like in your body? Can you remember a time you've felt that before? Where does it show up in your system? What color is it? What shape? Does it have a texture? Or a smell?

What action could you take to help you move up the ladder and feel into those feelings now?

Lauren Armstrong is a 5/1 Self Projected Projector which, in English means she loves talking things out, creating offers based on what she is recognized for and solving the problems she is invited to help lead and guide others to solve. She has a unique way of seeing the world and loves mastering the system of coaching using her favorite tool...you guessed it! Human Design.

Her signature program is LEVERAGE: Human Design for Business where she helps coaches and course creators fill their purpose-driven programs without feeling pressured to build their businesses the way everyone else does. Lauren believes that we are all uniquely wired for what we are meant for in this life. If you'd like to learn more about how to finally drop the overthinking and comparison when it comes to your programs and offers you can visit purposewithoutpressure.com

She also runs a projector-specific 'mastermind' called Projector Playground helping projectors lean into their energy type and create a sustainable business by their design.

Lauren is certified as a Human Design Business Consultant through the International Human Design School. She also holds certifications in neuro-linguistic programming and time techniques, is trauma-informed and is a clinical hypnotherapist, reiki practitioner, retreat leader and speaker.

Outside of Human Design work you can find Lauren travelling with her soon to be husband Jeremy and spending all the time she can get at the beach in San Diego where she lives and likely, taking a new certification to help her clients create the futures they are designed to live into.

Connect with Lauren at hello@createdfutureacademy.com and on social media:

Instagram: https://www.instagram.com/laurenearmstrong

Clubhouse: https://clubhousedb.com/user/laurenarmstrong

Book Resources: https://www.laurenarmstrongtraining.com/book-resources

CHAPTER 22

LEADING WITH SOUL

STEP INTO YOUR PURPOSE AND UNLEASH YOUR WEALTH POTENTIAL

Sabine Messner, M.A., Certified Human Design Specialist

"It's not the fault of the wood when it wakes up one morning as a violin."

- Arthur Rimbaud

MY STORY

WAKING UP IN THE MATRIX

Have you ever wondered what your life would look like if you didn't have to rush off to work every day? Do you feel stuck in an unfulfilling career rather than excelling in your dream life? Are you too busy paying the bills instead of exploring your dormant talents and skills? Are you sad that you spent countless years giving work all of your focus with little or nothing to show for yourself?

If similar questions are swirling in your head, this chapter will bring you a new perspective. Our busy society doesn't readily provide answers to our quandaries and quests for a more meaningful life. It's all too easy to go back to what's familiar, which is going about your day, working hard, and hoping someday you'll get a break.

I recently met a woman during a Human Design workshop I was co-hosting. The workshop's premise was to make Human Design more practical by encouraging participants to ask any question they're currently struggling with. One of the participants, a lawyer who for decades had been working for a government agency, said: "I think every day about how I can't wait to retire and get out of this job. But my pension is not enough to pay the bills. My problem is, I don't know what else I can do. I'm really getting tired of this."

Though I had never met this woman before, I saw her journey through the lens of Human Design. For me it's like reading a person's Soul DNA. I can see it all so clearly. I responded, "Oh my gosh, how are you surviving your job? You are divinely designed to be an adventurer, not sit in a cubicle all day. Just the monotony alone is torture for your Soul. If you could live like a nomad moving periodically from place to place or being on the road for part of the year, you'd be the happiest. It would be immensely satisfying and stimulating for you to immerse yourself in other cultures, climates, and environments."

As I described her authentic inner landscape, she was instantly moved to tears. I'm not implying her legal career isn't a fit. Instead, mundane repetition depletes her life force and causes emotional exhaustion. The lawyer is no exception. Sadly, her dilemma is the norm. Most people can't even imagine making it anywhere close to retirement age in their careers. I've worked with plenty of clients in their 20's and 30's who've wondered how they would escape the trap.

To change predictable outcomes, we must open ourselves up to higher potentials. Easier said than done, especially if you've lost the user manual for your own life along the way. You see, in the 3rd dimensional reality, we consciously or unconsciously trade our time and life force energy for the ability to pay for our livelihoods. That's why it's called "making a living."

The promise is, if you work hard and save enough money, you will eventually re"tire" and then have all the time you've ever wanted. Not only is this model flawed to no end. It's a grand illusion. What creativity and life force energy do people have left once they make it to their goal? And do they even know what to do with all their so-called "free time?" Statistics show that people die within three to five years after retiring. To survive retirement cannot possibly be the purpose of our existence or is it? Have we all but forgotten how to live our lives?

To make matters worse, our economic safety nets are getting challenged to the core. Since the world woke up in a global lockdown in 2020, millions are forced to search for new ways to make a living. Will they find new jobs? Hundreds of thousands of professionals are now working from home and will likely never return to their old offices. Perhaps deep down in their Soul, they're also seeking relief from chronic overworking, overdelivering, and overstressing? Something more fulfilling, more meaningful, less mechanical. But is that even possible for them? As unwanted, unexpected, and traumatizing this whole ordeal is, it creates an evolutionary crisis of meaning.

ACTIVATING YOUR HIGHER POTENTIAL

It's no surprise that I'm encountering more people from all walks of life who truthfully don't want to go back to the old normal. As uncomfortable as it is at first to admit, the great time-out makes them question their jobs, careers, relationships, and lifestyles. As they explore new opportunities, the biggest and by far most daunting questions are, "What happens if I pursue these crazy ideas I've been having? How will I pay my bills and keep my income level? How will I take care of my family?"

When the 3rd-dimensional world collapses, higher guidance must take the lead. This is usually the junction where I step into the picture and help facilitate a paradigm shift. People know they need to evolve but don't know where or how to begin. That's when I open up inner and outer wealth potentials for businesses and individuals alike. The result is more authentic self-expression, more life force energy, more freedom, and naturally more money.

Thankfully, in times of crisis, the Soul finds its way into the foreground. Perhaps you, too, have been tapped on your shoulder by God, Creator, your Higher Self, or whatever you may want to call this higher impulse to lift your limitations. You may feel the pressure on a cellular level:

- It's time for truthful expression and more deliberate use of your life force energy.

- It's time to shatter your financial glass ceiling.
- It's high time to get your life on purpose!

Before I tell you how I utilize Human Design to provide people with the map for their new purposefully aligned lives and prosperous ventures, I must first tell you my story.

HOW MY SOUL TOOK THE LEAD

Since my earliest childhood memories, I've always had a strong connection with my Soul. I grew up in Germany's Black Forest, living an idyllic, magical, and mystical childhood. However, it all changed at the early age of 17 when I watched my father gradually transition during a coma. As devastating as his tragic death was, it entailed the greatest gift of my life. I witnessed the metaphysical departure of his Soul from his body. I saw a ball of light with my inner eye as he slowly left through his heart and then hovered above his body and eventually floated to a cross of Jesus on the wall. From there, he looked down upon my mom and me, assuring me that he was fine and all is well.

Amid my unspeakable pain and sorrow, I experienced the gift of Grace, an angelic and heavenly archway that opened up my Soul sight and gave me the ability to see through the veils of this dimension. Decades later, I would learn that Grace (Gate 22) plays a significant role in my Human Design. During his funeral, I made a powerful pledge to myself, not realizing it would change the trajectory of my life forever. I pledged that I would live a life in which I could die any day, knowing that I had fulfilled my highest purpose. This pledge catapulted me out of the ordinary world and led me to pursue the extraordinary.

From that moment on, I took charge of my destiny by reverse-engineering everything, and I mean everything. As a 3-5 Manifesting Generator with the life theme of Transference, I've always intuitively known that I am manifesting my reality, which means I go full steam for my most significant dreams (Gate 30 Desires). And I surely never cater to mainstream as I'm much more interested in lifting the confinements of mediocrity to create bountiful uniqueness and beauty (Gates 8-1 Creative Role Model Channel).

Soon after my Soul awakening, I landed my dream of attending the University of Arts in West Berlin. I studied Visual Communication, immersing myself for years and years in painting, drawing, photographing, sculpting, and tutoring. All along, I used my extensive training and education to not just become a classic visual artist or graphic designer but to be the Creator of my Life.

My Masters of Arts was an elaborate art installation called "Fishing for the Heavenly Body." In it, I correlated the seven stairs to heaven with the seven ISO layers of the Internet. An interactive computer animation at the center of the room simulated the World Wide Web years before its official inception. I intuited and visualized everything we take for granted today, such as having virtual conversations across the globe and sharing thoughts, words, and images (Gates 64-47 Abstract Mind Making Sense Channel). I've always been able to see the future and tend to be years ahead of the Zeitgeist. That's a huge part of having the Soul sight.

My relentless quest for innovation (Gate 35 Progress) led me to San Francisco, where the founders of Wired Magazine hired me on the spot to co-design the very first online magazine in the world. It was called Hotwired, and it launched two weeks after the inaugural Internet browser Netscape was released in October 1994. We pioneered the future that we now live in.

This is how I landed my very first job, and boy, was it out of this world! I continued to create out-of-this-world professional and personal opportunities. I landed more dream jobs, landed in the arms of my dream husband, and woke up one fine morning in my dream business. Opening higher potentials for myself and my clients is at the heart of my life's work.

My Alchemist channel (Gates 2-14) enables me to morph an undeveloped potential into a higher materialized state, like turning lead into gold or taking a vague idea and making it real. That's why I excel in launching start-ups. The entire transformational experience is such a thrill for me. I welcome all creative challenges and love to collaborate and co-create for the benefit of all (Gates 40-37 Community Seeking One's Larger Family Channel).

I've helped countless Silicon Valley companies, brick-and-mortar businesses, and innovative solo entrepreneurs to either start their venture or reinvent themselves by literally transporting them from the overwhelm of too many rough ideas to the consolidated finished vision or product. I use branding as the alchemical art form to initiate the state change. It works like a charm even if clients don't exactly know what they want or how they could become their next highest version.

Years before I learned about Human Design, I claimed my life's work with my trademarked Soul Purpose Branding® process that anchors people in their calling and lets others easily understand what that they're all about. Soul Purpose Wealth™ opens a person's inner and outer wealth potential. Soul Purpose Wealth is not just about financial freedom, though that's a significant aspect. It's a multi-faceted way of living that brings about Soul-fulfilling experiences, answers, connections, relationships - all calibrated to your unique purpose and precisely aligned with whatever brings you joy and abundance.

HOW HUMAN DESIGN CONFIRMED WHO I AM AT THE CORE

Human Design has brought me instrumental validation. While my Soul has always guided me, it felt gratifying to receive my first Human Design reading by Human Design expert Chetan Parkyn, who later became my beloved mentor. I'm honored to be one of his personally certified students. Human Design unequivocally confirmed who I am at the core and how I am here to serve. Moreover, it helped me refine my business model, get out of Generator mode and be more on point as a Manifesting Generator. And it elevated my coaching practice and showed me how I can even better serve by expanding into my "deservability" (Gate 45 The Queen).

In my experience, if a person is following their Soul guidance, there tends to be a great match to their Human Design. It's like a glorious affirmation and celebration of their authentic self. If a person is lost in the 3rd dimension, Human Design is a sure-fire shortcut to get their life on track. That's why I love Human Design so much. It reveals who you are at Soul-level and therefore equally serves people on their path and those looking to discover their purpose, perhaps for the first time in their life.

Human Design gives me the knowledge to powerfully assist people at this critical junction of the Old Earth crumbling away while simultaneously the New Earth is emerging. These are challenging times, and helping people make deliberate changes that shift their entire trajectory in this lifetime is beyond words. Because of the significant instability of these transitory decades, people tend to cling to their routine jobs, identities, and predefined roles in family and society. That shrinks their potential. Whenever we let fear and worry lead the way, more limitations are the consequence.

That's why I use Human Design to create a massive shift in one's self-perception towards deserving more abundance, love, and universal support. By clearing out unconscious self-limitations, economic opportunities manifest quickly. It's like lifting a veil and shattering the old conditioning. Then I use branding and positioning to reorient people and companies to own their higher, most prosperous identities.

YOUR SOUL HOLDS THE BLUEPRINT FOR YOUR BEST LIFE

As I'm writing this chapter, I am assisting a postal worker in initiating her Soul Purpose Brand. Yes, you read correctly. She is a mail carrier who received the divine shoulder tap years ago. She's been channeling a stunning light language in visual and auditory codes to assist and empower humanity. It turns out she is a highly advanced Soul with the life theme of Alpha Leadership.

Imagine our joy as we're translating her innate abilities into a business, complete with a branded eCommerce website so she can attract and serve her ideal clients. Soon she won't recognize her old life, and all sorts of new opportunities will come her way. It's exhilarating to partake in a person's liberation that positively affects all aspects of their life and everyone in their world.

I love assisting people of all walks of life and financial backgrounds. Equally rewarding, I love working with highly successful business owners and multi-millionaires on their next-level expression, whether it's personal or business-related. Often, they've experienced substantial Soul loss as they pursued their goals and garnered impressive worldly success.

Regardless of where a person is at, my priority is always to serve their Soul. Because of my multi-dimensional seer skills, my Human Design readings are said to be very different. I call them "Human Design Soul Activations." I tap straight away into the blueprint of the Soul's evolutionary journey and connect the dots to the purpose of their incarnation. I customize my explanations and transmissions accordingly. A Human Design Soul Activation is a priceless, timeless paradigm shift for those ready to lift off.

I hope this chapter inspires you to let your Soul lead the way.

MY TOOL

TUNING INTO YOUR INFINITE WEALTH POTENTIAL

"Who would you be, and what would you do if money was not an issue?" You've probably heard this question before. It's a classic transformational inquiry that gets to the heart of our 3rd-dimensional condition. On a deep dive, this question is not easy to answer. It goes beyond the superficiality of typical "winning the lottery" answers and what money can buy.

In the 3rd-dimensional reality, **"Time is Money."** We're wired to look at our lives linearly, which locks in the future as an unknown ever changing variable. Meanwhile, we're surely running out of time and money. To break through this dimensional barrier a shift in perspective is required.

In the 5th dimensional reality and beyond, **"Time is Art."** It's the measure by which we calculate galactic time in the Eternal Now, the realm of Soul. The Eternal Now is the simultaneous existence of past, present, and future. Changes in one affect the others.

Would you like to experience this space? Then pull out a journal and close your eyes. Now imagine that your Soul has an Infinite Trust Fund when you come into this world. Imagine that you don't have to work at all, not one single day, and your Infinite Trust Fund continually replenishes. There are no bills to pay, and you don't have to prove your worth. There's also no performance pressure. Only a blank canvas and the freedom to create and Self-express.

Imagine waking up every day to that beautiful canvas creation purely for your Soul's pleasure and sacred reflection. All that the Universe wants from you is your most significant contributions as a way to sing your song and add your unique, irreplaceable signature frequency to the cosmic symphony. As you create your day, you create your reality and, ultimately, your world. You are eternal Soul.

Does your Soul show you a picture, a feeling, or a sensation? Perhaps you see yourself in a different dimension, era, or even on another planet? Can you sense an emerging and expanding feeling, like a warm embrace? Can you capture your experience with words or sketches? Perhaps you're inspired to set up an Infinite Trust Fund wealth altar to remind you daily of your birthright to receive abundant support as you return to the Creator realms.

Keep tuning into your Infinite Trust Fund and expand your wealth frequency over the next days and weeks. The more you can bring this higher energy through into your every day life, the more you'll be guided in the direction of your greatest fulfillment and joy. This is what I call Soul Purpose Wealth. It's an incredibly exciting and rewarding journey to be on!

WHAT SOUL ART WILL YOU CREATE WITH YOUR LIFE?

There's a blank canvas waiting. Let's co-create together!

For additional Soul embodiment tips and resources, join us at www.SoulPurposeWealth.com/overflowing

Sabine Messner is a visionary Futurist and 5D Branding & Business Consultant, showing individuals how to be in business with their higher calling. Combining her new paradigm branding approach with her cutting-edge strategic guidance, Sabine turns emerging leaders into extraordinary luminaries thriving as sacred stewards and entrepreneurs alike.

On an individual level, her clients range from spiritual leaders, financial insiders, corporate executives, PhDs, doctors, and alternative healing professionals to well-known coaches in the expert industry. She also delivers innovative, holistic branding to start-ups and established companies with higher ambitions.

On a collective level, Sabine's work assists in the awakening of humanity and the planet by liberating and anchoring the Prosperity Consciousness locked in the human potential. Blending her 30+ years of experience and education in the fields of arts, visual communication, and marketing with her extensive studies of cross-cultural energy modalities, Sabine's approach is as enlightening and profoundly empowering as it is down to earth.

Sabine holds an M.A. in Visual Communication from the Berlin University of the Arts and is the founder and creator of Soul Purpose Branding® and Soul Purpose Wealth™. As Wired's Senior Designer, she was instrumental in launching the world's first online magazine in 1994. Equally groundbreaking, Sabine served as a Cyber Crime Marketing VIP for America's inaugural identity theft resolution provider.

Having a knack for collective trends, she added a thorough Human Design certification training to her eclectic tool belt to assist her clients in ascending into 5D and navigating it. If she's not traveling the world or hosting international retreats, Sabine lives blissfully in Phoenix, Arizona, with her Soulmate husband in their mid-century ranch home turned urban sanctuary.

Connect with Sabine at SoulPurposeWealth.com

CHAPTER 23

WORK WOUNDS

ALIGNING YOUR WORK SELF WITH YOUR TRUE SELF

Nancy OKeefe, MBA, MS

MY STORY

What am I going to do? In an instant, I was a widow with two children to raise. I sat in the hospital waiting room, shocked, numb, like I was living in a nightmare, a million panicky thoughts coursing through the confusion in my head. *How could this happen? He's only forty-seven. How am I going to tell the kids? How am I going to pay the mortgage?* I couldn't make my mind slow down. *What about mowing the lawn? What if something breaks? No! Stop! Any minute now, they're going to come out and tell me it has all been a terrible mistake.* But no one came. I was there alone in the hospital, and the person I always turned to for help was gone.

I told the kids, handled the funeral and all the relatives. I wiped tears, comforted, and explained. I kept a brave face while I tried to keep everything normal. *Normal. What is that? Nothing was normal, not one thing, not one plan*, but I assured everyone we would be alright. I didn't believe it. I was exhausted, and I was scared to death.

I did a great job convincing everyone we would be fine. Even the kids believed me. They missed their dad terribly, but they were able to move forward. Little by little, I watched the miracle of their adaptation amid their grief. I felt so proud of them, proud and envious at the same time. I had no life to go back to. I sat alone with my thoughts day after day, going through the motions, partially present. I had a full-time job, but it didn't pay anywhere near enough. I had a high school education and a few college courses but no career prospects. As the mailman delivered the bills, I knew I needed to make more money. I needed a career.

There were not many women with careers to model myself after, so I started to pay attention to the men who worked in my office. I learned the unspoken rules of business. Unfortunately, I wasn't accepted, so I was forced to remain a quiet observer soaking everything up like a sponge.

My company had tuition reimbursement, so I signed up for a class at the university. "Thank God," I told myself, "A way to get ahead." I worked during the day, went to class in the evening, helped with homework, and did homework between loads of laundry at night. Most evenings, I went to bed after the *Late Show* and rose with the sun to do it all over again. I learned what to wear, what to say, how to act, how to look, how to think, and gradually was recognized and promoted.

Most of the women in the office didn't know what to make of me. Many stopped the friendly exchanges, and I knew I was *the* topic of conversation at lunch. Most of the men felt the same, but I was lucky to find a few who respected me for supporting my family. "That's okay if the girls don't ask me to lunch on Fridays anymore," I told my mother. I had no time for a social life, even if I had money to go.

I felt so totally alone everywhere in my life. Our couple friends stopped calling. "I'm still here!" my heart screamed. But the only thing I felt coming from the people we spent every Saturday night with was pity. I was struggling to fit in somewhere, anywhere. I turned to earning a living. "I had no choice," I told myself, "I have to do whatever it takes. My family depends on me." That helped me explain away everything else that I lost.

I completed my degree. I was promoted, putting my family on solid financial footing. With success in my sights, I became the cold corporate woman, dressing, talking, and acting the part every step of the way. My male co-workers started accepting me, not as one of the boys but occasionally invited me into the club. I conformed and learned how to succeed. I did the long commute into Boston in one and a half hours of bumper-to-bumper traffic each way. I worked the ten hours a day that was expected. I expected my now older children to pick up the slack at home. I brought work home on the weekends to get ahead in between cooking for the week, cleaning the house, and helping the kids with what they needed. I changed jobs a few times and rose to the level of Vice President. I was officially on the treadmill now, voraciously going after more success.

I applied to graduate school. My kids were in college now too. I earned my MBA at a school renowned for its entrepreneurship program and started my own multi-seven figure business. My kids started lives of their own too. Always pushing myself was a habit now, easier in some ways because it became a way of life. I landed one big client after another until 2008 when the housing market crashed, the stock market crashed, and I crashed into the realization that I had spent two decades running away from the life and the dreams I lost in the hospital that day. Suddenly, I didn't want the life I pushed so hard to build anymore. I gave it all up. I was done.

I spent the next few years experimenting to find something I was passionate about, but I was burnt out from decades of pushing to accomplish and prove myself. Tired and perhaps even a little depressed, I wanted to do something fun and creative. I learned home staging and decorating and did color consultations. I explored painting, even had a few of my watercolors accepted in a local gallery. I played golf and tennis, made new friends, had a social life, and spent lost time with my children and their children a few times each week. I did everything I could find that was opposite from the business life I lived, trying desperately to find myself. For the first time in a long time, I felt happy and relaxed, enjoying my life again. But no matter what I pursued, I felt a nagging feeling that I was repeating a pattern just in a different direction. *I'm still missing something, I thought, and I need to find it.*

In my quest to find myself, I stumbled upon Human Design. The first time it showed up on my radar, I dismissed it as something akin to astrology and of no real interest. It seemed too complicated, and I had enough of complicated. But it kept showing up in my life, and finally, I took the hint and began to explore it. I attended an online class that went right over my head. I looked at the Human Design bodygraph that was supposed to represent me and couldn't make any sense of it. The instructor was an expert, but she was so far advanced she couldn't dumb it down enough for a novice like me. Finally, desperate to understand myself, I had a Human Design Reading. It changed my life.

Suddenly, everything in my life made sense. Every experience, every struggle, every success had meaning. I felt so validated. For the first time in my life, I understood my purpose. I knew what it meant to be me, and I felt relieved and re-energized at the same time.

As I learned about the energies in my design and how I was living them, I realized the high cost of pushing the way I did. I realized how far I drifted from who I truly am and how many wounds I had from the work I thought it was so important to do. The conditioning, even brainwashing you experience as you work to be a good fit for your job and employer, is mind-blowing. All the wonderful training I received had trained me to do what I needed to do, but it also trained me to be someone I wasn't.

At first, my discoveries made my blood boil. *Had I wasted the bulk of my life? Sacrificed time with my kids and my friends for nothing?* Human Design helped me see that I was meant to have a life filled with experiences. I am an experimenter. "Well, I certainly got that part right," I mused. My energy type is a Generator. Generators are workers. Generators are like the Energizer Bunny, and work is a Generator's world. "So that's how I managed to keep up with everything on four hours of sleep a night!" I exclaimed. I could see in my chart how I fell into the over-achiever trap, desperate to prove myself. I could see how much of who I am I hid in the name of earning a living. The awareness was eye-opening. So many times, I felt at odds with what I was doing but pushed my feelings down deep, ignored my gut, and did it anyway.

We live out the energies in our Human Design. We can't help it. These are the personal characteristics, skills, and talents we come into the world with. How we live them, express them, use them is the key. Energies have what I'll call a light and a shadow side, and I was in living out the shadow side of many of my energies each time I made choices that weren't aligned with who I truly am. The revelation was startling. And yet, I knew it wasn't about shedding my work self. There are lots of things about that me that I like. It's about aligning your work self with your true self. It's about shifting how you use your energies and your gifts, not hiding them to fit in. It's about allowing yourself to honor what makes you different and unique. It takes a lot of energy to be something you aren't. Over time, it drains the life right out of you, and we don't have to live that way to be accepted and fit in.

"Okay, I get it; this is huge!" I said out loud, knowing that this explained how I felt, "But how do I change? How do I start living the light side of my energies? How do I get comfortable making different choices? How do I express who I really am?"

We are taught how to think. We are taught to think things through, weigh the pros and cons, and use logic to make decisions. We are taught this in school, and it is reinforced everywhere in life. Here is a news flash! We are not meant to make decisions with our heads! Our thinking is designed for curiosity and questioning, for examining possibilities, not for making decisions. Each of the five energy types in Human Design has a unique decision-making center. Making aligned choices, choices that keep you on your true life path, choices that help you express the light side of your energy must be made using your energy type's decision-making center. And no type has a decision-making center in the head! *Wow*, I thought. *Everything I thought I knew about making decisions is wrong.*

I began to question my every thought and peel back the layers of who I had been taught to be to get at who I truly was. Have you seen the movie *Runaway Bride* starring Julia Roberts and Richard Gere? In this movie, Julia's character claims to like whatever type of eggs her current fiancé likes. Richard Gere's character challenges her, saying she doesn't know what type of eggs she likes but is conditioned to fit in by giving up her true choice and settling for each fiancés choice. We all do this every day in the name of being accepted and loved. When she realized Richard Gere was right, she sampled every way to cook eggs until she remembered what she truly liked best.

Where did I settle for something less than what I really wanted in my life? That is the first question I needed to answer to peel back those layers and find the real me. *Where am I still settling?*

I started by making a list. At first, it was difficult to separate the "had to" things from the "want to" things. The list was short, and I was frustrated by my lack of progress. Societal and work conditioning go deep, and I knew I had to keep at it if I was going to stop repeating the patterns that didn't feel good to me. Then one night, I was lying in bed reliving the day's events and thinking about what I had to do tomorrow when it came to me. *I don't have to do anything tomorrow but breathe!* I pulled out the paper and pen from my nightstand, and in the darkness of my bedroom, I wrote three words: *freedom, heart, and inspire.* I felt peace wash over me. I closed my eyes and fell soundly asleep, pen and paper still in my hand.

I knew those three words had been given to me to help me find myself. Freedom is my core value, and after continuing my journey into my Human Design, my purpose has everything to do with being true to my heart and inspiring others. I am a 6/2 Profile in Human Design, Role Model/ Hermit. My purpose is to be myself, have experiences, and share what I have learned to inspire others to see the possibilities in their own lives. I'm here to question what is possible and to help others think differently. Force fitting into a box, like a box work creates with its rules, norms, and expectations, can dampen your spirit and put artificial boundaries around what is possible for you, but it can't extinguish your spirit. The truth of you is always inside, and it is never too late to open the box and bring your spirit into the light. I spent most of my career cultivating talent and helping people see new possibilities and new ways of doing things. Unconsciously and unaware that this is my purpose, I still managed to flirt with my true life path.

I continue to explore my Human Design and work with its energies to master living in the expression of the light side of those energies. My work wounds are a part of me. I am not throwing away the woman I have become through all my experiences, good or bad, but rather, I continue to question how I feel about each experience, incorporating what feels right and letting go of what doesn't. I am surrendering to my true self. I am confidently following my path in the direction it feels right to go. I am no longer hiding my differences but proudly display them as part of aligning and living my truth. It is a gift to be on this journey. I love the woman I have become. It feels good to be who I am.

THE TOOL

WORK WOUNDS JOURNAL PROMPTS

How well do you know yourself?

Where are you hiding or settling?

Where have you sacrificed yourself in the name of fitting in?

Use these journal prompts to help you begin to peel back the layers of who you have been taught to be and align your work self with your true self.

MANAGE YOUR ENERGY

We only have so much energy, and it varies by our Human Design Type. We need to manage our energy to do all the things in life that we want to do and be fully expressed as the individuals we are.

Do you know when enough is enough?

How Do You Tell?

TRUST YOURSELF

Only you know what is right for you. You are hard-wired to know. It is your inner wisdom.

How does your inner wisdom speak to you?

STRENGTHEN YOUR COURAGE

We all have fears. You can't stop your fears, but you can learn to walk through them and live courageously.

What have you been stopped from doing because of your fear?

CHOOSE WISELY

Learn to make decisions that are aligned with who you are. Aligned decisions are about whether it feels right.

Where have you made a decision you regretted?

STAND IN YOUR SELF WORTH

You are unique. You have a unique role to live out in this world. You are a valuable piece of the puzzle we call the Human Story.

Where do you judge your self-worth by the standards set by others?

RECEIVE AND GIVE LOVE

We all need love and support from others. Allow yourself to give and receive the gift of love.

What situations in your life lack love or are toxic and prevent you from giving or receiving love?

MANAGE YOUR EMOTIONS

Practice Emotional Intelligence by learning to control your own emotions and be empathetic and compassionate with others.

What triggers your emotions (frustration, anger, upset)?

BE EMPOWERED

You came into this world with a purpose and a set of gifts, skills, and talents to support you in fulfilling your purpose. You are divinely designed to be unique, and you are powerful.

What keeps you from feeling empowered to go after your dreams?

BE AUTHENTIC

Be Yourself. That is the best version of you, the version the world needs.

Where are you living inauthentically in your life?

For more insight and additional journal prompts, download the complimentary, full version Work Wounds Journal Tool here: Work Wounds Full Journal Prompt Tool (Bit.ly/workwoundsjournaltool).

Nancy OKeefe is a consultant, intuitive coach, and compassionate transformer who helps people peel back the layers of who they have been taught to be to reveal who they truly are so they can live their inner truth, go after their deepest desires, and create a life filled with success, satisfaction, and joy.

Nancy has been developing and coaching people for over 25 years, helping them bring out their best qualities, build confidence, and feel empowered to go after what they want in life. She helps CEOs create cultures where people can share their unique gifts and workplaces where the best talent wants to work.

Nancy is a Certified Executive Coach from the College of Executive Coaching, holds an MBA from Babson College in Entrepreneurship, and an MS in Process Improvement from Anna Maria College. She is a Certified Quantum Human Design Specialist, Certified Career Transition Coach, Fascination Advantage® Adviser, and Certified in Conversational Intelligence®

Nancy can be found at NancyOKeefeCoaching.com where you can download her free gift, 3 Sacred Gifts You Can Learn from Your Human Design Chart, so you can learn more about your Human Design.

CHAPTER 24

CREATING A WORLD-CLASS CAREER

FROM EXHAUSTED AND UNFULFILLED TO THE CAREER OF YOUR DREAMS

Jacqueline Martinez

MY STORY

Up until a certain point, I was focused on doing everything "right," until I wasn't anymore.

As a little girl, I believed that the American dream should be my life goal.

"You'll never make any money as a teacher," I heard from naysayers. "Why don't you think about becoming a doctor or lawyer?" was the advice I received.

So I set my sights on having a large family, a successful career, and anything else society deemed suitable for my life to have meant something.

So I grew up checking the boxes, making the grades, getting the promotions, and perfecting my role as daughter, wife, mother, and successful employee.

I took on several personas focused on helping others and doing my best to be "the best." Many people recognized and rewarded this throughout my early life and college in the form of accolades, scholarships, job opportunities, and fast-track mentor programs, where I received personalized development and advice to get where I wanted to go, faster. I remember giving myself one rule early on: to do what I enjoy rather than climb a corporate ladder.

As a genuine and ambitious young woman, I stepped into each opportunity with a heart full of optimism, a sparkle in my eyes, and a determined focus on helping others while being successful.

Sounds perfect, right?

From the outside looking in, it certainly was cookie-cutter. But by the ripe old age of 23, I found myself in the rat race, working long hours and going against my personal rule about the corporate ladder. I was dazzled by the paycheck, which seemed significantly higher than my other entry-level peers' offers.

What's the worst that could happen? I thought.

I remember stepping into my first role as a human resources leader for a large retail organization, and the district leader pulled me aside. He said, "Jacqueline, it will be a tough challenge to turn this place around, but I believe that you can do it."

I felt my face turn red, and my heart start to race. *What did he mean by that? What did I get myself into?* I nodded in agreement, not knowing what to say. *Well, of course I can do it—challenge accepted.*

It didn't take long for me to realize 1. people and culture transformation was the challenge ahead of me and, 2. I had a lot to learn.

This isn't impossible, I told myself. *I can figure anything out. Let's do this.* And that was the moment I initiated myself into 60-hour workweeks.

I poured my blood, sweat, and tears into the team there, and I'm so thankful I did because my passion for people at work and understanding how to create better work environments grew tremendously in that role. On top of that, my metrics reflected all of the late nights, early mornings, and skipped meals from putting so much into creating results and supporting this team for two years, which I was thrilled about! But I clearly lost myself in the chaos, and my new marriage wasn't benefitting from this lifestyle. So I took the opportunity to find another company that would allow me to build a supportive environment for its people and hopefully find time for "me" again.

And so, I made the leap to support another growing organization that needed transformational leadership and long hours, this time in manufacturing. And then another. And while I was making these exciting and next-level career moves, my motivation was to help build a solid culture where people loved coming to work and regularly empathized with one another. But the longer I worked in HR and saw how people and companies related to each other, the more friction and hopelessness I witnessed. So for years, I worked to build people processes, suggest more empathetic ways to lead, and help people see their part in the culture we were building.

"Your ideas will never work at this company," I remember a mid-level manager saying to me. "All that happy talk and people acting with integrity - yeah, you can forget it. Good luck, though."

Seriously?! My blood boiled. I could feel my face getting hot. *How do you know if you don't try? Things could be different if we all worked together on it—even just a little.*

"Thank you - appreciate it," I muttered, unenthused. And I walked on.

I remained hopeful and optimistic, but it started to wear on me. My big efforts showed little return, and the autonomy I thought I had to build the company I dreamed of was leaving my line of sight.

Physically, emotionally, relationally—I was drained. My personal relationships suffered, and I found myself no longer seeing a vision for myself in the town I lived in, the few friends I had, and even the marriage I was in. As a person who loves people, my loss of joy was a red flag for me.

I kept pressing forward, looking for the thing that would bring me joy again. I took on new projects at work, started running again, and even started the adventure of becoming a mother to my beautifully perfect daughter.

Still, *I* remember sitting in my cubicle at work, looking out the window beyond the cube farm in front of me, thinking, *how did I get here? Is this all there is? I know I'm meant for something else. There has to be more for me.*

"Hey, you okay?"

"Yeah, I'm okay. Why what happened?"

"You were staring out the window again. Just wanted to make sure."

"Oh yeah," I laughed so I didn't cry. "Thank you. I'll be right back," I said as I stood up from my cube and power walked to the bathroom, fake smiling at everyone I passed so they wouldn't notice the tears that were welled up in my throat, bound to burst through my eyes at any minute. After what seemed like the longest walk of my life, I busted through the door to the women's restroom, ran to the stall, and started sobbing. *I can't do this anymore. Nobody gets it. Nobody gets me.*

"Oh no, are you okay?" I heard another familiar voice from the next stall over. *Oh my gosh. Can this get any worse?!*

At the time, I didn't have a clue how to get back on track, back to joy, or back to me.

I didn't want to make any wrong moves or choices at first. But then, I realized this rule I had for myself, the rule that I needed to do things perfectly, was the very thing throwing me off.

So I threw it out the window.

And I made changes. I tried to pay attention to what I wanted in everything I did and to choose that instead of what others dictated.

I found ways to get in touch with what lit me up. Then, I started moving away from the things that didn't.

I did hard things, made big moves, and after a divorce, split custody, a year, a new city, and a new relationship later, I had tons of practice in being imperfect and unbecoming everything that wasn't me.

I know it's easy for me to glaze over the hard parts, so I won't. Starting a rebellion in my life wasn't a clean process. It was messy, uncomfortable, and it hurt like hell. I lost people and experienced the tremendous emotional pain of release while knowing in my gut it's what I needed to create space for the people and things that supported my lit-up, multi-passionate self.

Actually, at the time, I didn't know that good things were coming. I felt as if I was walking through the jungle with a machete, paving my own path. Only it was dark, and I didn't have a light.

I did know that if I kept showing up every day as the best mother, leader, and figure-outer I could with the energy I had, then I trusted that what was for me would show up, and as it did, my confidence increased. Every day I felt a bit freer—a bit more like myself.

As I grew and continued to take imperfect action, I continued to focus on building transformational leadership cultures in organizations. As I experimented with different techniques and methodologies, I noticed everyone around me reaping the benefits. A few key themes in my work in HR and leadership arose after hundreds of hours in conversation coaching employees and management, alone and together.

I learned the most transformational leaders were 1. Self-aware, and 2. Willing to practice empathy consistently. Everything else, I noticed, was personal style, and all people, whether they had a team or not, were leaders as long as they chose to lead themselves first.

Without self-leadership, managers could not be transformational leaders. My passion for supporting transformational leadership grew.

The same month I had this personal ah-ha, I was introduced to Human Design, which I instantly resonated with. With a background in psychology, personality assessments and conversations were my guilty pleasure. But, for me, Human Design superseded every framework I had ever learned due to its ability to support each individual person specifically.

All of the other personality and team assessments grouped people into a type, so one group description may or may not accurately describe each member inside it. I found it refreshing that Human Design is all about sharing the specific individual's patterns, personality, talents, and authority. Naturally, I dove in to learn anything I could about something so powerful.

When I decided to go down the HD rabbit hole, I tried piecing together the information I grabbed from various websites to learn enough to make a difference. I stumbled upon a strategist who made it her job to interpret charts for people, and I raced to book a time on her calendar, seven days out. I was practically counting down the hours until our session, anxiously awaiting the magic she would find in my chart.

When our time to meet over Zoom finally came, I sat perfectly still, hanging on to every word she said. After our session ended, I stared at her on the screen, not knowing what to say. I said something to the effect of, "Wow, I love your job." She laughed at me.

I turned off my camera and just sat there with tears. At the time, I remember feeling two distinct feelings. The first one was exposed: *How in the world did she know these deeply personal things about me? We've never met!*

Secondly, I felt understood. *Finally,* I thought, *someone sees my inner world. I feel seen. Someone gets me.* It was a feeling I'd been seeking for far too long.

Whether or not she actually got me wasn't the point. For me, I finally saw myself. I was absolutely blown away by the specificity and accuracy of a logical system and enrolled in a course suggested by a new friend to learn everything I could. Class after class, I was lit up and amazed by the blueprint being laid out in front of me.

This is the prescription for people looking to live authentically, like me, I thought. I knew this information, if lived out, would give people the framework to become their best selves and, in turn, transformational leaders. It was all right here!

As much as I desired to help everyone else, I knew the key to real growth for those around me was to focus on my own. A common statement by my favorite author and speaker, Brendon Burchard, rang in my ears. "Common sense doesn't always mean common practice," he'd mention regularly.

With joy and curiosity, it was fun for me to learn and experiment in iterations with the patterns I was learning about myself and others. I still remember the moment my confidence shot through the roof. I was learning and practicing what Human Design calls my decision-making strategy: wait until I'm emotionally clear before making decisions.

Seriously?! I thought. *My whole life, society has suggested emotions don't belong at work. But you're saying I'm here to use them to make decisions?!*

I laugh now at that moment, but it was deeply affirming for me to be correct, just as I am, as my authentic self.

Up until that point, being authentic was foreign to me. Even when I thought I was my real self, I was always stuffing little parts of myself away because it "didn't belong" or was different from others. Honestly, I had to practice being authentic. I didn't learn or start to use this information about myself 100% every day with world-changing results. Moment-by-moment, I noticed how I was responding to life, my desires, and my emotions. Over time, it became the default and very clear to me what the term alignment meant because I was living it!

A few examples:

I was asked to do a project that didn't light me up. After waiting it out, did I say yes? No. But my former self would have.

Even in response to writing this chapter, I was completely afraid and worried that I didn't have the time. Yet, I was lit up and excited even as time passed, so I took the leap and said yes! (I'm glad I did because here you are reading, and I hope parts of this resonated with you).

Alignment didn't mean perfect. And I'm so glad for that because there is so much pressure that comes with perfection as the standard. Alignment, for me, is knowing what my fundamentals are and intentionally coming back to them every moment that I remember to.

There's no pressure. There's no performance. There are a lot of amazing opportunities, though.

After passing on my Human Design knowledge to dozens of friends and clients looking to align themselves in their careers and organizations, I've seen some wonderful opportunities come my way. I've now stepped into a leadership role with a company that surpasses my expectations of people treatment, autonomy, and collaboration. Friends and mentors with similar values have come into my circle. This extends well beyond work. My family and my marriage are better off due to the personal alignment we've found for ourselves. I could go on and on here, so I'll proceed by showing you what I mean.

And it all started with getting clear on where I was and was not headed. You heard from my story how easy it was to stray from my desires. Without a clear direction, I was headed everywhere, and it left me exhausted and unfulfilled. There's no reason to beat yourself up if you have ended up there now or in the past. What's important now is taking the brave and bold move to envision the direction you want to go instead and pivot in that direction.

THE TOOL

If there is one simple foundational tool that I could suggest to someone in a place where they feel unfulfilled and potentially burned out, it's the Ideal Day Exercise.

The intention of the Ideal Day Exercise is to help you determine what you want to keep in your life and what you would like to do without.

The outcome: you will have a list of things you want to add or reinforce in your life and a list of things you're going to get rid of eventually, even if not right away. This allows you to freely dream while also creating a filter for yourself. As you start to make changes, you can evaluate your decisions by using your decision-making strategy in Human Design while also double-checking against the list of things you've determined you don't want more of in your life. (Don't say yes if it's not a heck yes!)

THE IDEAL DAY EXERCISE

Take a moment to relax. Take a deep breath in and hold it. Now slowly let it out. Are you ready? Here we go. You're going to brainstorm what you want your ideal day to look like.

1. On a separate sheet of paper, draw a large "T" with the intention to draw a line vertically down the paper.
2. On the left side of the paper at the top, write "My ideal day:"
3. On the right side of the paper at the top, write "I no longer want:"
4. Get ready to dream. You'll be brainstorming, without pressure, the first things that come to mind for each column. On the left side, answer the question, "What do you want your ideal day to look like?" Feel free to write down everything, big and small, from what you're wearing to who you're talking to and what kind of work you're doing. What is your commute like? What are you eating? What activities do you engage in? Add in a focus on career if that's you. This is your life—create it.
5. On the right side of the page, make notes of everything you currently experience in your day that you would like to release. Do you desire

a more supportive environment? Is your commute longer than you'd like? Nothing is too small or too big.

6. Now, look at each item you wrote on the left side of the page. For everything you desire, start to visualize what that will look like for you.
7. On the right side, feel free to file it away and use it as awareness as you are making decisions for yourself to create an ideal version of yourself and your life/career.

This is just the beginning. The first step to becoming more you is a big one. I would absolutely love to support you or recommend someone in your journey! Feel free to visit www.offtherecordhr.com for tools and resources on creating your own world-class career. I'm rooting for you.

Jacqueline Martinez is a Human Resources and Talent leader by day and Career Coach by night who is passionate about helping people discover their personal leadership capability and potential. In her free time, she hosts audio and video podcasts about growth and leadership. Jacqueline is a life-long student; after graduating from Purdue University with a BS in Psychology + Communication, she earned two HR Certifications and continues her studies in Human Design for Business through the BG5 Institute alongside other self-awareness and healing methodologies. Jacqueline is a 6/3 emotional Manifesting Generator in Human Design.

When she's not actively empowering people to become the best versions of themselves or adding books to her wishlist, Jacqueline spends time cooking whole-food dishes, hiking through the woods, and playing outside with her family. Jacqueline lives an active life in Indianapolis, IN, with her husband, Rudy, and three kids, Draven-14, Mira-10, and Aubrey-6.

Connect with Jacqueline at Jacqueline@offtherecordhr.com and on social media:

LinkedIn: Jacqueline Martinez

Instagram: @Jacqueline.Hepburn

Youtube: The Modern Woman Show

Spotify or Apple Podcast: From Coffee to Wine

CHAPTER 25

WEALTH MINDSET

THE ALIGNMENT YOU NEED FOR THE LIFE YOU WANT

Julianne Joy

Are you ready to enjoy your journey and the process of unfolding who you came here to be? You cannot create new experiences by doing the same things you've always done. Different results require different actions. Change requires alignment with who you want to become, even before you ever get there. Imagine stepping into who you want to be or what you want to have *now*, even though you're not there yet. Act as if you already have the abundance you are seeking or the experience you are desiring. Think about what the new you would do and move in that direction. Dress up and play the part. Start taking some action to get you closer to the life you want. It takes time to change the way you behave. It takes commitment to reprogram a lifetime of outdated patterns, but small changes can lead to big shifts. When you make these small changes, it's like you're telling the Universe who you want to be. It requires grit and resilience to move in a direction that may be uncomfortable for you. But it can be much easier when you have a roadmap. *Cha-Ching!*

MY STORY

What if a blueprint or an energetic roadmap could show you how to live in alignment and enjoy your best life? Along my journey, I had a longing to know my life purpose. Have you ever felt like you just needed to understand what it is you're here to do?

As I'm searching for my purpose like a penetrating investigator, I'm looking into every possible resource and digging into the depths of information and even my psyche to uncover my hidden truth. Enter Human Design: soul shifting system to understand myself!

I ask for guidance in my morning meditation. As I'm driving to work, I see a word on a license plate; I notice the red-bellied bird playing just outside my window, and I keep seeing the same numbers everywhere I look. I am receiving signs and symbols from the Universe and begin writing them down, researching, and interpreting the hidden meanings. Now I know that this is guidance for me. And the more I notice and write them down, the more I receive these synchronicities. Everything is a code that is guiding me along my journey! As an alchemist, I have a magnetic aura that attracts opportunities to me. To follow my strategy and authority, I need to wait to respond to the right opportunities. I need to use my body's inner GPS to make decisions and not my mind.

Now I get it! I am not meant to initiate; instead, wait to respond. And I only need to say yes to opportunities that are in alignment. In between the opportunities, I can practice self-care and do activities that I enjoy to stay in alignment. All my life, I was conditioned to take action and initiate, to push through with force to get things done. That is not my way of being, and it leads to burnout when I serve from an empty cup.

It's tax season, again. As I continue to work long, late hours and feel the pressure and overwhelm of deadlines, my body is screaming at me. *How can you do this to me again? When are you going to listen to me and stop this incessant behavior? Take a break and go for a walk already! Be nice to me or else!* As my body is yelling at me, I'm feeling the stabbing pain in my side. I can't stop because I need to meet my deadlines. My brain is telling me *just a few more tax returns, just a few more days*. Everyone is on edge around me about their deadlines too. I try to remain cool and calm, but inside I'm screaming and ready to cry at the drop of a hat like a two-year-old child.

As I step away from my desk and head out into nature for a walk, I can immediately feel my chest lifting and begin to breathe again! My body knows when I'm taking *her* for a walk. She is completely content now as I recharge. Until I began practicing self-care, I kept repeating this scenario over and over. I'm designed to find balance with work and rest and never serve from an empty cup. Since I pick up and amplify the pressure from everyone around me (based on my undefined root center), I learned I need to be vigilant with my self-care practices. This allows me to stop overworking and start overflowing. And this not only benefits me but ultimately everyone around me!

Human Design taught me how to be in alignment by following my strategy and authority to make decisions. My emotions are my inner compass to guide me along my path (my GPS). Now I know when to say yes and, more importantly, when to say no, which makes it easier for me to choose the life I want to live. When I say yes to things that don't bring me joy, it drains my energy. Recently I was invited to an event. They said, "You should attend this networking event." *I feel the pressure to say yes like I have before, but then I remember how I felt the last time I went. My energy is draining just thinking about it!* I check my calendar, hoping I have a conflict, but I'm available and feel compelled to say yes. I respond, "Sure, I can attend."

As I arrive at the event, I make my way to the venue. Once again, I don't see any familiar faces, and I can feel the energy of competition in the room. I muddle through the uncomfortable networking session, and we're finally seated. The speaker begins his presentation, and it's all I can do to pay attention and pretend I'm engaged. My boredom is a sign that I'm not fulfilled or in alignment. Instead, I need to follow my inner compass to find joy. I now realize I don't need to go to every event I'm invited to if it doesn't activate my joy. Since we attract opportunities when we are in a state of joy, there is no point in attending when we are out of alignment. I made a commitment to myself that I would say no to those meetings in the future. And now, I also know that I need to ride my emotional wave before committing to a decision. So I say, "I will check my calendar and get back to you within a few days." By following my strategy and authority, I can move into being the person I came here to be that is aligned with my values. Alignment unlocks the key to prosperity and wealth. And part of the new wealth consciousness is health and internal wealth (mindset).

RELEASING OLD PATTERNS TO UNLOCK YOUR BLOCKS

My undefined root center is a pressure center where I get all the pressure from the people around me and amplify it. I end up working really fast to relieve that pressure, only to realize that it is still there, even when I am done! I'm in my office, and the telephone rings. "What time are you coming home tonight?" I respond, "I will be on time tonight." He asks, "What would you like for dinner?" You could have heard a pin drop in the complete silence. I couldn't think of anything I wanted. There were too many ideas running through my head!

Once again, I was drawing a complete blank. Then I remember why I can't decide; I need a few options to respond to. So I ask him, "Do you have any ideas about what you might want?" We agree on something through the process of elimination with yes/no questions (we both share this strategy to respond). Then I proceed to finish up my work. As I look up at the clock, my heart begins to race, and I panic. *Holy crap! How can it possibly be 6 pm already! I am late, again! You just said you would be home on time, and once again, you broke your word and will be late! How can this be happening to me? Sabotaged yet again by the open root center!* It is so important to set boundaries. *Like, how about setting the alarm on my phone?!* Releasing these old patterns and saying no made space for more goodness to come into my life.

STRENGTHEN YOUR BELIEF SYSTEMS

Have you ever wondered why certain patterns keep playing out in your life? The endless chatter of your mind telling you that you can't do something, that you're not good enough, and stirring up extravagant fear stories stored in your DNA, which are probably coming from lifetimes ago! I was doing the work to release shame, guilt, fear, and not being enough, but for some reason, the patterns wouldn't stop. I experienced triggers that came up, and these patterns would just start running again on autopilot in the background of my mind. And no matter how aware I was of the pattern from my mind's eye, I was unable to stop them.

It's time for bed, and I start thinking about all the work I need to get done tomorrow. My heart begins to race, and I can feel the pressure mounting in my chest from overwhelming deadlines and struggling to find the answers to issues I am currently having. Here comes the fear again. My mind says I need to do more, I need to figure it out, or I won't be good enough, and then what will happen to me next, and on and on with endless negative self-talk. And now I can't sleep. It felt like I was in the movie, *Groundhog Day*, reliving those patterns over and over like a negative feedback loop. And I don't know about you, but I was always waiting for the other shoe to drop. Do you have this happening in your life? If you do, keep on reading because I have answers that lit me up with excitement once I discovered them. They provided me with the realization and awareness that these patterns can be changed! *Hallelujah!*

There are three levels to these patterns. They are made up of the conscious mind (which is your mental awareness), the subconscious (where you store suppressed feelings like past trauma and fear in some part of your body), and the unconscious (the deepest area which is based on an energetic or soul level.) And each level requires different tools to release those patterns. So, for example, even though you may do therapy sessions that uproot the patterns and bring them into your mental awareness for your mind to see, there are still two deeper levels to clear. The subconscious and the unconscious are still running those patterns in the background of your life. *No wonder! I had self-sabotage patterns of self-worth that were running my life and creating my reality.*

Every time you feel a negative emotion from an experience, you can observe the emotion without judgment. Your mind can replay emotions over and over, which causes suffering. *Bingo! This is exactly what was happening to me.* And all the fear and anger in society can manipulate your emotions, but when you stay in a state of compassion, you do not invest your energy and therefore cannot be manipulated. However, until you do the deep inner work required to feel and release these emotions, they will continue to run your life! *OMG, light bulb moment!*

You have the capacity to choose to release the beliefs that make you feel like a victim of life. You can step out of victimhood once you realize that everything is happening for you and not to you. This was such a pivotal point for me and allowed me to take back my power simply by changing my perspective! You have the power to create your own reality and rewrite your story.

BRINGING IN THE NEW LIFE YOU WANT

So how do you release these patterns? Although there are several tools you can use, I recommend you start with a simple meditation to get grounded into the present moment. You can gently train your brain to quiet down and be still. Over a period of time, you have the capacity to grow new neural pathways. You can use any meditation you like, or you can listen to my free meditation at www.juliannejoy.me/wealthflowcodegifts.

You can use the manifesting tool below to focus on what you want to bring into your life by having clear visions and goals. It will help you be intentional with what you want to create in your life. Remember to surrender to the "how." The Universe knows the best way, and you may limit yourself if you are attempting to figure out the "how." You can also track what you want to grow (like your money by using a budget or your health by using a self-care journal) because whatever you focus on grows. Think of this tool as your mental magic wand; it's that simple!

ALIGN WITH YOUR DESIRES TOOL

This is a seven-step process to align with your desires. The first step is below. If you would like the next six steps, you can access the free download at www.juliannejoy.me/sosogifts.

Before you get started, do a meditation practice to ground your energy and get into the present moment using your breath. Go into nature whenever possible.

With your feet flat on the ground and sitting up with your back straight, breathe in through your nose and expand your belly out, hold your breath at the top for a few seconds and then breathe out through your mouth and push all of the air out of your body and bring your belly button flat to your spine. Do this two more times. Now connect to the earth, envisioning roots growing out from your feet down into the earth and wrapping around the planet. Then visualize golden white light coming down from the sky and into the top of your head. See the golden white light flowing down through your crown to your third eye, past your throat, your heart, and down into your solar plexus until it reaches your sacral chakra and finally your root chakra. Imagine that the roots coming up from your feet are connecting with the golden white light coming down through your head at your heart space. Feel the love and compassion and oneness of everything in the Universe. You are connected above and below like a bridge.

I call this heaven on earth. This is how you can get out of your head and drop into your heart. As above, so below.

You can listen to a free meditation at
www.juliannejoy.me/wealthflowcodegifts.

Then set an intention by making a decision or commitment that you are passionate about (and do not worry about the *how*). Then just be curious and wonder how it will show up for you. Be playful with it so you can activate the creative side of your brain during your intention-setting process.

You can use this ritual with an Epsom salt bath adding essential oils, candles, music, and add crystals around the bathtub to hold and magnify your intention. Music will inspire you as you focus on your new thoughts and trigger new ways to think, feel and dream. Writing helps you manifest because when you write what you want to experience, you are focusing your energy and attention. Then you can put your written intention under your crystal to amplify its power or even create a crystal grid bringing in the shapes of sacred geometry. Crystals are also a great visual reminder of your intention. Each crystal stone holds its own energy, so use your intuition when choosing your crystals, and don't overthink it. If you choose a crystal necklace or bracelet, you can wear it as a reminder of your intention. If you choose a crystal gem tree, you can even imagine the intention getting grounded through the tree's roots.

EXERCISE: Now, draw a picture of your intention. You can even use this as a meditation practice as if you are praying for the intention to come to life and then write your intention out 11 times. In the process of doing this, you will activate your intention on an energetic level, and your unconscious mind will be at work behind the scenes helping you to co-create your desire. Have fun and play with it!

To learn the next steps of the Align with Your Desires tool, go here to download the free resource at www.juliannejoy.me/sosogifts.

ALIGNING TO YOUR NEW WEALTH MINDSET

It's time to unlock your blocks and rewrite your story! Stop waiting to be ready because you will never be ready. Be willing to do it now, even though you may be feeling shaky and afraid. Create a desire and embody your dream and your new routine *now*. Develop a new way of *being*. This is how the Universe will see you, and it will organize accordingly to your new normal. Let's get you set up for success by clearing the path and training your mind so you can release limiting beliefs and create a new identity that matches your desires. And when you are in alignment, prosperity flows more freely to you.

Julianne Joy is a best-selling published author and Certified Public Accountant (CPA). Throughout her 30+ year career, she has built her practice based on the foundation of relationships and serves her clients with the ultimate goal of seeking to do what is best for each client.

Julianne is the author of her best-selling book *The Wealthflow Code: Finding Focus, Freedom and Balance in a High-Stress Career*. She is also a contributing author to two books in the best-selling New Feminine Evolutionary Series, *Set Sail: Shine Your Radiance, Activate Your Ascension, Ignite Your Income, Live Your Legacy* - "10 Ways to Cultivate Resilience, So You Can Flow with Change" and *Practice: Wisdom from the Downward Dog* - "Yoga: A Pathway to Inner Peace."

Most of all, Julianne enjoys writing, nature, and spending time with her family and Chinese crested dog, Isadora.

For more information and resources, visit www.juliannejoy.me

CLOSING CHAPTER

ALIGNED BY DESIGN

SHIFTING FROM OVERWORKING TO OVERFLOWING

Kristi H. Sullivan

If working hard paid off for everyone the same, then wouldn't more of us be happy, healthy and wealthy?

Can you believe that to achieve success, you don't have to work as hard, or be as worn out, struggling or overwhelmed, as you might be now?

Can you consider the potential that working less for more success is possible, and that authentically living your best life could be a lot easier and feel effortless?

I hope you have discovered these possibilities after reading the transformational stories in this book.

It would be great if we could just easily read a book to achieve success and manifest abundance, but alas, it's now time to do the inner work to reach awareness, acceptance and alignment of our design, in order to live our best lives.

Let's look a little more into the rabbit hole.

All of us have received conscious and unconscious conditioning from numerous influencers, such as family, including parents and ancestors, along with teachers, authority figures, advertising spokespersons, and even celebrities. This 'brainwashing' often encourages a one-size-fits-all in areas like education, work, habits, attitudes, and life in general. However, the Human Design theory helps us understand our unique energetic blueprint, how we each were naturally encoded at birth, and how our energy operates, differently from others.

Another important concept from Human Design is that the mind is not the best place for solving problems or making decisions. In fact, thinking can often produce confusion, indecision and resistance. While the head invaluably takes in inspiration, visualizations and concepts for research and processing, it's our wisdom in the body (below the head) where our innate decision making resides in the form of intuition, gut feelings or emotions. This means that getting out of the head and into the body is critical for tapping into our deeper wisdom, beyond the intellect.

Human Design is a 'how to manual' for de-conditioning ourselves, and accessing the wisdom that exists outside of the mind and deep within oneself. To access this, daily self-care activity is essential for releasing beliefs or habits that don't serve us, and tapping into our wisdom centers in the body. Daily self-care is essential not only for well-being but to align your energy. The more we make self-care a priority, the more we align to our true selves, including our guidance and inner wisdom that leads to our success.

Our ability to manifest this success is a direct result of aligning our effort and energy with our true, natural design. By living in alignment with our unique Human Design, we create more opportunities and invitations for success and abundance.

In my Human Design experiment, it seems that the less hard I work, the more effortless things become - as long as I recognize my energetic design and make the effort to stay aligned. Self-care is a priority for me to help this happen. The work is on the inside, not the outside!

Self-care is personalized and looks different for every person/design. Inside this book, you hopefully found a few new tools that may be a beneficial addition to your self-care routine.

Unlearning our conditioning and living in an unconditioned way is a new formula, and to do so is a daily practice and takes consistent self-care. With this new formula, I transitioned from working hard, and stepped more fully into following my passion in wellness and self-care, along with teaching Human Design. And this new career feels effortless and in alignment with my true design - a life-changing transformation!

My mission is to help you Stop Overworking & Start Overflowing!

Please don't hesitate to reach out to me or other practitioners in this book to help guide you on this transformational journey!

GRATITUDE

This book was made possible thanks to many great minds and wise souls!

In 2020, I had opportunities to join three collaborative book projects with fellow coaches, healers and practitioners to inspire readers with our stories and tools for well-being. Those wonderful experiences planted the seeds and inspired me to create my own anthology.

I first and foremost give thanks to the amazing 25 authors who leaned into their Human Design authority and decided with their innate wisdom that this was the right opportunity for them. These amazing authors as well as a few other contributors who accepted the invitation to this collaborative book journey are "badass" (as our fearless publisher would say).

Speaking of our publisher, my immense gratitude goes to Laura Di Franco, who most definitely works tirelessly to create an incredible publishing empire and supports world-changing healers, coaches and practitioners to truly change the world with their written words and stories. My thanks also to the great team behind the scenes who helped produce and promote this book.

I send heart-felt appreciation to several like-minded, supportive communities that I've met this past year along my personal journey, including incredible entrepreneurs, inspiring mentors/teachers, and divine, wise souls. By the way, it's in my design to connect and collaborate, so networking is natural for me and has led me to so many great opportunities.

And special thanks to my family, especially my soul-mates Scott (my husband) and Cacy (my fur-baby/cat). They have been by my side all along usually as sounding boards to hear my unique ideas, provide space for my out-of-the-box thinking, and support my spiritual journey.

Last, but not least, I dedicate this book to my mother and to my father (in spirit) who both inspired the journey of my wellness and personal growth — and always cheered me on for my success and accomplishments in life.

To our readers, my departing wish for you:

> To be your unique self and always be aligned.
>
> To accept your design and the uniqueness of others.
>
> To embrace the limitless potential in each of our designs.
>
> To understand that while we are all unique, we are also deeply connected.

ABOUT THE AUTHOR

Kristi H. Sullivan, is a Human Design and self-care expert, author, and speaker on a mission to help busy women Stop Overworking and Start Overflowing. She hosts a virtual community for personal development junkies (like herself) to create better wellness, improve relationships, shift mindsets, and manifest more success, wealth, and freedom—to live their best lives.

Her journey and passion for mind, body, and spiritual development began nearly two decades ago as a yoga teacher (RYT200). During COVID, Kristi "retired" from a 25-year marketing communications career and became a full-time solopreneur, developing her business online where she connects her community to resources and support for transformation. She encourages her clients and students to be inspired and empowered—to authentically align with your true self to manifest abundance and live your best life.

Kristi is an international teacher, retreat leader, and influencer on the topics of Human Design and self-care. She has been featured on dozens of podcasts, workshops, and conferences, including the Women in Business Summit, Women Future Conference, Wealthy Healer Conference, Coping with Trauma Summit, Forgiveness Summit, and Awakening to a New World Summit. She also has hosted several retreats and webinars focusing on wellness, self-care and Human Design.

Stop Overworking and Start Overflowing is the first collaborative book project that she has led with 25 Human Design practitioners and launched with her publisher, Brave Healer Productions, in 2021. Kristi is also co-author of three best-selling books written and published on Amazon during the 2020 pandemic: *The Ultimate Guide to Self-Healing, Volume 2; The Great Pause: Blessings & Wisdom from COVID-19; and Transformation 2020.*

To connect with Kristi and her offerings to help you get aligned and authentically live your best life:

- VISIT www.KristiHSullivan.com
- FOLLOW @KristiHSullivan on Instagram
- JOIN her on Facebook at www.facebook.com/groups/kristihsullivan/
- INVITE Kristi as a podcast guest, workshop/conference presenter, or retreat leader
- BOOK a Human Design reading with Kristi to understand your unique energetic blueprint (based on your birthdate) and learn how to make a few transformative shifts in your life
- ENROLL in her 1-hour self-guided digital course to learn an overview of Human Design and how to create personalized self-care
- GET her free PDF to create a personalized self-care plan
- GIFT another copy of *Stop Overworking and Start Overflowing* to share with a friend!

Made in the USA
Monee, IL
24 October 2021

80400098R00146